What Would Drucker Do Now?

Solutions to Today's
Toughest Challenges from the
Father of Modern Management

RICK WARTZMAN

New York   Chicago   San Francisco   Lisbon   London   Madrid   Mexico City
Milan   New Delhi   San Juan   Seoul   Singapore   Sydney   Toronto

The McGraw·Hill Companies

2 3 4 5 6 7 8 9 10 11 12 13 14 15   QFR/QFR   1 9 8 7 6 5 4 3 2 1

ISBN   978-0-07-176220-5
MHID   0-07-176220-5

e-ISBN   978-0-07-176311-0
e-MHID   0-07-176311-2

Library of Congress Cataloging-in-Publication Data

Wartzman, Rick.
    What would Drucker do now : solutions to today's toughest challenges from the father of modern management / by Rick Wartzman.
         p.   cm.
    ISBN: 978-0-07-176220-5 (alk. paper)
        1. Management.   2. Twenty-first century—Forecasts.   3. Drucker, Peter F. (Peter Ferdinand), 1909–2005.   I. Title.

    HD31.W3347   2012
    658—dc22   2011009174

Permission to reprint The Drucker Difference columns granted by *Bloomberg Businessweek*.

For Randye, because I love you madly

And for Mom and Dad,
whose strong sense of values infuses these pages

Contents

Foreword

I grew up with Peter Drucker. My father spent 25 years in human resources management at General Electric and another decade leading HR at Chase Manhattan Bank. He met Peter at GE's Crotonville training center in the 1950s and always had Peter's books in his study at home. When I was in college, I would occasionally flip through classics like *The Effective Executive* and *The Practice of Management*.

But I didn't get serious about Drucker until I was in my mid-20s and responsible for the Navy Exchange Service and retail operations at the U.S. air base in Atsugi, Japan. This was my first real business job, and I needed a business education fast. Drucker was it.

Almost 30 years later—after the navy, Harvard Business School, and more than 22 years as a manager at Procter & Gamble—I took the initiative to meet Peter personally. It was 1999, and I had just returned from a five-year stint running P&G Asia. The company was in the midst of what was arguably the most ambitious strategic and organizational transformation in its then 162-year history.

I was responsible for P&G's North America region, the company's home market, and for creating a new global beauty and personal care business. I called Peter and asked if he would see me. A week later, I found myself sitting in his modest Claremont, Calif., home talking about a world he had thought about for 60 years (and I had worked in for 25).

I had hoped for an hour of his time. We chatted for four. For every question I posed, Peter had two or three more to consider. That exhilarating first exchange provided the themes that he and I would return to again and again over the next six years: the customer, innovation, strategy, and leadership.

A flood of memories from those conversations came back to me as I read this collection of columns by Rick Wartzman. Rick hits on many of the same subjects that Peter and I discussed, and he brings these principles to life by applying them to current topics. Each column is like a mini-case study, written in a style that, like Peter's own, is pragmatic and accessible (and simply fun to read).

As I spent more time with Peter, we ultimately took up a topic that he turned to in the last years of his life: the unique work of the CEO. His final column for *The Wall Street Journal*, which ran in December 2004, about a year before he died, explored this subject. My May 2009 *Harvard Business Review* article, "What Only the CEO Can Do," combined Peter's thinking with my actual experience in that job at P&G in the first decade of the twenty-first century.

As CEO, I was a shameless disciple of Peter Drucker. He said, "The purpose of a business is to create and serve a customer." Plain and simple. At P&G, the consumer was boss, and consumer-driven strategy, brands, and innovation drove our business and financial growth. We focused on delighting current customers and attracting new ones by providing offerings that better met their wants and needs. We understood that the smartest way to conduct consumer research is to actually experience what the customer does. That's why, whenever I traveled, I personally went into the homes of our customers. It was essential to understand how these people—mostly women—used our brands and products. I also shopped with them, so I could experience how they made their purchase choices.

Peter insisted on the practice of management. He had little patience for detached theory or abstract plans. "Plans are only good intentions unless they degenerate into hard work," he liked to say. I focused on the few strategic choices that would give P&G sustainable advantage. I also focused on consistent, excellent execution, because I knew that the only strategy our customers (and even competitors) would ever see was what we executed in the store and in the home every day.

Peter also insisted on leaders taking responsibility: "Management is doing things right; leadership is doing the right things." As P&G CEO, I knew we needed consistently good everyday management. But we also needed leaders. Leaders were the difference maker in our company, and leadership was a core value expected of every P&Ger.

Of course, as CEO, I had a special leadership responsibility as Drucker saw it—namely, to shape the values and standards of the entire company, as well as to be a role model in terms of morals and ethics. This responsibility is only going to become more important in a world of ever-increasing demands and expanding company constituents.

More broadly, Drucker maintained that the CEO was the "chief external officer" for the corporation—"the link between the inside, where there are only costs, and the outside, where the results are." For many reasons, businesses and other organizations invariably become inwardly focused. Peter argued that the CEO must counterbalance this tendency; he or she has primary responsibility for bringing the voices of the market, customers, competition, partners, and shareholders into the company. I always wanted the "hot breath" of a globally competitive, unpredictable, and volatile marketplace to be felt in the corridors of P&G. I wanted us to come to grips with the reality of the outside world—to see things as they actually were, not as we wanted them to be.

Peter's ideas remain as relevant and important today as they always were. They are simple but powerful—and eminently practical. Clearly understood and well executed, Drucker delivers results.

What better way to understand the relevance and importance of Peter Drucker than to read this collection of "Drucker Difference" columns. Rick applies Peter's teachings to current real-world challenges and opportunities. His clear writing and thinking demonstrate the practice of good management the way Peter would have wanted.

As Peter said, "A time of turbulence is one of great opportunity for those who understand, accept, and exploit the new realities." This collection is like a road map for those who are intent on doing just that.

A.G. Lafley

Preface

The title of this volume notwithstanding, I really have no idea what Peter Drucker would do. The truth is, nobody does. Charles Handy, the British social philosopher, remarked that Drucker "revels in surprising you." The writer Jeffrey Krames has observed that Drucker had a penchant for coming up with "counterintuitive ideas," while one of his former Ph.D. students explained it like this: Drucker was "frequently unpredictable and almost always provocative and original."

Nevertheless, for nearly four years now, I have written "The Drucker Difference" column for *Bloomberg Businessweek* (formerly *BusinessWeek*) online, in an effort to provide a sense of how Drucker might react to issues dominating today's headlines.

To say that mining Drucker's 39 books, along with his countless magazine and newspaper articles, has been a privilege would be a gross understatement. I love crafting "The Drucker Difference" in what I've come to regard as a biweekly attempt to achieve some kind of mind meld with one of the greatest minds of the twentieth century.

I must confess, however, that I took up the column somewhat reluctantly. When I first became executive director of the Drucker Institute in 2007, after a 20-year career as a reporter and editor at *The Wall Street Journal* and *Los Angeles Times*, I wrote a piece on spec for *BusinessWeek* on what Drucker might have thought about China's spate of product recalls for lead paint and other dangers. Frankly, I did this because, at the time, I wasn't quite sure what my new job entailed; writing was the one thing I felt qualified to do.

As it turned out, the essay was a hit. It attracted more eyeballs than any other that weekend on *BusinessWeek*'s website and elicited a string of thoughtful responses. Clearly, Drucker's views or mine—or, more precisely, this combination of the two of us—had resonated with readers.

The next week, John Byrne, then *BusinessWeek*'s executive editor, called me and asked if I'd like to contribute a regular column based on Drucker's teachings. "Absolutely," I told him. This was, after all, a coup. What else was I going to say?

Inside, though, I was incredibly nervous. My mind, if not my heart, was racing: How long could I keep this gig going? Did Drucker (who died in 2005, just shy of his ninety-sixth birthday) really have enough to say, especially on contemporary subjects? Would it seem strange to be channeling a dead guy?

Nearly 100 columns later—and with the help and support of two terrific editors, Patricia O'Connell and Rebecca Reisner—I am happy to report that all my fears have long been laid to rest. Not only have I been able to sustain "The Drucker Difference," but I've been able to use it to cover an extraordinary amount of terrain.

I've tackled the collapse of Lehman Brothers; the federal bailout of General Motors; Toyota's sticky-accelerator problems; and innovation at Apple, Google, Wikia, and Sony. But I've also been able to write about the service and volunteering movement, the complexities of race in America, the soaring cost of college tuition, President Obama's health-care plan, women in the workplace, the role of spirituality on the job—even music, art, and baseball.

The reason for this range is simple: The breadth and depth of Drucker's body of work are nothing short of remarkable. Much more than a management thinker, Drucker inhabited and helped shape "the world of ideas," as Warren Bennis has described it. He adds that unless this is truly appreciated, "we risk placing Drucker in too narrow an intellectual context and will fail to do full justice to his unique contribution."

Indeed, because of Drucker's scope—and the 10,000 book pages he left behind—I've actually been able to compose all of these columns without using the same quotation twice. (OK, I goofed once and belatedly discovered that I'd accidentally duplicated a quote.) Drucker had so many insights to share, there's no need to repeat myself.

As for drawing so heavily on the work of a person who has passed away, that hasn't been odd in the least. There are three reasons for this. First, Drucker's writing is so foundational—he was, as *BusinessWeek* declared, "the man who invented management"—that his work possesses a timeless quality. Kenneth Wilson, a Nobel Prize–winning scientist and education reformer, once told me that what Newton was to mathematics, Darwin to biology, and Einstein to physics, Drucker was to our understanding of organizations and society.

Second, Drucker was so farseeing, we're just beginning to get a handle on many of the topics he wrote about toward the end of his life, including what it means—from multiple dimensions—to live in a knowledge age.

Third, there is my own strong connection to Drucker. Above all, our values are in sync. What's more, although Drucker wore various hats, including professor and consultant, he considered himself a writer first and foremost; that's an identity I share.

I should point out that I never had a chance to meet Drucker. But, as you might imagine, I feel as if I knew him. Through his words, he has certainly taught me more than anyone else.

Of course, I am hardly alone in expressing this sentiment. "A goodly share of productive organizations worldwide are led by men and women who consider Drucker their intellectual guide, if not their personal mentor," noted T. George Harris, the former editor of *Harvard Business Review*.

He has similarly inspired new generations of scholars, who see him as their exemplar. As Gary Hamel and C.K. Prahalad once put it: Drucker "has been an unfailing beacon, lighting the way toward the management issues of tomorrow." I hope "The Drucker Difference" is helping to keep that light alive and making it shine just a little brighter.

1

Management as a Discipline

Peter Drucker: Timeless, Ubiquitous

A few Sundays ago, I was sitting in my home office, working on an outside writing project—a historical narrative that has nothing to do with my day job as director of the Drucker Institute. The think tank's mission is to advance the teachings of the late Peter Drucker, the man widely hailed as "the father of modern management."

My stack of reading this day included a 1939 article from *The Nation* magazine that explored a long-forgotten pension scheme, popularly known as Ham and Eggs, which failed twice at the ballot box in Depression-era California. I was breezing right along—that is, until I got to the penultimate sentence, which contained these six words: "as Peter Drucker has pointed out." I shook my head, burst out laughing, and raced downstairs to tell my wife about my serendipitous discovery. "Geez," I said, "this guy's following me everywhere."

In the weeks since, though, what has struck me as most remarkable is not that I stumbled upon Drucker in a nearly 70-year-old magazine story. It is that hardly a week passes when a major publication somewhere in the world doesn't invoke him in the very same manner: "as Peter Drucker has said," "as Peter Drucker has pointed out."

The Big Idea

How many people can you name whose ideas—and ideals—were being discussed in 1939, in 1969, in 1999, and will be, undoubtedly, in 2039? Likewise, how many people can you cite whose counsel was requested and (to varying degrees) followed by both General Electric Chief Executive Jack Welch and United Farm Workers leader Cesar Chavez? How many get credit for inspiring an organization such as the Girl Scouts while also helping guide a financial giant like Edward Jones?

Drucker's extraordinary staying power and his wide reach speak to several factors: the depth and breadth of his insights, an uncanny ability to anticipate the future, and a prose style that is as clear as mountain water.

But perhaps most of all, he remains highly relevant two years after his death at age 95 because he reminded us again and again that responsible management is not about buzzwords. It's not about fads. Ultimately, it is not even about developing new products or fattening the bottom line (although he believed those things are important).

Rather, it is about far more fundamental tenets—a philosophy that grew directly out of Drucker's experience as a young writer who had witnessed the rise of Nazi Germany (which in the early 1930s banned and burned the Austria native's work).

Drucker wrote that management, at its core, "deals with people, their values, their growth and development—and this makes it a humanity. So does its concern with, and impact on, social structure and the community. Indeed, as everyone has learned who . . . has been working with managers of all kinds of institutions for long years, management is deeply involved in moral concerns—the nature of man, good, and evil."

Every couple of weeks, this column will endeavor to tie Drucker's teachings to events in the news. It will also, from time to time, feature the latest thinking of scholars and practitioners who have been strongly influenced by Drucker. There is no shortage of these folks around, from Procter & Gamble Chairman and Chief Executive A.G. Lafley to best-selling author Jim Collins, who has said that his book *Built to Last: Successful Habits of Visionary Companies* might well have been called "Drucker Was Right."

"What Would Peter Say?"

I am neither presumptuous nor foolish enough to suggest that I can possibly write with Drucker's prescience or perspicacity. That's not the intent of this column. All that any of us can do is simply ask, "What would Peter say?" and then try to connect the dots between his body of work and some of the issues making headlines now: the mortgage industry meltdown, thorny questions about globalization, immigration and income inequality, the blurring of nonprofits and profit-making enterprises in the social sector, the government's handling of a disaster like Hurricane Katrina.

Fortunately, there is a vast amount to draw from. Drucker wrote 39 books and countless articles.

He didn't always hit the mark and was occasionally criticized for being loose with the facts. But many of the concepts that Drucker introduced in the 1940s, '50s, '60s, and beyond have been built into the DNA of the world's top companies and embraced as second nature by a generation of social entrepreneurs. Among them: "There is only one valid definition of business purpose: to create a customer." "The business enterprise has two—and only these two—basic functions: marketing and innovation." "The shift from manual workers who do as they are being told—either by the task or by the boss—to knowledge workers who have to manage themselves profoundly challenges social structure." "Innovation and entrepreneurship are . . . needed in society as much as in the economy, in public-service institutions as much as in businesses."

These are but a few of his principles, and they lead to what could be called the Drucker Paradox. His imprint is everywhere, so much so that his contribution has become, in many ways, imperceptible. Yet, at the same time, there are lots of people in business, government, and the nonprofit realm who forsake his wisdom each and every day. The need for effective management and ethical leadership—the need for Peter Drucker—has never been more pressing.

September 13, 2007

Muhammad Yunus:
The Unlikely Disciple

There is no shortage of people who exemplify Peter Drucker's principles and practices—a multitude of middle managers and top executives responsible for many millions, if not billions, of dollars in economic activity. Yet the most Drucker-like of all may well be a man who launched his enterprise with a series of transactions totaling 27 bucks.

Nobel Peace Prize winner Muhammad Yunus, who pioneered the concept of microcredit—providing the poorest of the poor with tiny loans to start their own moneymaking ventures—is promoting a new idea these days. He calls it "social business," and in his just-released book, *Creating a World Without Poverty*, he contends that it promises to relegate destitution across the globe to where it belongs: inside a museum.

His notion is to foster a whole class of companies capable of competing in the marketplace but whose primary aim is to meet a clear social need, not to maximize profits.

These firms are meant to earn money. But they pay no dividends. Instead, explains Yunus, "any profit stays in the business—to finance expansion, to create products or services, and to do more good for the world." (Microsoft Chairman Bill Gates recently shared a somewhat similar, though not identical, vision in Davos, Switzerland, with his plea for "creative capitalism.")

And what might Drucker have made of all this?

Any business, he asserted in *Management: Tasks, Responsibilities, Practices*, "exists for the sake of society." In *The Effective Executive*, he added: "An organization is not like an animal, an end in itself, and successful by the mere act of perpetuating the species. An organization is an organ of society and fulfills itself by the contribution it makes to the outside environment."

No Political Boxes

This is not to say Drucker pushed for corporations to focus specifically on the needs of the indigent as Yunus has. But I think he would have greatly appreciated Yunus' model, for it is an overt expression of Drucker's conviction that "psychologically, geographically, culturally, and socially," the business community must be part of the wider community.

Interestingly, it's tough to stick Yunus in any particular political box. His Grameen Bank "supports less government . . . is committed to the free market, and promotes entrepreneurial institutions," he pointed out. "So it must be far right." At the same time, Grameen is "committed to social objectives" and does not advocate a system of pure laissez-faire; rather, it would like to see policy incentives that encourage "businesses to move in directions desired by society." Yunus noted: "All these features place Grameen on the political left."

Surely Drucker could relate, once suggesting that, as he sought out the proper balance between continuity and change in society, he could see himself "sometimes as a liberal conservative and sometimes as a conservative liberal but never as a 'conservative conservative' or a 'liberal liberal.'"

Motivated by More than Dollars

Drucker, too, would have no doubt been sold on Yunus' basic premise: People are motivated by a variety of impulses—not simply a desire to get filthy rich. The existing system, said Yunus, has "created a one-dimensional human being to play the role of business leader. . . . We've insulated him from the rest of life, the religious, emotional, political, and social. He is dedicated to one mission only—maximize profit."

Drucker—whose own writing draws heavily on sociology and psychology, on history and art and religion—once remarked that his work was likewise predicated on the belief that "people are diverse, often unpredictable, always multidimensional."

In the end, though, it is not just Yunus' theories Drucker would have admired; above all, it's his effectiveness. Two things are behind it.

Challenge Conventional Wisdom

The first is a willingness to punch holes in conventional wisdom. "Despite their importance," Drucker wrote in *Management Challenges for the 21st Century*, "the assumptions are rarely analyzed, rarely studied, rarely challenged—indeed rarely even made explicit."

Yunus thrives on challenging assumptions. He's doing it now, as he tries to reframe what most people imagine a business can be. And he did it before, when he established Grameen.

Indeed, had he listened to the many reasons that offering credit to poor people was supposedly a fool's errand, Grameen never would have grown from that first $27 in loans, made 32 years ago straight from Yunus' pocket to 42 Bangladeshi villagers, into what it is today: a financially self-reliant bank that has given $6 billion in loans to millions of Bangladeshis, boasts a 98.6 percent repayment rate, and has put a huge dent in that nation's level of poverty. (It also has become the centerpiece of a network of two dozen socially driven companies with interests in education, health care, apparel, telecommunications, and much more.)

Avoid Lofty Philosophy

The second factor that makes Yunus so effective is that, even though there is more than a hint of idealism in his efforts, he consciously tries "to avoid grandiloquent philosophies and . . . take a pragmatic approach." To that end, Grameen backs its actions with sound market analysis, nurtures its employees, actively seeks out customer input, and continually improves its products and services.

This, of course, is classic Drucker. Despite "the romance of invention and innovation," Drucker advised, "'flashes of genius'" don't get terribly far. What does carry a business forward is "hard, organized, purposeful work."

See for yourself. Check out Yunus' new book and, if you missed it, his first: *Banker to the Poor*. Not only are they inspirational, they are highly informational—fantastic case studies on how to manage a business the right way. Which is to say, the Drucker way.

January 31, 2008

Wide-Angle Thinking

Charles Handy has been called "the Peter Drucker of Britain." But in a sense, pinning Handy to a particular place misses the whole point. In the last year alone, this venerated thinker and writer on organizational behavior and society has left his home near London to spend time in Hong Kong, China, Romania, Spain, Italy, Denmark, Sweden, and India. He's also made three trips to the U.S., where he just wrapped up a five-week stay as a scholar-in-residence at Claremont Graduate University's Drucker School of Management and the Drucker Institute, of which I am the director.

It was there that I had the pleasure and privilege of watching Handy up close and discovering a couple of lessons that all of us would be wise to heed—for ourselves as well as for the institutions we manage.

Handy, as you might imagine, was a magnet during his stay. All sorts of people—students, faculty, and members of the larger community— were eager to pick his brain. And he gave generously, whether in the campus lecture hall, in small meetings, in countless one-on-one sessions, or during the weekly commentaries he crafted for public radio's *Marketplace* while in Southern California.

The Art of Listening

But what I noticed most is that Handy didn't always command the spotlight. Often he'd retreat a bit and discreetly survey the interaction of others around him, playing the role of bystander, just as Drucker loved to do. And when Handy did find himself at the center of a conversation, he didn't just answer questions; he asked them—lots and lots of them.

Surely, Drucker would have applauded. "Too many think they are wonderful because they talk well," he once pointed out. "They don't realize that being wonderful with people means listening well."

Yet it wasn't just Handy's ability to open his eyes and ears so wide that struck me. It was that he tilted them in as many directions as possible—

toward academics, corporate executives, those active in the social sector, and, most avidly, toward artists of all kinds.

"You've got to get out of your own box," says the 75-year-old, whose newly published autobiography, *Myself and Other More Important Matters*, traces his career as a Shell executive, cofounder of the London Business School, official of the Church of England, BBC broadcaster, and best-selling author. "Otherwise, you stop being creative."

Broadening Perspectives

To this end, Handy and his wife, Liz, a photographer with whom he often works, abide by a handful of rules when they travel. One is that they use public transportation wherever possible; it serves as a great window into everyday culture. Another is that they always arrange to gather with a group of a half-dozen or so thirtysomethings so that they can get their take on the local scene and, says Liz, "hear their dreams."

It's clear why soaking in civilization this way would be of interest to a self-described "social philosopher" such as Handy. It should also be clear why all of us, on a personal level, would benefit from seeing more of the world. What may be less obvious, though, is the need for institutions—whether public, private, or philanthropic—to broaden their perspectives as well.

The first step, of course, is for those running the enterprise to emerge from behind their desks and observe. There are no shortcuts. As Drucker noted more than 40 years ago, "Decision makers need organized information for feedback. They need reports and figures. But unless they build their feedback around direct exposure to reality—unless they discipline themselves to go out and look—they condemn themselves to a sterile dogmatism."

Looking Beyond Traditional Boundaries

The next step is to be smart about where to look. As Drucker recognized, this often requires peering into less-than-familiar arenas. Through the 1800s and the first half of the 1900s, he wrote in *Management Challenges for the 21st Century*, "it could be taken for granted that technologies outside one's own industry had no, or at least only minimal, impact on the industry. Now the assumption to start with is that the technologies that are likely to have the greatest impact on a company and an industry are technologies outside its own field."

Handy goes even further, advising that companies should roam far beyond their traditional bounds to better understand not just technology but myriad practices and processes. Say, for instance, a manufacturer needs to tap a team of top talent for a project that will be disbanded after a relatively brief period. Handy's suggestion: Arrange a visit to one of the Hollywood studios. They manage high-end, short-term work all the time.

Get Out There and Listen

Similarly, Handy says, an outfit such as Penguin Books might well be positioned to teach a high-tech company how to outsource intellectual capital more effectively. After all, a publisher's entire business rests on this model. There are insights to be gleaned, as well, from peeking inside hospitals, theaters, and arts organizations. "Too many companies benchmark themselves against others in their industry," says Handy. "They should be comparing themselves to totally different organizations."

Gaining access, he adds, is not as hard as you might suspect: "If you're not a direct competitor, companies love to tell you how successful they are—and how they do it."

All you have to do is get out there and listen.

February 28, 2008

Dusting Off a Managing Tome

O
f all of Peter Drucker's achievements—advising captains of industry and heads of state, coining the term "knowledge worker," winning the Presidential Medal of Freedom—the most remarkable may be this: In 1974, his 800-plus-page tome, *Management: Tasks, Responsibilities, Practices*, vaulted past *The Joy of Sex* on the national best seller list.

Last week, HarperCollins released a revised edition of *Management*. And regardless of whether it winds up eclipsing *Bonk*, the latest hot-selling volume on the physiology and psychology of sex, I can tell you this: It deserves a spot on every manager's shelf, much as the *Physicians' Desk Reference* can be found in every doctor's office.

The new edition of *Management*—slimmed down, though still not exactly svelte at nearly 600 pages—contains updated facts and figures and examples. But more important, it has been tailored to reflect the evolution in Drucker's thinking and writing in the three decades between the book's initial publication and his death in 2005.

Devoted Protégé

The person who filled in the gaps is Joseph Maciariello, a professor and longtime colleague of Drucker's at Claremont Graduate University and the academic director at the Drucker Institute, which I run. As Maciariello describes it, the project was a true labor of love, with an emphasis on the word "labor."

"This was Drucker's magnum opus," he says. "But even though I just tagged along, it is also the biggest thing I've ever done."

Maciariello first happened upon Drucker's work in the early 1960s when he was helping to design management systems at Hamilton Standard, the old aerospace giant. After a few trips to the corporate library to investigate what had been written about the general discipline of management, Maciariello discovered that it was pretty much a canon of one:

Drucker's 1954 landmark, *The Practice of Management*, was about the only thing available on the topic.

Maciariello later went on to study economics at New York University. Drucker was teaching there at the time, "but I couldn't get into his classes," Maciariello recalls. "My schedule didn't work out."

In 1973, Maciariello received his doctorate. That same year, *Management* was published. Maciariello's wife, remembering his admiration for *The Practice of Management*, bought him the new book. He devoured it.

"Drucker was trying to bring *The Practice of Management* up to date," Maciariello says. "But I began to see that in spirit, it was the same." What resonated in particular for Maciariello was Drucker's "deep, deep concern for the human being."

A Couple of Epiphanies

In another book, *The Ecological Vision: Reflections on the American Condition*, Drucker recounts being at a 1934 lecture in Cambridge delivered by John Maynard Keynes. "I suddenly realized," he wrote, "that Keynes and all the brilliant economics students in the room were interested in the behavior of commodities while I was interested in the behavior of people."

Reading *Management*, Maciariello had a similar epiphany. It struck him that the subject he had been focusing on—economics—"lacked flesh."

"I felt like I was dying in economics," Maciariello says. "This is not to disparage it. Peter used a lot of economics. . . . But his work was really about bringing out the best in people. This was powerful stuff. It was inspired."

In 1979, Maciariello came to teach in Claremont, where Drucker was by then on the faculty. The two became friends, and over the years they began to collaborate. In the late 1990s, when Drucker started to cut back on his hours in the classroom, Maciariello developed a Drucker on Management course. They later worked together on two books, *The Daily Drucker: 366 Days of Insight and Motivation for Getting the Right Things Done* and *The Effective Executive in Action: A Journal for Getting the Right Things Done*.

It was during the editing of the latter—about six months before Drucker passed away—that Maciariello broached an idea he had long been contemplating: How about revising *Management*?

Drucker didn't hold back. "That," he said in his thick Austrian accent, "is going to be a lot of work."

Road to Redux

And so it was. Just scrubbing the facts in *Management* was an arduous process. Despite Drucker's reputation for being loose with them—"I use anecdotes to make a point, not to write history," he once said—Maciariello found that he was accurate at least 95 percent of the time.

More daunting, Maciariello says, was trying to understand, in a careful and considered way, the major themes Drucker had concentrated on in the years after *Management* had first come out. During a nine-month sabbatical, Maciariello pored over the more than 20 books and hundreds of articles that Drucker had written since *Management*'s debut.

The result is that the redux edition weaves together a lot of original content with Drucker's later writings on innovation and entrepreneurship, the imperative for each individual to "manage oneself," the crucial role of the nonprofit sector, and, especially, the significance of "knowledge work." Tellingly, Chapter 4 of the new book is titled "Knowledge Is All."

An "Overwhelming Sense of Responsibility"

From the opening words of Chapter 1—"Management may be the most important innovation of [the twentieth] century . . ."—the book blends theory and practical application, reminding us that effectiveness is a skill that can be learned and that the health of society depends upon our institutions functioning ably.

"Organizations are far from perfect," Drucker concluded. "As every manager knows, they are very difficult; full of frustration, tension, and friction; clumsy and unwieldy. But they are the only tools we have to accomplish such social purposes as economic production and distribution, health care, governance, and education. And there is not the slightest reason to expect society to be willing to do without these services that only performing institutions can provide. Indeed, there is every reason to expect society to demand more performance from all its institutions and to become more dependent upon their performance."

In the end, says the 66-year-old Maciariello, the hardest part of revamping *Management* was "the overwhelming sense of responsibility, bordering on fear, that I not do harm to Drucker's legacy."

On this, Maciariello has more than met his objective. He has not only protected Drucker's legacy, he has enhanced it for a new generation.

April 24, 2008

AIG and Drucker's Glimpse
at a Very Dark Place

Soon after I was hired as the director of the Drucker Institute a couple of years ago, one of my board members passed along a short piece that he described as "the keystone" of Peter Drucker's work and told me to pay close attention to what it said.

It was the preface to the 1973 edition of *Management: Tasks, Responsibilities, Practices.* Drucker entitled the composition "The Alternative to Tyranny."

I read it over a couple of times and then zipped off a note to Bob Buford—a cable-TV pioneer, social entrepreneur, author, and a dear friend of Drucker's—thanking him for having shared the essay with me.

But the truth is, I didn't really appreciate what it was all about—at least not until this week, when the firestorm erupted over AIG.

Trusting "Large Organizations"

"Our society has become, within an incredibly short 50 years, a society of institutions," Drucker wrote. "It has become a pluralist society in which every major social task has been entrusted to large organizations—from producing economic goods and services to health care, from social security and welfare to education, from the search for new knowledge to the protection of the natural environment.

"To make our institutions perform responsibly, autonomously, and on a high level of achievement is . . . the only safeguard of freedom and dignity" in a society like ours, Drucker added. "But it is managers and management that make institutions perform. Performing, responsible management is the alternative to tyranny and our only protection against it."

Frankly, this last passage had always struck me as more than a little over the top. Sitting in sunny Southern California, the prospect of totalitarianism seemed awfully remote. I couldn't even begin to fathom how we'd ever slip into such a state.

But then AIG, the insurance giant bailed out by Uncle Sam, decided to pay out $165 million in bonuses to many of the same employees who'd wrecked the company's fortunes in the first place and nearly undermined the nation's financial system in the process. Suddenly, Drucker's words made sense.

"Appalled by the Greed"

Let me be clear: I'm not at all suggesting that we're about to fall into the grip of some twenty-first-century strain of Stalinism. Let me be equally clear that what AIG did—making "all kinds of unconscionable bets" on the housing bubble, as Fed Chairman Ben Bernanke has put it, and doling out these outrageous "retention payments"—should not be countenanced in any way.

And I am confident that Drucker would have felt the same. "I am appalled by the greed of today's executive," he declared in 2000, referring to those more interested in generating short-term gains than building sustainable businesses.

Yet Drucker, I think, would not only be disgusted by AIG's conduct; he would also cast a nervous eye at some of the reaction to it.

Indeed, the fact that so many have been clamoring for the government to abrogate unilaterally the contracts covering those AIG bonuses (maddening as they are); that Representative Barney Frank (D-Mass.), the chairman of the House Financial Services Committee, asserted we should "forget about the legal matter here for a second"; that armed guards have been posted at AIG's offices in the face of death threats; that a U.S. senator (Charles Grassey—R-Iowa) has called on AIG executives to "resign or go commit suicide"—it all goes to the heart of what Drucker was getting at. When managers are irresponsible, when major institutions fall apart, we as a society leave ourselves open to unforeseen and sometimes extreme responses.

"Crisis of Belief"

Drucker's unease grew straight out of his early experiences in Europe, where he watched the Nazis rise to power. His first major book, 1939's *The End of Economic Man*, explored how "a society built around the market (the major social institution of the nineteenth century) . . . had failed, and that this had 'destroyed the belief in capitalism as a social system,'" Drucker's biographer, Jack Beatty, has noted. "The Great War and Depression made this crisis of belief a reality for millions."

Wrote Drucker: "These catastrophes broke through the everyday routine which makes men accept existing forms, institutions, and tenets as unalterable laws. They suddenly exposed the vacuum behind the façade of society."

Looking for a miracle, the masses turned toward what Drucker termed the "abracadabra of fascism."

The U.S., as I said, is certainly in no real danger of sliding into dictatorship. But this week, we got the tiniest glimpse of what Drucker was writing about in that preface to *Management*—and a warning about what could happen if we keep going down the road we're on.

If nothing else, we'd be fools to take for granted that our way of life will always be here, undisturbed. "We are learning very fast," Drucker said in a far-seeing 1996 interview, "that the belief that a free market is all it takes to have a functioning society . . . is pure delusion."

For me, the AIG debacle has made it plain: As our managers go, as our institutions go, so goes the health of our economy—and maybe our democracy, too.

March 20, 2009

Management as a Liberal Art

————————

I've had the opportunity to take part in several conferences and symposiums this summer revolving around topics at the center of Peter Drucker's teachings: innovation, marketing, service, and volunteering. But it's the gathering where I am now—surrounded by novelists and poets, instead of corporate executives and social entrepreneurs—that I believe Drucker would have relished the most.

Here, at the Squaw Valley Community of Writers, amid the natural splendor of the California Sierra Nevada, Drucker would have felt truly at home. He considered himself a wordsmith first and foremost. And with 39 books to his name, who could argue? In addition to works such as *The Practice of Management* and *The Effective Executive*, Drucker authored two novels: *The Last of All Possible Worlds* and *The Temptation to Do Good*.

Yet he also would have loved this place, with its nightly readings of fiction and memoir and social history, because he believed that management, when done right, incorporates lessons from all of these disciplines and many more.

Action and Applications

Management "deals with action and application; and its test is its results. This makes it a technology," Drucker explained in *The New Realities*. "But management also deals with people, their values, their growth and development—and this makes it a humanity. . . . Management is thus what tradition used to call a 'liberal art': 'liberal' because it deals with the fundamentals of knowledge, self-knowledge, wisdom, and leadership; 'art' because it is practice and application."

"Managers," Drucker continued, "draw on all the knowledge and insights of the humanities and the social sciences—on psychology and philosophy, on economics and on history, on the physical sciences and on ethics."

That too many corporations and other institutions have lost sight of this is painfully obvious today. This is not to imply that if more CEOs and regulators had merely studied Aristotle's warnings about "the unlimited acquisition of wealth" or digested Dickens' *Little Dorrit*, the financial crisis or the Madoff scandal would have been averted. But pausing to consider such wisdom surely couldn't have hurt.

It's not that people have stopped writing; by one estimate, a new book of fiction is published in the U.S. every 30 minutes. It's not that people have stopped reading, either (though more and more are doing so online). The National Endowment of the Arts released a survey last January showing that for the first time in more than 25 years American adults are consuming more literature.

The Nitty-Gritty

The problem is that the broad world of ideas has become largely separated from the world of business.

"What Drucker wanted was for knowledge to 'no longer be ornamental—to be consumed to refine oneself or to impress others,'" says Joseph Maciariello, the academic director at the Drucker Institute, which I run. "Rather, knowledge is to be brought down to the grimy earth, where we all work, and integrated so that work can be made more productive and more humane."

Maciariello is spearheading an effort to bring the concept of "management as a liberal art" into the nation's colleges and universities. The goal is to have business professors integrate the humanities more fully into their classes, while liberal arts majors contemplate "not just applied reasoning and ethics but virtuous living," as Maciariello puts it, rooted in real results. Ultimately, the intention is for these ideals to transcend the academy and reach the realm of practice.

In the meantime, the creative souls at Squaw Valley have, unbeknownst to them, underscored a few things that all managers would profit from thinking about. For starters, there's the Community of Writers itself. Founded 40 years ago by novelists Blair Fuller and Oakley Hall, the organization is thriving, thanks in large measure to a strong sense of self. "Community" is not just a throwaway word in the name here, but the very essence of the place. The authors on staff, many of them highly acclaimed, are unfailingly unpretentious and nurturing of the young writers they teach.

"Any organization . . . needs a commitment to values and their constant reaffirmation, as a human body needs vitamins and minerals," Drucker wrote. "There has to be something 'this organization stands for,' or else it degenerates into disorganization, confusion, and paralysis."

Brilliance Is Not Enough

What has also been made clear at Squaw Valley this week is that work of value never comes easy. "I do not believe in genius," Dorothy Allison, the best-selling author of *Bastard Out of Carolina* and *Cavedweller*, declared the other night. With that, she implored everyone trying to get his or her first book published to keep honing the manuscript—through 19 drafts, if need be—until it's just right.

Managers could benefit from the same basic advice. "Brilliant men," Drucker noted, "are often strikingly ineffectual; they fail to realize that the brilliant insight is not by itself achievement. They never have learned that insights become effectiveness only through hard systematic work."

Finally, and most importantly, there are the books. As I've sat and listened to Allison, Dagoberto Gilb, Lynn Freed, and others read from their latest narratives, I've been reminded how much literature can shed light on a subject that lies at the very heart of management: the human condition. "I am rereading each summer—and have for many years—the main novelists," Drucker wrote to a friend in 1997. Among them, he said, were Austen, Thackeray, Trollope, and George Eliot. "I never read management books," Drucker added. "All they do is corrupt the style."

I can, of course, think of at least one management writer whose work qualifies as a great exception.

August 7, 2009

Reflecting on Prahalad
Reflecting on Drucker

Peter Drucker liked to ask all kinds of penetrating questions, but in the end, none cut to the core as much as this: "What do you want to be remembered for?"

Among those who surely could have answered with great conviction was C.K. Prahalad, who passed away last week at the age of 68 following a brief illness. Although I didn't know Prahalad well, my interactions with him left a strong impression: He was a man as gracious and good-humored as he was stimulating and smart.

Among management scholars and practitioners, Prahalad was a giant. An expert on corporate strategy, he advised major companies across the globe. With Gary Hamel, he coined the term "core competencies." Perhaps his most lasting legacy will be his pioneering work in identifying the poorest of the poor as an untapped market worth as much as $13 trillion. Underlying this insight was Prahalad's deeply held belief that every business must have a social purpose as it produces a profit.

Not surprisingly, given his extraordinary intellect and influence, *The Times of London* ranked Prahalad, a professor at the University of Michigan, as the leading management mind in the world.

But tellingly, Prahalad placed another name at the top of his own list of the most important contributors to the field. "We have to pay attention to Drucker," he told an audience in Vienna last fall. "No other person has had as much of an impact on the practice of management."

Drucker Distilled

From there, Prahalad deftly distilled Drucker's decades of writing, an exercise that felt a little like Stephen Hawking breaking down the theories of Albert Einstein or Albert Pujols analyzing Babe Ruth's swing. The intent, Prahalad explained, was to challenge academics to reconsider the ways in which they research and teach management. Drucker, Prahalad couldn't help but observe, was so scorned by his business school colleagues that it's a wonder he ever got tenure.

Yet the handful of lessons Prahalad shared that day weren't just applicable to those trapped in the ivory tower; he offered plenty for executives to chew on, as well.

The first thing that characterized Drucker's work, according to Prahalad, was its constant focus on the future. "It's all about 'next practice,' not 'best practice,'" he said. To figure out what lies ahead—that is, what companies should be doing, not what they are doing—"means you have to amplify weak signals," Prahalad added. "You have to see new patterns, both of problems and of opportunities."

For his part, Drucker maintained that he never predicted the future. Rather, he said, "I just look out the window and see what's visible but not yet seen"—an orientation that makes a lot of sense for thinkers and doers alike.

A second quality of Drucker's that Prahalad highlighted was his emphasis on results. "Good words are not enough," Prahalad said. "You must perform." Or as Drucker himself put it: "The best plan is only good intentions unless it degenerates into work."

"Action Bias"

When Drucker would get together with a consulting client, he'd often end the session with a challenge: "Don't tell me you had a wonderful meeting with me. Tell me what you're going to do on Monday that's different." How many of our own meetings end with what Prahalad called "an action bias"?

Drucker's conception of leadership also caught Prahalad's eye. Drucker, he stressed, was interested in the tasks of leaders, not their personalities. And the ultimate task is unmistakable: to lift all of those in the organization to higher heights. Today, said Prahalad, the central question is, "How do you influence people who are . . . knowledge workers—not people who will be pushed around because you have power?"

Another attribute of Drucker's to which Prahalad pointed admiringly was the way he would "look beyond the corporate world" to art, sociology, history, theology, literature, and a host of other subjects to help shape his views. "He was a master at synthesis," Prahalad said. Although few can match Drucker's erudition, the message was plain: Most of us would do our jobs better if we stepped outside their limited confines and drew on other areas for information and inspiration.

The trick is to do this without getting tied up in knots. Indeed, as Prahalad remarked, Drucker had a trait that all of us, whether we're college professors or corporate managers, would do well to emulate: communicating clearly. "Peter tried very hard to make ordinary people understand nuanced, complex ideas," Prahalad said, noting that most of us, by contrast, take simple ideas and make them needlessly complicated.

Shared Values

Prahalad went on to explore several other themes, including the weight that Drucker placed on innovation and entrepreneurship. But one in particular jumped out at me: Drucker "had constancy of values," Prahalad said.

Many of these values Prahalad shared. Some have criticized Prahalad's assertion that the most impoverished people on the planet represent a lucrative market. But this notion was rooted in the unwavering principle that social responsibility lies at the heart of every business. "The bottom line is simple," he wrote. "It is possible to 'do well by doing good.'"

As he concluded his talk, Prahalad called Drucker "a gift to the world." So, too, was Coimbatore Krishnarao Prahalad.

April 23, 2010

Avoid the Economist's Folly

Peter Ducker was often said to be an economist. He wasn't. He sometimes referred to economic theory—along with history, sociology, philosophy, theology, art, and literature—as he honed his management principles. And he admired, in particular, the great Austrian economist Joseph Schumpeter, with his entrepreneurial concept of "creative destruction."

"It is becoming increasingly clear," Drucker wrote in a 1983 essay, "that it is Schumpeter who will shape the thinking and inform the questions on economic policy for the rest of this century, if not for the next 30 or 50 years."

But Drucker, whose own doctorate was in international law, couldn't help but poke fun at practitioners of the dismal science for often being hopelessly out of touch. "In all recorded history," Drucker once said, "there has not been one economist who has had to worry about where the next meal would come from."

Get Out of the Clouds

Drucker's dig sprang to mind recently when I read World Bank President Robert Zoellick's own pointed comments challenging economists to pull their heads out of the clouds so as to help combat global poverty with greater effectiveness. "Economics, and in particular development economics, must . . . build on its recent focus on empirical evidence . . . but not allow itself simply to chase data down narrow alleyways," said Zoellick, who is not an economist.

Zoellick's remarks have stirred up something of a fuss within the field. But his challenge need not be seen merely as an indictment of a single profession. Embedded in his speech, delivered Sept. 29 at Georgetown University, were several Drucker-like lessons that can—and should—be applied to virtually any occupation or organization. One is that we must focus not on activities but on results. Another is that good ideas are not enough; they must be scalable.

But perhaps Zoellick's most important insight is that we must approach whatever we do with a healthy dose of humility. "Modern portfolio theories," he noted, "claimed to master the uncertainty of our world." But as the subprime crisis has made plain, this was utter nonsense. "According to its risk model," Zoellick pointed out, "one investment bank suffered a loss on several consecutive days that should have occurred only once in 14 life spans of our universe."

From Successful to Smug

For Drucker, this episode would surely have reminded him of when, as he wrote, adherents of John Maynard Keynes came to regard themselves as "economist-kings" who were "infallible." They believed that "playing on a few simple monetary keys—government spending, the interest rate, the volume of credit, or the amount of money in circulation—would maintain permanent equilibrium with full employment, prosperity, and stability."

Yet it's not just economists who suffer such "righteous arrogance," as Drucker put it. Many times, he said, "innovators are so proud of their innovations that they are not willing to adapt them to reality." Other times, past performance can make an organization haughty and lazy. Companies are always at risk of "living smugly off the accumulated . . . fat of an earlier generation," Drucker warned in his 1954 classic, *The Practice of Management*.

Last week, at the World Business Forum in New York, Jim Collins echoed this notion, reminding the thousands of executives in attendance that past triumphs can be a dangerous narcotic. "It is when success leads to hubris," he said, "that the fall begins."

Open Your Ears

One manifestation of overconfidence is that you begin to close yourself off to different ways of thinking. Zoellick, for one, implored economists to take into account what others have to teach them. "We need to recognize that development knowledge is no longer the sole province of the researcher, the scholar, or the ivory tower," he said, urging theorists to open their ears to health-care workers, school officials, and business owners who are toiling on the ground in poor nations.

Drucker couldn't have agreed more. "Far too many people, and especially people with high knowledge in one area," he wrote, "are contemptuous of knowledge in other areas or believe that being 'bright' is a substitute for knowing" what's actually going on.

Being cocksure can be perilous in another way, too: It makes us stop questioning things. "We must ask ourselves: Have we become trapped by our received wisdoms?" Zoellick said. "Has certainty blinded us to opportunity?"

Outside of economics, Drucker saw many a manager slip into the same trap. "Don't go by what 'everybody knows' instead of looking out the window," he advised. "What everybody knows is usually 20 years out of date. In political campaigns the ones who look so promising at the beginning and then fizzle out are usually the ones who go by what they believe everybody knows. They haven't tested it, and it turns out that 'This was 20 years ago.'"

For those with status or in positions of authority, humbleness doesn't always come easy. But Zoellick couldn't have been more forceful about what's needed in economics—and, by extension, in a host of other arenas, too. "Above all," he declared, "we must be honest about what we do not know." Drucker, who knew many, many things, would have been the first to say, "Amen."

October 12, 2010

Drucker Does Spirituality

Considering that this is the month in which Jews observe Hanukkah, Muslims mark al-Hijra, Buddhists commemorate Bodhi Day, and Christians celebrate Christmas, it is the perfect time to explore a topic that makes many people squirm: the role of religion in the workplace.

Peter Drucker, for his part, never shied from the subject. On one level, he viewed theology as he did most any other discipline, be it art or literature, history or sociology, philosophy or psychology. Because these fields shed light on the way human beings interact, it is incumbent on managers to learn lessons from all of them.

Drucker, for example, turned to the New Testament to explain how difficult it can be to get a message across to someone if it goes against the person's values or aspirations. "Even the Lord, the Bible reports, first had to strike Saul blind before he could raise him as Paul," Drucker wrote. "Communications aiming at conversion demand surrender."

He also found that certain religious institutions were showcases for efficiency and effectiveness. "No other organization to this day equals the Catholic Church in the elegance and simplicity of its structure," Drucker remarked in an article published in the late 1980s. "There are only four layers of management: pope, archbishop, bishop, and parish priest. Armies have 10 layers, and General Motors close to 20. And what in business is called the 'central staff overhead'—for the most transnational of all organizations and one serving close to a billion members worldwide—numbers 1,500 people in Rome, far fewer than are employed in the headquarters of the large American corporation."

A Role for Compassion

But it's on a much deeper level, Drucker asserted, that religion can have a positive influence on the world of work and, indeed, on the world at large. "Society needs a return to spiritual values—not to offset the material but to make it fully productive," Drucker wrote in his 1957 book, *Landmarks of Tomorrow*. "However remote its realization for the great mass of mankind, there is today the promise of material abundance or at least of material sufficiency.

"Mankind needs the return to spiritual values, for it needs compassion," Drucker continued. "It needs the deep experience that the *Thou* and the *I* are one, which all higher religions share."

Bringing such ideas into the office can be difficult, of course. Some, feeling offended, will undoubtedly push back or run away. "Americans are increasingly concentrated at opposite ends of the religious spectrum—the highly religious at one pole, and the avowedly secular at the other," Robert Putnam and David Campbell note in their new book, *American Grace*. (I myself am a semiobservant Jew, who is struggling to make the grand leap from pure reason to true faith.)

Kierkegaard Influence

As for Drucker, he grew up in an Austrian home in which, as he once described it, "the Lutheran Protestantism . . . was so 'liberal' that it consisted of little more than a tree at Christmas and Bach cantatas at Easter." As a young man, he was deeply moved by the Danish religious philosopher Søren Kierkegaard's *Fear and Trembling*; after reading it, Drucker determined "that my life . . . would have to have an existential dimension which transcends society." When he got older, he became a practicing Episcopalian while expressing appreciation for the pastoral megachurch, which he identified as "surely the most important social phenomenon" in late twentieth-century America.

All along, he wasn't one to call much attention to his own spirituality. But many see it as a strong thread through his work. Drucker's "practical wisdom" and his unwavering "urge for moral purpose" are "deeply rooted in Christian faith," concludes Timo Meynhardt, managing director of the Center for Leadership and Values in Society at the University of St. Gallen in Switzerland, in a paper published earlier this year.

Perhaps nowhere is this more evident than in the way Drucker counseled organizations to treat their employees—namely, as assets possessing tremendous value. Big companies "must offer equal opportunities for advancement," Drucker wrote in *Concept of the Corporation*. "This is simply the traditional demand for justice, a consequence of the Christian concept of human dignity."

Akin to the Golden Rule

In a piece that appeared in the magazine *Spirituality & Health* in 2005, just a few months before Drucker died, Procter & Gamble executive Craig Wynett and T. George Harris, the former editor of *Harvard Business Review*, suggested that the fundamental Drucker principle, "the marketer is the consumer's representative," is built on the Golden Rule, which many trace to sacred sources such as the Torah.

Drucker found religious inspiration, as well, when talking about tolerance and the need to encourage multiple points of view—another hallmark of the best organizations. "I've always felt that quite clearly the good Lord loves diversity," Drucker said. "He created 2,500 species of flies. If he had been like some theologians I know, there would have been only one right specie of fly."

With that in mind, I wish everyone a wonderful holiday season, no matter what you believe in, or choose not to.

December 17, 2010

2

The Practice of Management

Google: A Druckerian Ideal?

Google turned out quite a dazzling display of data recently when it released its third-quarter results: Profit jumped 46 percent. Revenue soared 57 percent. The company's shares shot up $6.14, to more than $639 each, on the news. But it's another set of figures that most impresses me: 17, $0, and 20 percent.

These refer, respectively, to the number of cafés at Google's Mountain View (Calif.) campus; what it charges employees for all the meals and snacks eaten there; and the amount of time it encourages its engineers to carve out each week to tackle company-related projects that interest them personally but aren't part of their core assignments.

More than any enterprise I know of, Google has built a working environment that can only be described as Druckerian—early Druckerian, to be precise.

Beginning with some of his first major writings in the 1940s, Peter Drucker wanted "work to reflect social values like opportunity, community, solidarity, and individual fulfillment, not just business values like cost and efficiency," explained the late management philosopher's biographer, Jack Beatty.

Of course, plenty of companies (as well as other types of organizations) espouse these tenets, and many observe them to varying degrees.

The difference is that Google applies them to the fullest, and not simply through its much-vaunted list of perks, which includes—in addition to free gourmet food and the encouragement to dream—on-site haircuts and oil changes (which aren't gratis); medical checkups; subsidized exercise classes; film series and lectures; gatherings for all sorts of hobbyists; shuttle-bus service throughout the Bay Area; parties and family events; weekly TGIF "town halls" and schmooze-fests where top executives Larry Page, Sergey Brin, and Eric Schmidt are regularly present; and hefty cash rewards for referring someone to work for the company or when buying a hybrid car.

A Self-Governing Village

Indeed, more than any one of these things, it's the overall atmosphere that the Internet company has cultivated—Google's gestalt—that puts it in step with Drucker's early belief that "the corporation is not only an economic tool but a social institution."

More specifically, his industrial-age vision called for the establishment of a "plant community" in which line workers would govern many of their own affairs and, in doing so, reap rewards that went well beyond their paychecks. Drucker, in his 1949 book, *The New Society*, wrote of workers' demand "for good and close group relationships with their fellow workers, for good relations with their supervisors, for advancement, and above all, for recognition as human beings, for social and prestige satisfactions, for status and functions."

At Google, there is no "plant" per se. But employees use language strikingly similar to Drucker's when describing their high-tech home. "It's like a village," says Dan Ratner, a mechanical engineer who joined the company about two years ago.

The lunches and dinners served at Café Pintxo, a tapas joint, the pan-Asian Pacific Café, and any of the other eateries around Googleplex (as headquarters is known) are supposed to be pretty terrific. But what most whets Ratner's appetite is the camaraderie and brainstorming that occur between bites.

It is not uncommon, he says, for a mealtime conversation to develop into a serious collaboration, often involving fellow employees he may never have met before. Once that happens, Ratner is likely to be off and running, using his 20 percent time to zip to Home Depot (where he can charge Google, without managerial approval, for basic supplies), build a prototype of his idea with some of his colleagues, and begin measuring its effectiveness.

A Dividend-Yielding Culture

The best innovations find their way in front of a supervisor and, if they make the cut, can ultimately win formal project status and funding. The ones that aren't so hot fade away—usually very quickly. "It's a real competitive place," Ratner says. "It's not all touchy-feely."

Google won't disclose what it spends on its myriad employee benefits, and a spokeswoman says that, in spite of the company's computational prowess, it can't quantify their effect on productivity. Clearly, however, the culture yields dividends. Among the projects that have emerged from 20 percent time are Gmail, Google News, and the Sky feature on Google Earth.

For Ratner, though, even the ideas that flame out have a tremendous value. The mere act of pursuing them, he says, speaks to "the entrepreneur, the artist" that tends to reside in many of Google's 15,000-plus employees. It fulfills the "need in every human to create," he adds.

What If the Going Gets Tough?

It must be noted that all of these offerings are relatively easy to provide when almost everything seems to be going without a glitch and the financial picture is so bright. Should Google's swagger give way to a big enough stumble—as has happened with countless other firms that once seemed invincible—its commitment in all these areas will surely be tested.

Over time, Drucker himself gave up on the notion of a "plant community," convinced, sadly, that most companies were consumed with the bottom line and little else. It also became more difficult to promote the corporate-community paradigm with job security in the U.S. and elsewhere growing ever more elusive. By the late 1980s, he had begun to look toward the nonprofit sector as the one that "gives people a sense of community, gives purpose, gives direction."

Perhaps he abandoned the model of workplace-as-social-institution too soon. Then again, who could have guessed that the world's most forward-thinking company in 2007 would have so boldly adopted a concept that Drucker framed more than half a century ago?

October 25, 2007

Has Toyota Lost Its Way?

The Toyota Way might just as well be called the Drucker Way. As much as any company anywhere, Toyota Motor eagerly embraced many of the key principles that Peter Drucker first laid out in the 1940s and '50s: that corporations must move away from a "command and control" structure and cultivate a true spirit of teamwork at all levels; that line workers must adopt a managerial outlook and take responsibility for the quality of what they produce; that the enterprise must be steered by a clear set of objectives while giving each employee the autonomy to decide how to reach those results.

Though widely accepted now, plenty of U.S. companies at the time dismissed these notions as dangerously radical, if not downright loony. By contrast, they were "almost immediately translated into Japanese, eagerly read and applied," Drucker wrote decades later.

Indeed, "Drucker deeply influenced Japanese management thinking," Pascal Dennis noted in his 2002 book, *Lean Production Simplified*. "Companies like Toyota," he added, organized their manufacturing operations by soaking in and then "refining Drucker's ideas."

So what might Drucker say now that Toyota finds itself hitting a particularly rough patch of road?

I believe that his advice would, in the end, be quite simple: Slow down, even just a tad, in the quest to be the world's largest automaker.

Quality Slips

In the last few months, Toyota has been beset by a variety of troubles, including departures from its North American unit by several top executives; slumping sales (though things picked up again in October); and condemnation from environmentalists, who've challenged the company's commitment to fighting global warming.

Most serious have been rising concerns over the reliability of Toyota's vehicles. In October, *Consumer Reports* said quality had slipped so badly, it would stop giving Toyota's new or redesigned models an automatic stamp of approval. A series of high-profile recalls in the last couple of years have also tarnished the Toyota Production System, long the envy of the world.

Toyota has downplayed many of its problems, contending that as it continues to expand and prosper, more and more people are quick to criticize it. "The nail that stands highest gets hammered," a company spokesman told one reporter recently, invoking an old Japanese proverb.

Without a doubt, there is some truth to that. But make no mistake: It's shoddiness, more than schadenfreude, that's really the issue here.

Growth Can Make You Vulnerable

Toyota is bent on becoming the top-selling car company in the world, and as it hits the gas pedal on growth, it's obviously finding it tough to maintain its usual standards for quality. The company shouldn't be surprised by this. Perhaps, though, this was the one lesson from Drucker that Toyota somehow missed.

"Growth at a high rate and for an extended period is . . . anything but healthy," Drucker declared in *Management: Tasks, Responsibilities, Practices*, his 1973 classic. "It makes a business—or any institution—exceedingly vulnerable. It makes it all but impossible to manage it properly. It creates stresses, weaknesses, and hidden defects which, at the first slight setback, become major crises."

In fairness, it's General Motors, even more than Toyota, that seems caught up in the game of who's the biggest. After Toyota took over as the world's leading seller of automobiles earlier this year, GM Chief Executive Rick Wagoner sounded like a kid who'd just lost his marbles at recess. "I like being No. 1," he said. "And I think our people take pride in that, so it's not something that we're going to sit back and let somebody else pass us by." (GM has since reclaimed the crown—at least for the moment.)

Yet Toyota hasn't been above a bit of grandstanding of its own. Several years ago, for instance, it announced plans to ramp up global production and seize market share under the slogan "We Can & We Will." Last August, Toyota President Katsuaki Watanabe predicted that the company would sell 10.4 million vehicles in 2009—smashing GM's industry record of 9.6 million sold, set in 1978.

Continuous Improvement

Nobody is accusing Toyota of being reckless. Watanabe has spoken repeatedly of the company's need to be extra-attentive to the dependability of its products as it keeps growing, and executives have imposed even tougher quality-control methods in light of its recent difficulties. Hubris, it's safe to say, won't destroy Toyota.

"Breakthrough innovation is only one aspect of" the company's culture, Jeffrey Liker concluded in his book *The Toyota Way*. "Possibly the most important aspect is Toyota's relentless application of the more 'mundane' process of continuous improvement"—*kaizen* in Japanese. The company has proven, Liker continued, that it's adept at "learning from its mistakes, determining the root cause of problems, providing effective countermeasures," and "empowering people to implement those measures."

For all these reasons, it's a darn good bet that Toyota will restore its reputation for quality in the next couple of years and also get where it's trying to go, distancing itself from GM to become the undisputed king of the auto industry.

But in the meantime, the few dents it has suffered of late serve as a useful reminder for all managers. As Drucker put it: "The idea that growth is by itself a goal is altogether a delusion. There is no virtue in a company's getting bigger. The right goal is to become better. Growth, to be sound, should be the result of doing the right things. By itself, growth is vanity and little else."

November 26, 2007

Wikia's People-Powered Engine

As I sat down to work on this column, I couldn't help but feel as if I should be lending my voice to the "Wikia Search stinks" chorus. After all, the Internet search engine, rolled out this month by Wikipedia cofounder Jimmy Wales, didn't seem to be doing much to enhance the standing of my organization, the Drucker Institute.

When I typed our name into the search field, I got reasonably close: The top result that popped up was the Web site for our affiliate, the Peter F. Drucker & Masatoshi Ito Graduate School of Management. But our own site was nowhere to be found.

After sifting through the first 100 returns—including off-the-mark links to an organization of jewelry appraisers, a group of Scrabble enthusiasts from Canada, violinist Eugene Drucker, and the Virginia Peninsula Chamber of Commerce—without seeing www.druckerinstitute.com, I gave up. (On Google, by contrast, we were in our usual spot: No. 1 on the list.) No wonder Wales has been upbraided across the blogosphere. "Wikia Search Is a Complete Letdown," howled the headline on TechCrunch .com. At SearchEngineLand.com, the review was just as blunt, characterizing Wikia's offering as "crappy."

Still, I can't help but think the man whose ideas my institute is advancing, Peter Drucker, would have loved what Wales is attempting: having people play more of a role, and computers less of one, when it comes to interpreting information and spreading knowledge.

Will User Input Improve Search?

"The strength of the computer lies in its being a logic machine," Drucker wrote in *The Effective Executive*, first published in 1967. "It does . . . what it is programmed to do. This makes it fast and precise. It also makes it a total moron; for logic is essentially stupid. It is doing the simple and obvious. The human being, by contrast, is not logical; he is perceptual. This means that he is slow and sloppy. But he is also bright and has insight.

The human being can adapt; that is, he can infer from scanty information or from no information at all what the total picture might be like. He can remember a great many things nobody has programmed."

Wales's vision is to improve the potency, accuracy, and ingenuity of his search tool over time largely through the input of users, as opposed to the algorithms that drive searches on Google, Yahoo, and Microsoft. There are several ways folks can participate in the process, including by rating search results on a five-star system (complete with a note about why a particular link received the score it did). They can also write "miniarticles" to discuss results in an open-ended forum.

Wales has acknowledged this won't happen overnight. It's going to take time "for the humans to come in and start building" these functions, he told TechCrunch. Many are skeptical—and rightly so—that Wales's effort will ever snatch meaningful market share from Google, home to nearly 60 percent of all Internet searches in the U.S., according to Nielsen/Net Ratings. (Its closest rival, Yahoo, accounts for about 18 percent.) Nevertheless, Wales's instincts about what is needed in the world of search (and, indeed, across many areas of the high-tech universe) are right on, at least from Drucker's perspective.

Birth of the Knowledge Worker

Long before most anyone else had begun to glimpse it, Drucker recognized we were in the midst of a historic transformation. He came to call the age we had entered the "postcapitalist society"—an era in which labor, land, and capital are less important and "the main producers of wealth have become information and knowledge." The denizens of this new world are, of course, "knowledge workers"—a term Drucker coined in 1959.

But Drucker wasn't always so enamored of the way knowledge was being cultivated. For one thing, he suggested information technology was, by and large, too focused on the "T"—that is, the collection, storage, transmission, and presentation of data—and not focused enough on the nature of the "I." As he put it, "What is the meaning of the information? What is the purpose?"

What can get at those questions, he wrote in 1999's *Management Challenges for the 21st Century*, is not "more data, more technology, more speed." What's required is to step back and figure out what kind of information would best help tackle the task at hand—a determination in which living, breathing creatures have a clear advantage over cold calculations.

People Connect the Dots

Drucker also taught that those using information should assume active roles in shaping it. "Only individual knowledge workers . . . can convert data into information," he counseled. "And only individual knowledge workers . . . can decide how to organize their information so that it becomes their key to effective action." To leave it to the technology wizards, in other words, is a big mistake.

Finally, humans may well be better equipped than computers to do something else Drucker deemed crucial: connect the dots between highly specialized disciplines or, as he described it, "to mobilize the multiple knowledges that we possess."

Whether Wikia can do all this in a search context remains to be seen. Certainly it has a long way to go. And yet by early this week, my institute's Web site had magically soared to the second slot on the list, evidently propelled there by the thing Drucker believed in most: people power.

January 17, 2008

What Can Microsoft Offer Yahoo?

You'd be hard-pressed to find many things to which Peter Drucker was as openly hostile as the hostile takeover. In his book *The New Realities*, he went so far as to call the gobbling up of companies in this fashion "the most serious assault on management in its history—a far more serious assault than any mounted by Marxists."

Mind you, he made these comments in 1989, when all too many real-life Gordon Gekkos were commanding center stage. What rankled Drucker was the tendency of these corporate raiders to quickly dismantle the enterprises they'd just gotten their hands on, as if they were stolen cars, "sacrificing long-range, wealth-producing capacity to short-term gains."

Of course, the unsolicited takeover proposal dominating the news these days—Microsoft's $44.6 billion bid for Yahoo—doesn't fit this mold. Microsoft hopes to strengthen Yahoo's core assets, not strip them.

Still, that doesn't mean Drucker wouldn't have viewed Microsoft's attempt as fundamentally flawed. The reason: I suspect he would have questioned whether the software giant actually brings enough to the party.

What may happen next is unclear. Yahoo, having spurned Microsoft's overture, is reportedly in talks with News Corp. about some alternative alliance. Microsoft, meanwhile, seems to have two choices: raise its offer in the hopes that Yahoo will yield, or launch a proxy fight and take its case straight to shareholders.

Cash: Not Enough

But what is its case, exactly? Contrary to the way many people tend to look at such propositions, Drucker believed it's incumbent on the purchaser—not the entity being purchased—to add value. In his Jan. 31 letter to the Yahoo board, Microsoft Chief Executive Steve Ballmer focused primarily on one advantage that a combination of the two companies' Internet operations would create: "scale." In fact, he used the word no fewer than five times in his missive.

There's sound logic behind that. No one doubts it's going to take considerable heft at this stage to even try to challenge Google, the undisputed industry leader. As Ballmer noted, this means possessing a sufficiently large online advertising platform, as well as having the "expanded R&D capacity" to drive innovation.

The issue is: What specific pluses, besides sheer size, would result from a Microsoft-Yahoo marriage? By definition, the union of any two big companies will help achieve scale; that's simply a function of arithmetic. What Drucker suggested is if a takeover is going to work in the long run, it needs to be predicated on much more than that.

"An acquisition will succeed," he wrote in *The Frontiers of Management*, "only if the acquiring company thinks through what it can contribute to the business it is buying, not what the acquired company will contribute to the acquirer, no matter how attractive the expected 'synergy' may look.

"What the acquiring company contributes may vary," Drucker added. "It may be management, technology, or strength in distribution." The one thing it can't be, according to Drucker, is the one thing that Microsoft has lots of: dough. "Money alone," he said, "is never enough."

Two-Way Street

A collection of case studies, written by Drucker and updated by my Claremont Graduate University colleague Joe Maciariello, cites the 1998 merger of Citibank and Travelers—a transaction initiated by Sandy Weill, then chairman of Travelers—as an example of how to do this right. At the time, Citibank enjoyed a strong presence around the globe. Travelers, for its part, boasted a terrific portfolio of financial products and services.

"What Travelers saw itself as being able to contribute," Drucker and Maciariello explained, "was to greatly increase the volume of business the superb Citibank worldwide distribution system . . . could sell, and at little or no cost."

So what would Microsoft provide if it were ultimately able to snap up Yahoo? Some analysts say plenty. Imran Khan of JPMorgan Securities has pointed, for instance, to Microsoft's international reach. "If you look at Yahoo," he says, "it is very strong in the United States, but it's not very strong outside the U.S., whereas Microsoft has a . . . stronger position in the European market."

Notably, however, most observers have zeroed in on the benefits that Yahoo would deliver to Microsoft—not the other way around. Among them: a share of online advertising revenue that's more than double that of Microsoft's MSN; advances Yahoo has made in online advertising auction theory and data-mining; and, as Jeffrey Rayport of the consulting firm Marketspace has put it, "features with the kind of sex appeal Microsoft itself could never achieve."

No Simple Execution

Takeovers, even friendly ones, are rarely easy to execute. Top talent often flees, if it isn't fired first. Cultures can clash, resulting in an ugly Us vs. Them dynamic. "Sometimes," wrote Drucker, "it takes a whole generation before these invisible but impenetrable barriers come down."

If Microsoft does wind up swallowing Yahoo, it may well have to sort out many such problems. But first, there is a more basic question for the boards and shareholders of both companies to ask themselves: What does Microsoft really offer Yahoo beyond a bucketful of cash? If there's no good answer, count this as a deal Drucker would have discouraged.

February 14, 2008

Buffett's Plan
for Successful Succession

A couple of weeks ago, Berkshire Hathaway Chairman Warren Buffett officially put the kibosh on what many an investor must have regarded as the ultimate succession plan: "I've reluctantly discarded the notion of continuing to manage the portfolio after my death—abandoning my hope to give new meaning to the term 'thinking outside the box,'" Buffett, 77, wrote in his annual letter to shareholders.

Despite his tongue-in-cheek approach, Buffett touched on one of the most important issues an enterprise faces: figuring out who's the right person to one day take the reins.

A company's very "survival," Peter Drucker wrote in his 1946 book, *Concept of the Corporation*, depends on the ability "to develop independent leaders below the top who are capable of taking top command themselves, and to devise a system under which succession will be rational and by recognized merit rather than the result of a civil war within the institution and of force, fraud, or favoritism."

Drucker's thinking on many topics evolved over the course of his long career. This wasn't one of them. In *Management Challenges for the 21st Century*, published in 1999, he echoed what he had concluded more than 50 years earlier: "Succession has always been the ultimate test of any top management and the ultimate test of any institution."

Failed Succession Planning

What's amazing is how many organizations are, by this measure, outright failures. The Human Capital Institute, a professional association and research group, estimates fewer than 50 percent of North American companies with revenue of more than $500,000 "have any meaningful CEO succession planning in place."

Even some of the biggest corporations have been caught flat-footed. After Stan O'Neal was ousted as Merrill Lynch's chief executive last year, his predecessor, Daniel Tully, decried the fact that the investment bank was forced to look outside for a successor. Previously, "we spent days, months talking about succession planning," Tully said in an interview with a Bloomberg reporter. In what he called the "hit-by-the-bus scenario," names were continually collected in case "something happened to the chairman."

The philanthropic universe isn't any better. A 2006 survey by DRG, an executive recruitment firm that works exclusively with nonprofits, found that 58 percent of social-sector chief executives and their boards hadn't discussed succession—even though 40 percent of CEOs intended to leave their job within two years. Size mattered not. "Organizations, large and small, are equally challenged and equally unprepared for leadership changes," notes DRG's managing partner, David Hinsley Cheng.

How does this happen?

Some of it is the result of fear—specifically, a fear by certain leaders (or "misleaders," as Drucker labeled them) of having smart, self-assured colleagues around them. "An effective leader knows, of course, that there is a risk: Able people tend to be ambitious," Drucker wrote in 1992's *Managing for the Future*. "But he realizes that it is a much smaller risk than to be served by mediocrity. He also knows that the gravest predicament of a leader is for the organization to collapse as soon as he leaves or dies."

Grooming and Promoting

Indeed, there is powerful evidence that the best institutions constantly cultivate and elevate those within—and don't fall into the trap that says the only way to stimulate progress and change is to reach outside for new blood.

In their book *Built to Last*, Jim Collins and Jerry Porras reported that of 113 CEOs who had overseen corporations that were both outstanding and enduring—"visionary companies," in their words—only 3.5 percent came directly from somewhere else. This compared with 22 percent of the 140 CEOs at the other companies they examined, businesses that were deemed "good" but not great.

What's more, the most excellent organizations nurture their people up and down the line. Collins and Porras pointed to the financial publication *Dun's Review*, which once described Procter & Gamble's program for grooming managers as "so thoroughgoing and consistent that the company has talent stacked like cordwood—in every job and in every level."

When it comes to choosing who to promote, there is no shortage of advice out there. The management shelf is crowded with books on the subject. Drucker, though, kept things pretty simple. One hard-and-fast rule is that the leader heading for the exit should never select his or her own heir. He or she can be part of the process—but shouldn't control it. Otherwise, vanity is apt to override most every other consideration.

"We tend to pick people who remind us of ourselves when we were 20 years younger," Drucker said. "First, this is pure delusion. Second, you end up with carbon copies, and carbon copies are weak."

Strength in Numbers

As for Berkshire Hathaway, it's evidently inclined to find different folks to put on the three hats Buffett wears: chairman, chief executive, and chief investment officer. Buffett has indicated that his son, Howard Buffett, will become chairman—a way to help preserve the company's distinctive culture. Three internal contenders are being eyed for the CEO gig. (One of those widely thought to be in the running, David Sokol, just last week modified his duties at Berkshire's utility unit, leading some to speculate he may be the favorite.)

For the investment job, Buffett said he has identified four outside possibilities, and "all wish to work for Berkshire for reasons that go beyond compensation." Earlier, Buffett had suggested he might bring in a potential successor or two in this area—"a younger man or woman"—in something of an understudy role.

Meantime, Drucker would no doubt be delighted the billionaire is so clearly determined to meet his definition of true greatness: "the leader who himself has strength and leaves behind strength."

March 13, 2008

Exxon Mobil Needs a Longer View

John D. Rockefeller has been described in many different ways: as greedy and cutthroat; as munificent and caring; as "solitary, taciturn, remote, and ascetic," in the words of author Daniel Yergin. But as a manager, perhaps Rockefeller's most indispensable quality was this: He was uncompromisingly forward-looking.

It was Rockefeller, more than any single figure, who helped revolutionize the way people in the nineteenth century illuminated their homes, hastening the shift from costly whale oil to kerosene—a fuel that was, as he put it, "cheap and good."

Rockefeller's heirs recently evoked that history as they went public with their criticism of Exxon Mobil, charging the company with concentrating too much on short-term gains and not doing enough to cultivate cleaner, renewable forms of energy for the long haul. "They are fighting the last war, and they're not seeing they're facing a new war," griped Peter O'Neill, Rockefeller's great-great-grandson.

It's not that Exxon Mobil is doing nothing to pave a path to the future. Just last week—coincidently or not, given the Rockefellers' rebuke—the company announced it would spend more than $100 million to complete development and testing of a technology that could cut the expense of removing carbon dioxide during the production of natural gas.

A Change Will Do You Good

Still, the controversy highlights a challenge Peter Drucker believed every organization must face head-on if it is going to survive, much less thrive: deciding what to walk away from as it endeavors to move from yesterday to tomorrow.

"To call abandonment an 'opportunity' may come as a surprise," Drucker wrote in his 1964 book, *Managing for Results*. "Yet planned, purposeful abandonment of the old and of the unrewarding is a prerequisite to successful pursuit of the new and highly promising."

It might sound simple. But Drucker recognized that human beings are loath to let go of things. Egos are inevitably bound up in whatever direction an institution is already headed. In many cases, fiefdoms have been established—and they are sure to be guarded zealously. Unless something has been an outright failure, it can be extremely difficult to convince folks that any change is warranted, that any existing operation should be pared back or altogether axed.

Hanging on Too Long

This is all the more true in enterprises where there is relentless pressure to get bigger and bigger. "Most common is the plea, 'We must grow; we cannot afford to shrink,'" Drucker noted, quickly adding that this argument is pure sophistry. "It confuses fat with muscle," he wrote, "and busyness with economic accomplishment."

Exxon Mobil, for its part, raked in $10.9 billion in profit during the first three months of the year—its second-best quarterly showing ever—because of skyrocketing crude prices. Yet even in cases where a particular line of activity seems to be going swimmingly, one must not get seduced into hanging on too long.

"Yesterday's breadwinner should almost always be abandoned on a fairly fast schedule," Drucker asserted. "It still may produce net revenue. But it soon becomes a bar to the introduction and success of tomorrow's breadwinner. One should, therefore, abandon yesterday's breadwinner before one really wants to, let alone before one has to."

Drucker's chief issue was resources. Any institution, be it a corporation, a nonprofit, or a government agency, has a finite amount of capacity to do anything: If you place more money and brainpower in one area, another will automatically get less.

Also-Rans and New Opportunities

With this zero-sum situation in mind, Drucker cautioned managers to be especially careful when determining what to do with the "also-rans"—products, services, and assorted efforts that "are neither clear candidates for concentrated major work nor candidates for abandonment." In this middling category, he explained, will likely fall "today's breadwinners."

The trick, Drucker said, is to ensure the also-rans don't command resources that should be steered to initiatives with richer potential. "Only if resources are left over after the high-opportunity areas have received all the support they need, should the also-rans be considered," Drucker advised. In general, he added, the also-rans will "have to make do with what they have—or with less. They are put on 'milking status': as long as they yield results, they will be kept—and milked. They will, however, not be 'fed.' And as soon as these 'milk cows' go into rapid decline, they should be slaughtered."

Of course, figuring out what to abandon is only half the equation. Deciding what to zero in on next requires the same kind of discipline, the same level of focus. When seeking out a new opportunity, "don't diversify; don't splinter; don't try to do too many things at once," Drucker counseled in his 1985 classic, *Innovation and Entrepreneurship*.

But, at the same time, what's most crucial is that you do try. As Drucker declared: "Of course innovation is risky. But . . . defending yesterday—that is, not innovating—is far more risky than making tomorrow."

May 9, 2008

Drucker's Take on Making Mistakes

Lyndon Johnson occupied the White House when KeyCorp first began raising its dividend. The Beatles topped the pop charts. Martin Luther King led tens of thousands of civil rights marchers through Alabama.

For 43 straight years, the company's annual payout climbed, "a record we were extremely proud of," in the words of KeyCorp Chief Executive Henry Meyer. That is, until earlier this month. The Cleveland bank, slammed by the weak housing market and an adverse tax ruling, announced that it would halve its dividend to 75 cents in a bid to save $200 million a year. It also said it would seek to raise $1.5 billion in capital.

"We think hope is a bad management strategy," Meyer explained. "We're trying to admit where we made mistakes."

Mistakes are part of life; they're part of business. But far too many enterprises spend time hiding them and running from them, rather than owning up to them.

Capitalizing on Candor

Given that, KeyCorp deserves much credit. Whether the company can now capitalize on its candor will depend, in large measure, on how management deals with those responsible for its stumbles. The smartest organizations, according to Peter Drucker, are those that turn lapses into learning opportunities.

"Nobody learns except by making mistakes," Drucker wrote in his 1954 landmark book, *The Practice of Management.* "The better a man is, the more mistakes he will make—for the more new things he will try. I would never promote a man into a top-level job who has not made mistakes, and big ones at that. Otherwise, he is sure to be mediocre. Worse still, not having made mistakes, he will not have learned how to spot them early and how to correct them."

Drucker's tolerance for mistakes shouldn't be confused with him cottoning to incompetence. There are plenty of occasions, he believed, when employees should be let go. "Management owes this to the enterprise," Drucker said. "It owes it to the spirit of the management group, especially to those who perform well. It owes it to the man himself, for he is likely to be the major victim of his own inadequacy."

But he cautioned against overreaching: "That a man who consistently renders poor or mediocre performance should be removed from his job also does not mean that a company should ruthlessly fire people right and left." And he made clear that those in charge can't just turn around and blame those who work for them. "Whenever a man's failure can be traced to management's mistakes," Drucker declared, "he has to be kept on the payroll."

Batting Average

Among management's most common errors is putting a good person into the wrong job. After all, Drucker noted, "there is no such thing as an infallible judge of people, at least not on this side of the Pearly Gates." Whenever such a slipup is made, Drucker counseled, it's incumbent on the boss to say: "I have no business blaming that person, no business invoking the 'Peter Principle,' no business complaining. I have made a mistake."

In the end, Drucker defined success not as being right every time. Rather, he wrote in his 1973 classic, *Management: Tasks, Responsibilities, Practices*, performance must be evaluated on terms more akin to a batting average. (Slugging percentage might even be a more apt way to look at it: Sometimes you hit a single or a double, and occasionally a home run. But other times, you strike out. Maybe even with the bases loaded.)

In Drucker's view, not always getting a hit is not only acceptable; it's part of what it takes to be an organization of excellence. "A management which does not define performance as a batting average is a management that mistakes conformity for achievement, and absence of weaknesses for strengths," Drucker asserted.

Different Performances

A batting-average mentality, he added, allows for companies to accommodate different kinds of talent. "One man will consistently do well, rarely falling far below a respectable standard, but also rarely excel through brilliance or virtuosity," Drucker wrote. "Another man will perform only adequately under normal circumstances but will rise to the demands of a crisis or a major challenge and then perform like a true 'star.' Both are 'performers.' Both need to be recognized. But their performances will look quite different.

"The one man to distrust, however, is the one who never makes a mistake," Drucker continued, "never commits a blunder, never fails in what he tries to do. He is either a phony, or he stays with the safe, the tried, and the trivial."

Drucker not only penned these words; he lived them. By the 1950s, Drucker had concluded there was only one way to manage people correctly: by assuming that all of them will be responsible and self-directed as long as they find their work fulfilling. In 1960 a competing theory was articulated, which held that managers treat each and every employee as if they are inherently self-centered, lazy, and resistant to change.

But then along came psychologist Abraham Maslow, who in 1962 maintained that, either way, a single approach is silly. Drucker was quickly persuaded. "Maslow's evidence is overwhelming," he wrote, that "different people have to be managed differently."

The bottom line for Drucker was that he and others who'd shared his one-size-fits-all view of human motivation "were dead wrong." If only more people had the courage to say that—and then learn from it—a lot more things would go right.

June 19, 2008

What Drucker Would Say
About Mervyns

Mervyns portrayed itself as a victim of the crummy economy and a miserable retail environment last week as it filed for Chapter 11 bankruptcy protection. But in truth, a key part of the department store chain went bankrupt long ago. It's what Peter Drucker called the "theory of the business."

Every organization rests upon a set of such premises—fundamental notions about customers and competitors, about technology, about a company's own strengths and weaknesses. When an enterprise fails, Drucker explained, it is often because "the assumptions on which the organization has been built and is being run no longer fit reality."

As obvious as this may seem, it can be surprisingly hard to see. Many times, managers become preoccupied with how they are doing things. But what's equally important—maybe even more important—is what they are doing in the first place. As Drucker noted: "There is surely nothing quite so useless as doing with great efficiency what should not be done at all."

In a 1994 *Harvard Business Review* article, Drucker asserted that when a valid theory of the business is "clear, consistent, and focused," it's bound to be "extraordinarily powerful."

Naming the Mission

It all starts with mission. Drucker cited, for example, Sears Roebuck, which "in the years during and following World War I defined its mission as being the informed buyer for the American family. A decade later, Marks and Spencer in Britain defined its mission as being the change agent in British society by becoming the first classless retailer."

Mervyns, launched in San Lorenzo, Calif., in 1949, once had its own compelling vision of what it should be: a store that would provide high-quality products at a good value, filling a niche between Sears and Montgomery Ward at the lower end of the market and fancier, white-glove merchants at the upper end.

Through the 1950s and '60s, Mervyns prospered under this formula, even in the face of heavy competition from J.C. Penney and others. In 1971, the company went public, and it soon boasted dozens of stores bringing in hundreds of millions of dollars in revenue. Seven years later Dayton Hudson (now Target) acquired Mervyns and pushed it into Arizona, Louisiana, New Mexico, Oklahoma, Oregon, and Washington. In 1983, Mervyns opened its 100th store. (It has 177 now.)

But all the while, its basic theory of the business stood still; in fact, Mervyns continues to tout itself as "the prototype for the midrange department store."

The trouble is, all around it, things changed. More and more players barged into the space that Mervyns had comfortably occupied—Kohl's, most prominently. Meanwhile, the whole idea of "midrange" had itself become blurry, as those considered lower-tier began carrying trendier goods and designer labels. "There is no middle anymore," says retail consultant George Whalin. "It doesn't exist."

Under such challenging conditions, what should Mervyns' theory of the business have become?

"That Emotional Connection"

There are no easy answers. But Tom Kelley, a branding expert with Concept Group USA who briefly worked at Mervyns, expressed little doubt when I posed the question to him. He believes that each store should have accentuated its "homespun feel," deeply integrating itself into the community where it operated. He would have recruited store managers from local colleges, encouraged them to be active in civic affairs, and had them serve as a highly visible and welcoming presence for shoppers. "It's all about building that emotional connection with your customer," Kelley says.

In a sense, this is a page from the past. Being community-minded was originally a big part of Mervyns' culture. In essence, it had been baked into its theory of the business from the get-go. But here, too, Mervyns faltered—so much so that it lost its distinctive identity both inside the organization and among consumers. "Think of Mervyns and what image comes to mind?" asked a 1997 newspaper piece on the company. "If you draw a blank, you're not alone."

Drucker pointed out that it's not uncommon for a company to slip in this way, to take its theory of the business for granted as time passes. Management grows "less and less conscious of it," Drucker wrote. "Then the organization becomes sloppy. It begins to cut corners. It begins to pursue what is expedient rather than what is right. It stops thinking. It stops questioning. It remembers the answers but has forgotten the questions."

It would be unfair to suggest that Mervyns has done nothing to try to remedy its sagging fortunes over the years. It has highlighted its California roots, featured $1 to $5 in-store shops, and fiddled with its mix of name-brand versus private-label goods. But none of this amounted to what the company needed most: a thorough overhaul of its theory of the business. And, as Drucker cautioned, "patching never works."

A Desultory Nature

In 2004, Target sold Mervyns to a consortium of investment firms. Since then, Mervyns has had four chief executives—another sign of its desultory nature when what is called for is decisive action.

The current CEO, a highly regarded Levi Strauss veteran named John Goodman, has spoken in recent months of taking a tack similar to the one Kelley favors: In an era of faceless corporate behemoths, he has indicated that he'd like to turn Mervyns into a real "neighborhood department store" by catering to Latino customers, making strategic hires and investments in staff training, and directing sourcing and buying accordingly.

My fear is that it's too little, too late—that Mervyns didn't recognize soon enough that when a theory of the business becomes obsolete, it is, as Drucker put it, "a degenerative and, indeed, life-threatening disease." And that requires surgery, not Band-Aids.

July 31, 2008

When Cutting Costs
Is Not the Answer

The layoff announcements are mounting by the day: 50,000 at Citigroup, 12,000 at AT&T, 6,000 at Sun Microsystems, 2,500 at DuPont, 1,200 at United Airlines, 850 at Viacom.

In all, major U.S. companies said in November that they were going to whack 181,671 jobs, the outplacement firm Challenger, Gray & Christmas reported this week. That was the most since January 2002 and brought the total number of reductions planned this year to more than 1 million. Earlier today, the Labor Department said nonfarm payrolls fell by a larger-than-expected 533,000, while the unemployment rate climbed to 6.7 percent, its highest point since October 1993.

Given the fragile state of the economy, it's not surprising that employers are more likely to hand their workers a pink slip than a turkey this Christmas. But perhaps bloodletting isn't the only answer. Certainly, it isn't the only one that Peter Drucker would prescribe.

Not that Drucker was blind to the need for keeping a lid on costs. Indeed, he taught that enterprises big and small should always be asking themselves not how to make a particular aspect of the business more efficient but whether it should exist at all. "The question should be: 'Would the roof cave in if we stopped doing this work altogether?'" Drucker explained. "And if the answer is 'probably not,' one eliminates the operation. It is always amazing how many of the things we do will never be missed."

What's important, Drucker said, is to make this a routine exercise—not something that happens only during downturns. "Businesses that actually succeed in cutting costs," he said, "don't wait until they have to cut costs."

Investing in Knowledge Workers

In the same way, Drucker believed in investing in productive assets as a regular, everyday function—and there was no doubt as to where he thought investment should be channeled in this day and age. "The most valuable assets of the twentieth-century company were its production equipment," he wrote. "The most valuable asset of a twenty-first-century institution . . . will be its knowledge workers."

One person who has acted on these words—with extraordinary results to show for it—is K.H. Moon, the former chief executive of Korean consumer-products maker Yuhan-Kimberly. (Full disclosure: Moon, who is now a member of the national parliament in Seoul, until recently served on the board of the Drucker Institute, which I run.)

It was during the late 1990s, amid the Asian financial contagion, that Moon looked around and was disgusted by what he saw. "At almost all companies," he recalls, "the management just followed the old wisdom—massive layoffs."

Yet Moon felt that simply to slash employment was irresponsible, and he began to persuade his colleagues that there was a better way to go—not just to survive but to grow and prosper. This "was not the time to lose jobs," he says, "but to build our capability, personally and companywide."

To get there, Moon took several bold steps. One was to accelerate a push to a new staffing system, moving from a three-crew, three-shift arrangement to a four-crew, two-shift model. By spreading out the work this way—Moon has likened it to "job sharing in Western countries"—the company figures it has been able to employ 25 percent more mill workers than it otherwise would have.

Lifelong Learning

Because of this setup, employees work fewer hours overall. But they're encouraged not to be idle. Yuhan-Kimberly pays for them to attend classes so they can improve their technical acumen as well as increase their general knowledge (through Chinese language instruction, for instance). It's all based on a philosophy of lifelong learning—what Yuhan-Kimberly Chairman D.J. Lee calls the company's "true source of competitiveness and sustainable growth."

"It comes down to what Peter Drucker wrote about again and again—to see people not just as cogs in the wheel," says Edward Gordon, author of *The 2010 Meltdown: Solving the Impending Jobs Crisis*, which commends Yuhan-Kimberly's "counterintuitive approach."

The upshot is that by providing a healthier work-life balance, by giving the rank and file the opportunity to enhance their skills continually, and by taking other steps to create a self-directed team culture, Yuhan-Kimberly has seen job satisfaction among its 1,700 employees soar. So has productivity (along with market share and revenue)—so much so that workers' wages have also risen substantially.

Moon, meanwhile, has helped set up the New Paradigm Center, a government-funded organization that is teaching other Korean companies how to be Yuhan-Kimberly–like.

This formula won't work for everyone; implementing it involves real costs and, thus, real risks. What's more, there's no avoiding the fact that layoffs are inevitable during a recession, no matter what is tried. Even Drucker, who so admired Japanese industry for its commitment to lifetime employment, recognized this ideal was bound to crack amid the unrelenting pressures of globalization.

But what Yuhan-Kimberly reminds us is that shedding thousands of positions doesn't necessarily have to be management's automatic response to a bleak economy. When things seem darkest, it's time to innovate, not just eliminate.

December 5, 2008

Ask "For What?" Before "Who?"

At Borders, you can buy a hardback version of the essay collection *Classic Drucker* for $24.95 or grab the paperback for 10 bucks less. Here's hoping that a few folks on the bookstore chain's board of directors had the good sense to pick up a copy and peruse Chapter 5 before selecting their new chief executive.

Had they done so, they would have gleaned a few insights into what may well be the most crucial call that any enterprise makes: hiring key employees.

Ask the Right Question

In "How to Make People Decisions," first printed in *Harvard Business Review* in 1985, Peter Drucker laid out a handful of guidelines for making a good hire. Among them: Look at three to five qualified candidates and make sure you perform adequate due diligence by checking out each with several former bosses and colleagues. "One executive's judgment alone is worthless," Drucker wrote. "Because all of us have first impressions, prejudices, likes and dislikes, we need to listen to what other people think."

But in many ways, the hardest principle to follow is Drucker's first: "Think through the assignment." Or, to put it another way, you can't answer "Who?" until you've first figured out, "For what?"

"When the task is to select a new regional sales manager," Drucker explained, "the responsible executive must first know what the heart of the assignment is: to recruit and train new salespeople because, say, the present sales force is nearing retirement age? Or is it to open up . . . new and growing markets? Or, since the bulk of sales still comes from products that are 25 years old, is it to establish a market presence for the company's new products? Each of these is a different assignment and requires a different kind of person."

Beware the Renaissance Man

Though most executives would surely agree with this logic, many violate it nonetheless. In their book *Who*, Geoff Smart (who studied with Drucker) and Randy Street warn against falling into "one of the most common hiring traps": getting seduced by somebody who seems to be able to do almost everything exceptionally well, thus promising to be a star no matter the situation.

"There is a tendency to gravitate to the best all-around athlete; you know—tremendous skill set, résumé that is knock-your-socks-off," the authors quote Nicholas Chabraja, the chief executive officer of General Dynamics, as saying. Chabraja goes on to recall that he once hired someone like that—a man whose broad talents and creativity made him "a splendid business developer." But what the company really needed at that point was an executive with a knack for running operations who could shrink a bulging backlog.

The Right Person for the Right Job

"I made the mistake of putting in place a guy who went on to put more orders in the backlog," Chabraja says. "Operating margins actually went down. It took me a couple of years to address the mistake. The moral of the story was that I later got a guy whose skill set exactly matched the job at hand. He did gangbusters for us. . . . The other guy went on elsewhere to a splendid career where his role matched his skill set."

Drucker could have easily guessed this would happen. The best business leaders, he wrote in his 1967 classic, *The Effective Executive*, "never talk of a 'good man' but always about a man who is 'good' for some one task."

Borders, in announcing this week that it had tapped Ron Marshall to be its new CEO, seems to have this very idea in mind. The beleaguered retailer, weighed down by a heavy debt load and trying to stave off bankruptcy, said it must move "more aggressively" to improve its cash flow. Marshall, who most recently served as the head of a private equity firm, has the kind of deep financial background that may well lend itself to the specific challenges Borders now faces. The CEO he replaces, George

Jones, came into the job with more of a reputation as an innovator than as a moneyman.

Not everyone views the who-vs.-what dynamic exactly the same. Jim Collins, in *Good to Great*, is adamant that building "a superior executive team" should be the first order of business for any company aspiring to be world-class. "Get the right people on the bus . . . before you figure out where to drive it," he advises.

But Collins also points out that you must get "the right people in the right seats"—a matchmaking exercise that's impossible without assessing, at least on some level, the specific work that needs to get done.

Effective Specialization

If all of this sounds as if we're saying companies need people who are specialists, Drucker wouldn't disagree. This isn't to suggest that employees shouldn't possess strong general traits: a good work ethic, high standards, and the like. But today's knowledge worker is "usually a specialist," Drucker wrote. "In fact, he can, as a rule, be effective only if he has learned to do one thing very well."

Given that, however, Drucker also believed it's essential for the specialist to understand how his or her job fits into the framework of the organization overall.

The goal of this "is not to breed generalists," Drucker said. "It is to enable the specialist to make himself and his specialty effective. This means that he must think through who is to use his output and what the user needs to know and to understand to be able to make productive the fragment the specialist produces."

All of which is to say: It's critical that every "who" grasp the "why," "when," and "how" behind his or her "what."

January 9, 2009

How Lack of Focus Hurt Detroit

Though it is sheer coincidence that Ford Motor, the only one of Detroit's Big Three automakers not seeking aid from Uncle Sam, builds a car called the Focus, it's hard not to appreciate the symbolism. Peter Drucker, for one, surely would have gotten a kick out it.

Drucker also wouldn't be surprised that Ford's rivals, Chrysler and General Motors, now find themselves struggling to survive. He had critical things to say about both of these companies over the years. As I've noted before, Drucker believed that since at least the 1940s, when he first studied GM, its top managers have resisted changing long-standing plans and policies—even as the world shifted around them. The upshot: a company that's had tremendous trouble moving forward, like a Chevy stuck in the mud.

President Barack Obama's auto task force zeroed in on that same weakness when it chided GM for being "far too slow" in doing what's needed to turn itself around. But there's another part of the task force's assessment that Drucker would have agreed with as well, for it highlights a principle that he held was essential to good management (yet gets violated time and again): Don't spread yourself too thin. "GM," the White House panel said, "has retained too many unprofitable nameplates that tarnish its brands, distract the focus of its management team, demand increasingly scarce marketing dollars, and are a lingering drag on consumer perception, market share, and margin."

To Drucker, one of the most important things that any organization can do is to adopt what he called a "rifle approach," eschewing "product clutter." "Economic results," he wrote, "require that managers concentrate their efforts on the smallest number of products, product lines, services, customers, markets, distribution channels, end users, and so on which will produce the largest amount of revenue."

Abandon Those Products

And yet as fundamental as this seems, Drucker added, many businesses foolishly "pride themselves on being willing and able to supply any specialty, to satisfy any demand for variety, even to stimulate such demands in the first place. And many businesses boast that they never, of their own free will, abandon a product." Thanks to this attitude, plenty of companies "end up with thousands of products in their product line—and all too frequently fewer than 20 really 'sell.'"

Assembling the workforce often gets handled with a similar lack of focus. "We build enormous staffs," Drucker asserted, "and yet do not concentrate enough effort in any one area to get very far." Then, during tough times, many companies pare expenses the same, ineffectual way: Rather than "pinpoint" cuts, as Drucker advocated, they resort to across-the-board reductions.

Drucker warned about this in a piece for *Harvard Business Review* in 1963. But it's just as prevalent a problem these days. John Sullivan, a management professor at San Francisco State University and the former chief talent officer at Agilent Technologies, figures that more than half of all companies cutting back in the current downturn are implementing across-the-board layoffs, pay freezes, and furloughs. The reason, he says: "They don't have the courage" to confront employees individually, and in many cases don't have the proper performance measures to even know where to target.

Drucker's basic message—"focus, focus, focus"—extended beyond the organization as a whole, right down to the individual. The best managers "do first things first and they do one thing at a time," he wrote more than 40 years ago in *The Effective Executive*. Such single-mindedness, he explained, is dictated by a simple reality: "Most of us find it hard enough to do well even one thing at a time, let alone two."

Concentration Is Key

"Mankind," Drucker continued, "is indeed capable of doing an amazingly wide diversity of things; humanity is a 'multipurpose tool.' But the way to apply productively mankind's greatest range is to bring to bear a large number of individual capabilities on one task. It is concentration in which all faculties are focused on one achievement."

Time magazine may have dubbed today's young people "the Multitasking Generation," with their seeming ability to do their homework, chat online, and listen to their iPods—all simultaneously—but Drucker (a man who wrote 39 books, taught, and consulted) assiduously avoided being sidetracked from the main activity at hand.

He even kept a stack of preprinted response cards at the ready, allowing him to politely, but quickly and firmly, decline all manner of potential diversions. "Mr. Peter F. Drucker appreciates your kind interest," the cards read, "but is unable to endorse or to review books, manuscripts, or proposals; to appear on radio or television; to join boards or panels of any kind," and so on and so forth.

In fact, the "secret" of people who "do so many things," according to Drucker, is that they knock them off one by one. "We rightly consider keeping many balls in the air a circus stunt," he wrote. "Yet even the juggler does it only for 10 minutes or so. If he were to try doing it longer, he would soon drop all the balls."

Or, perhaps, drive his company to the brink.

April 3, 2009

A Company Is More than Its CEO

It's hard to read recent issues of *The Atlantic* and *Harvard Business Review* and not see one as a counterpoise to the other: "Do CEOs Matter?" asks a headline in the former. "What Only the CEO Can Do" trumpets a headline in the latter.

At a glance, there appears little question as to which of the two essays Peter Drucker would have found most persuasive. The piece in May's *HBR* was authored by none other than A.G. Lafley, the chief executive of Procter & Gamble and a Drucker disciple. Indeed, many of Lafley's insights are based on what he learned from Drucker.

But it's doubtful that Drucker would have dismissed the June *Atlantic* article out of hand. Written by Harris Collingwood, it asserts that "the American obsession with who sits at the top of the organizational chart has gone much too far."

We should be skeptical, Collingwood suggests, that the CEO possesses "supreme importance" and are right to challenge "the indispensability" of any single executive—even one as lionized as Warren Buffett or Steve Jobs.

What we've adopted as a culture "is Carlyle's Great Man theory of history, painted on a corporate canvas," Collingwood writes—and it's often used to try to justify inordinately "big pay packages."

Too Much for One Person

On all of this, Drucker surely would have agreed. At the very heart of his philosophy, after all, lies the notion that the magic of management is to "make people capable of joint performance." Running any enterprise is, inherently, a team sport. No one person, no matter how capable, can handle it alone. For one thing, there's simply too much to do. "An unlimited supply of universal geniuses could not save the one-man chief executive concept unless they could also bid the sun stand still in the heavens," Drucker wrote in his 1954 classic, *The Practice of Management*.

Beyond that, nobody—not even the CEO—is good at everything. "Strong people," Drucker pointed out, "always have strong weaknesses, too." In the end, then, having "chief executive" embossed on your business card is "not about being less or more important," Drucker wrote in his book *Managing in the Next Society*, "but differently important."

Which takes us back to the pages of *The Atlantic* and, in turn, *HBR*. For his part, Collingwood cites several academic studies that have concluded "external forces influence corporate performance far more than CEOs do." Yet for Drucker (and, by extension, Lafley), this is precisely the point: The first task of the CEO is to size up those external forces and decide how best to react to them.

"The CEO is the link between the Inside, i.e., 'the organization,' and the Outside—society, the economy, technology, markets, customers, the media, public opinion," Drucker declared in 2004. "Inside, there are only costs. Results are only on the outside."

Recalling these very words, Lafley says they helped him determine "which external constituency mattered most" for P&G—namely, the customer. While this may seem obvious, Lafley notes, P&G had started "losing touch with consumers" before he took the helm in 2000. At headquarters in Cincinnati, "employees were glued to their computers" and "mired in internal meetings with other P&Gers. . . . Too often we were working on initiatives consumers did not want and incurring costs that consumers should not have to pay for."

Now, Lafley explains, "everywhere I go, I try to hammer home the simple message that the consumer is boss. We must win the consumer value equation every day at two critical moments of truth: first, when the consumer chooses a P&G product over all the others in the store; and second, when she or a family member uses the product and it delivers a delightful and memorable experience—or not."

Information from "Outside"

To help maximize the chance for success, says Lafley, "almost every trip I take includes in-home or in-store consumer visits. Virtually every P&G office and innovation center has consumers working inside with employees. Our employees spend days living with lower-income consumers and working in neighborhood stores." Such activities capture beautifully what Drucker described as the second specific task of the CEO: "to think through what information regarding the Outside is meaningful and needed for the organization, and then to work on getting it in usable form."

Many businesses mistakenly view this exercise in parochial terms. "Toy makers tend to define the Outside as their toy-maker competitors," Drucker wrote. "But the most meaningful competitors for the toy maker are not other toy makers but other claimants on potential customers' disposable dollars. . . . Customer research, in other words, may be more important than market research."

It is only after the CEO has adequately assessed the Outside, according to Drucker, that he or she is poised to tackle the other aspects of the job: answering the fundamental questions, "What is our business? What should it be? What should it not be?"; judging which results are most relevant for the institution; deciding between "short-term yields and deferred expectations"; picking priorities—and resisting the incessant pressure "to do a little bit of everything"; and placing the right people in key positions.

So, go ahead and read Lafley's article to understand what being a CEO is all about. But just in case you find yourself intoxicated by the title, keep *The Atlantic* handy, too. It'll sober you right back up.

May 29, 2009

GM: Lessons from
the Alfred Sloan Era

L ast week's historic bankruptcy filing by General Motors has pundits pointing to places where the fallen car giant can learn important lessons as it seeks to revive its fortunes—rival Toyota, for example, or AT&T, which newly named GM Chairman Edward Whitacre helped turn into the world's largest telecommunications company.

But here's another, less obvious model of managerial success to consider: General Motors.

It was the GM of 60 years ago, after all, that helped define the discipline of management, having served as the subject of Peter Drucker's landmark book *Concept of the Corporation*. "When this book was being written . . . the corporation had barely been discovered and was totally unexplored—resembling somewhat the Africa of the medieval mapmaker, a big white space across which was written: 'Here elephants roam,'" Drucker remarked some four decades after the book's publication in 1946. "Books on the corporation itself and its management could have been counted on the fingers of one hand."

As noted previously in this space, *Concept of the Corporation*—and GM's head-in-the-sand reaction to its mild criticisms—foreshadowed an insularity that would ultimately prove crippling to the automaker.

Yet it's also worth recalling that Drucker found many, many things to admire about GM—and especially its chairman, Alfred Sloan. In an introduction to Sloan's autobiography, *My Years with General Motors*, Drucker credited the no-nonsense executive with being "the first to work out systematic organization in a big company, planning and strategy, measurements, the principle of decentralization," and more. Sloan's role "as the designer and architect of management," Drucker added, "surely was a foundation for America's economic leadership in the 40 years following World War II."

Defining the Professional Manager

Indeed, as Drucker saw it, Sloan was the pioneer who transformed management into a real profession, establishing the standard that the professional manager is duty-bound to put the interests of the enterprise ahead of his own. Sloan, Drucker wrote, also made clear that "the job of a professional manager is not to like people. It is not to change people. It is to put their strengths to work. And whether one approves of people or the way they do their work, their performance is the only thing that counts." Sloan's definition of performance, Drucker was quick to explain, meant much "more than the bottom line. It is also setting an example. And this requires integrity."

But of all the pointers Drucker picked up from observing Sloan, there is one in particular that today's GM might want to pay close attention to: reaching difficult decisions (Hummer or hybrid?) demands healthy dissent.

David Garvin, a professor at Harvard Business School, says one of GM's fundamental problems over the years—an inability to make the right strategic calls—has been caused, at least in part, by a dearth of open debate among top managers. Rather than frankly and candidly working through various options, executives would often line up needed votes before meetings, like a group of Chicago ward heelers, and gather privately at "premeetings" to eliminate any surprises at the regular session.

"All too many decisions were precooked," says Garvin, who wrote a 2004 case study on GM's process for determining policy. Garvin points out that Sloan's basic challenge was in some ways the opposite of that faced by his successors. He had to take a collection of highly independent, entrepreneurial car companies and coordinate their actions. As time has rolled on, GM has had the burden of figuring out how divisions scattered all over the world could tailor their lines to meet varying customer needs.

Test Opinions Against Facts

But whether you're talking about the Alfred Sloan era or the Ed Whitacre era, there are a couple of common denominators: First, the company must provide absolute clarity as to who is responsible for deciding what. This, says Garvin, got "fuzzier and fuzzier" at GM as the organization became "progressively more complex" and layered with bureaucracy.

Second, when the time comes for a major decision to be made, such as which products to pursue and which to abandon, all the alternatives must be vetted honestly.

"Gentlemen, I take it we are all in complete agreement on the decision here," Drucker quotes Sloan as saying. After everyone around the table nodded affirmatively, Sloan is said to have continued: "Then I propose we postpone further discussion of this matter until our next meeting to give ourselves time to develop disagreement and perhaps gain some understanding of what the decision is all about."

Sloan, Drucker wrote in 1967's *The Effective Executive*, "was anything but an 'intuitive' decision maker. He always emphasized the need to test opinions against facts and the need to make absolutely sure that one did not start out with the conclusion and then look for the facts that would support it. But he knew that the right decision demands adequate disagreement."

That said, perhaps we can all agree on this: The "New GM" would be wise to study up on the GM of old.

June 12, 2009

Manage Your Boss

The moment has come for workers everywhere to be put through the midyear microscope, as supervisors assess their employees' performances for the first six months of 2009 and gauge what they need to focus on in the future.

But this is also a useful time to remember one of Peter Drucker's most fundamental teachings: Your success depends not just on how well you do your job. It also depends, a great deal, on how well the person to whom you report does his or hers. And that means you must become adept not only at managing yourself and those who work for you but also at managing the boss.

"Few managers seem to realize how important it is to manage the boss or, worse, believe that it can be done at all," Drucker wrote. "They bellyache about the boss but do not even try to manage him (or her). Yet managing the boss is fairly simple—indeed, generally quite a bit simpler than managing subordinates."

That said, please don't take Drucker's insight as a license to suck up. He had no patience for brownnosers. "One does not make the strengths of the boss productive by toadying to him," Drucker declared in 1967's *The Effective Executive*. "One does it by starting out with what is right and presenting it in a form which is accessible to the superior."

Take a Letter

Among the best forms of communication, Drucker advised in his 1954 landmark, *The Practice of Management*, is a twice-yearly letter written to one's supervisor. The goal, Drucker explained, is for the employee to spell out not only his own goals but also what he sees as the boss's objectives. After that, the employee enumerates the "things he must do himself to attain these goals—and the things within his own unit he considers the major obstacles. He lists the things his superior and the company do that help him and the things that hamper him.

"Finally," Drucker continued, "he outlines what he proposes to do during the next year to reach his goals. If his superior accepts this statement, the 'manager's letter' becomes the charter" under which one carries out his duties—and, done right, it leaves little room for confusion or second-guessing. Said Drucker: "This device, like no other I have seen, brings out how easily the unconsidered and casual remarks of even the best 'boss' can confuse and misdirect."

The dialogue between superior and subordinate shouldn't stop there, however. Drucker also recommended that, at least once a year, every employee ask his or her boss (or bosses): "What do I do and what do my people do that helps you do your job? And what do we do that . . . makes life more difficult for you?"

Meanwhile, Drucker provided two other bits of counsel for managing upward. First, be mindful that nobody likes surprises—especially the boss. So keep him or her in the loop.

Second, never underestimate the person with the reserved parking space. "The boss may look illiterate; he may look stupid—and looks are not always deceptive," Drucker wrote. "But there is no risk at all in overrating a boss. The worst that can happen is for the boss to feel flattered." Yet if you underrate the boss, he may well "see through your little game and will bitterly resent it."

Candor and Trust

This doesn't mean that you should be cynical or insincere in the way you connect to those in the corner office. The key to managing people for whom you work, just as it is to managing people who work for you, is building relationships based on candor and trust—and recognizing, as part of that process, that everyone has his or her own strengths, weaknesses, and idiosyncrasies.

"Bosses are not a title on the organization chart or a 'function,'" Drucker remarked. "They are individuals and are entitled to do their work in the way they do it. And it is incumbent on the people who work with them to observe them, to find out how they work, and to adapt themselves to the way the bosses are effective."

If your boss is a reader, for example, give him reports in writing. If he's a listener, approach him that way instead.

Though Drucker began writing about managing the boss some 50 years ago, it is a subject that has particular resonance today. The more knowledge-driven that organizations become, Drucker noted, the greater the likelihood that a supervisor hasn't actually performed many of the specialized tasks for which his or her employees have been hired.

Like an Orchestra Conductor

The interplay that develops, therefore, "is far more like that between the conductor of an orchestra and the instrumentalist than it is like the traditional superior/subordinate relationship," Drucker wrote in his 1999 book, *Management Challenges for the 21st Century.* "The superior in an organization employing knowledge workers cannot, as a rule, do the work of the supposed subordinate any more than the conductor of an orchestra can play the tuba."

In turn, those down the ladder may hold more power than they realize. "Just as an orchestra can sabotage even the ablest conductor," said Drucker, "a knowledge organization can easily sabotage even the ablest, let alone the most autocratic, superior."

Be careful, though, before you do. Figuring out how to manage— rather than damage—the boss is very likely in your self-interest. After all, as Drucker pointed out, one of the surest ways to get ahead is "to work for a boss who is going places."

July 10, 2009

Innovation Isn't Just for Start-Ups

W e can all picture the scene: A couple of guys toiling away in a cluttered garage, perfecting the next innovation that will shake an entire industry. Meanwhile, the big corporate players in the market stand oblivious—fat, dumb, happy, and too bogged down by bureaucracy and conservatism to be innovative themselves.

It's a great image—one that has long persisted. There's just one problem with it: It's false. "The all but universal belief that large businesses do not and cannot innovate is not even a half-truth," Peter Drucker wrote in his 1985 classic, *Innovation and Entrepreneurship.*

Yet what is true, Drucker added, is that "it takes special effort for the existing business" to get beyond the temptation "to feed yesterday and to starve tomorrow."

I was reminded recently of the wisdom in Drucker's words when I had a chance to chat with Mike Shapiro, engineering director and chief technology officer for Sun Microsystem's Open Storage operation. As much as any story I've heard, Shapiro's demonstrates that, as Drucker put it, "innovation can be achieved by any business"—even the largest. But what Shapiro and his colleagues have accomplished also serves as a textbook example of Drucker's other insight: A major company must follow specific practices if it's to convert breakthrough ideas into real results.

Leaping Forward

Shapiro, his partner, Bryan Cantrill, and their small team are the brains behind a family of data-storage systems—the 7000 line—that Sun introduced late last year. It features oodles of capacity, a "killer app" that uses real-time graphics so that customers can observe and understand what their storage system is doing, and a pricing model that appears to blow away the competition. I'm more of a Luddite than a techie myself, but I can tell you that reviews in the trade press have been very strong, praising the products' speed, simplicity, and low cost.

So how can a corporation pull off something like this? First, it must focus "managerial vision on opportunity," Drucker wrote. This sounds simple, he noted, but most companies spend the bulk of their time concentrating on problems instead. And you can't exactly hit a bull's-eye if you never bother to look at the target.

At Sun, Shapiro and Cantrill made a conscious decision to hunt for opportunity. Highly accomplished engineers and close friends since their days together at Brown University, the two spent a decade working on Sun's Solaris operating system. A few years ago, they became intent on pushing Sun into an area where it hasn't tread much traditionally: making special-purpose appliances. This is opposed to general-purpose computer servers, whose underlying technology other companies have been able to exploit at times and turn into moneymaking products, leaving Sun with relatively little to show for all its high-tech prowess. (It is this vulnerability that helped lead Sun into the arms of Oracle, which is now waiting to complete its $7.4 billion acquisition of the company.)

Shapiro and Cantrill eventually settled on data storage as a particularly rich field to explore. But the duo didn't just lock themselves in a laboratory, examine the current state of storage technology, and dream up ways to improve upon it. Instead, they spent a lot of time acting as market researchers, hitting the road and talking with potential customers about what they were really looking for—a crucial step, according to Drucker.

"Because innovation is both conceptual and perceptual, would-be innovators must . . . go out and look, ask, and listen," Drucker wrote. "Successful innovators use both the left and right sides of their brains. They work out analytically what the innovation has to be. . . . Then they go out and look at potential users to study their expectations, their values, and their needs."

The Right Space

What Shapiro and Cantrill realized from this exercise was that they had to devise a genuinely "disruptive product"—not just a souped-up version of what was available. Because of the hassle and expense, customers weren't going to scrap their existing data-storage solutions unless Sun came up with something far superior. "We had to cost half as much and be twice as fast," Shapiro says.

The trouble was, Shapiro couldn't figure out how to create something like that within the confines of Sun. It wasn't for lack of talent. The concern, he says, was that "in large organizations, people's ways of solving problems are limited by the horizons that they see."

Shapiro also worried that his project, which by its nature needed to draw on resources from different parts of Sun, would give way to political infighting, with various vice presidents at the Santa Clara (Calif.)–based company vying for control.

Drucker certainly would have understood Shapiro's fears. "The entrepreneurial, the new, has to be organized separately from the old and existing," he asserted. "No matter what has been tried—and we have now been trying every conceivable mechanism for 30 or 40 years—existing units have been found to be capable mainly of extending, modifying, and adapting what already is in existence. The new belongs elsewhere."

In Sun's case, the elsewhere was downtown San Francisco, where Shapiro and Cantrill—with the full support of Sun's top brass—set up a separate organization inside an old office building. Dubbed Fishworks (the "fish" stands for fully integrated software and hardware), the venture was allowed to plug away largely under wraps.

Don't Reinvent Everything

At one point, Cantrill discovered a book called *Skunk Works*, written by the former chief of Lockheed's supersecret aircraft factory. Among the lessons it provided was that when Lockheed built the SR-71 spy plane, those in charge of the program didn't try to reinvent everything. They grabbed all the standard parts they could, ripping components out of old jets, so that they could direct their energy and attention to the SR-71's radar-absorbing skin and other groundbreaking advances. Shapiro and Cantrill adopted a similar strategy. "We decided we weren't going to rebuild the operating system," Shapiro explains. "That let us tease out the things that were truly innovative and disruptive."

Or, as Drucker counseled all innovators: "Don't diversify, don't splinter, don't try to do too many things at once."

He had another piece of advice, too: "A successful innovation aims at leadership" in a given market. If it doesn't boldly seek such a position, "it is unlikely to be innovative enough, and therefore unlikely to be capable of establishing itself."

With hundreds of customers out of the gate, the Sun Storage 7000 Series has definitely established itself—and Fishworks, which Shapiro continues to run, could well prove one of the hidden gems of the Oracle acquisition. In the meantime, the new product line stands as powerful proof of what Drucker preached: When it comes to innovation, it's smarts, not size, that matter most.

July 24, 2009

An Enthusiastic Thumbs Up
for Netflix

S ave for enjoying the occasional Charlie Chaplin or Buster Keaton send-up in his younger days, Peter Drucker was never much of a movie fan. Yet he certainly would have appreciated Netflix's efforts to upgrade its film recommendation system for its customers.

Netflix announced last week that it was awarding an international team of researchers and computer whizzes a $1 million prize for improving by 10.06 percent the online movie rental company's ability to predict what films its users will enjoy based on how they've rated other titles.

The winners, who bested tens of thousands of other teams from more than 180 countries, took nearly 36 months to reach the required 10 percent threshold as they labored to make technical advances in the field of taste prediction. By prompting scientists to wrestle with a huge data set of 100 million movie ratings, Netflix may well have spurred advances in large-scale modeling that will have widespread impact.

Achieving Concrete Results

But it was three underlying management principles, which Netflix embraced by setting up the contest in the first place, that would have earned an enthusiastic thumbs up from Drucker.

The first is that, by its very nature, a competition like this is all about achieving concrete results, not merely generating well-intentioned activity. And in the end, that's the most important thing for any organization to do. "Supplying knowledge to find out how existing knowledge can best be applied to produce results is, in effect, what we mean by management," Drucker asserted.

The second principle highlighted by the Netflix prize is that to be successful, companies must constantly strive to gain deeper insight into their customers' wants and desires. Nearly every business says that it does this, of course. But relatively few approach it with the discipline required—one reason that many corporations lose half their customers within five years.

"What the people in the business think they know about customer and market is more likely to be wrong than right," Drucker wrote in his book *Managing for Results*. "Only by asking the customer, by watching him, by trying to understand his behavior can one find out who he is, what he does, how he buys, how he uses what he buys, what he expects, what he values, and so on."

Going Outside for Information

Drucker worried that computers weren't terribly good for this job. The information they spit out "tends to focus too much on inside information," he explained, "not the outside sources and customers that count." While Netflix, Amazon, Google, and others have made great strides over the last decade in getting inside consumers' heads, most brick-and-mortar companies must still figure out how to use their IT networks for a similar purpose.

For whether your business is online or not, Drucker's maxim holds true: Outside "is where the results are. Inside an organization, there are only cost centers." Which brings us to the third principle showcased by Netflix: a bold willingness to open up in general to the outside.

This sounds much easier than it is. After all, "it is the inside of the organization that is most visible to the executive," Drucker noted. "It is the inside that has immediacy for him. Its relations and contacts, its problems and challenges, its crosscurrents and gossip reach him and touch him at every point. Unless he makes special efforts to gain direct access to outside reality, he will become increasingly inside-focused."

Gaining Traction

Still, more and more, some of the best-performing companies are getting beyond what Drucker termed this "degenerative tendency." IBM, Hewlett-Packard, Procter & Gamble, and others are engaging in collaborative research and open innovation. Intuit is devising ways, as cofounder Scott Cook has described it, for consumers, employees, sales prospects, and even those without any ties to the company to "volunteer their time, energy, and expertise to make life better for our customers." One example: a "Q&A community" that's embedded in Intuit's TurboTax software product, which provides users with a forum to learn from and share information with one another.

Meanwhile, the prize model is also gaining traction across the corporate arena as well as in the social sector. The X Prize Foundation, for instance, is promising eight-figure bounties to those able to make huge leaps in private space exploration, genomics, and alternative-energy vehicles. And sites such as InnoCentive allow companies to post challenges in product development or applied science, and then have outsiders vie for cash or other goodies as they attempt to solve them. Netflix, for its part, is already dangling another monetary prize for those who can create an algorithm that uses demographic and rental history information to predict the taste of users who haven't rated any movies.

But what every manager should keep in mind is that you don't need to stage a contest to mirror Netflix's commitment to attaining results, its attentiveness to the customer, and its eagerness to reach beyond its own walls to find and cultivate the best thinking from anywhere.

By doing these things every single day, your business will be the real winner.

October 2, 2009

Getting Toyota Out of Reverse

Shoichiro Toyoda, the honorary chairman of Toyota Motor, once recounted a conversation between two Japanese educators—Atsuo Ueda, an expert in the management practices of Peter Drucker, and Masatomo Tanaka, who was responsible for teaching about the automaker's vaunted production system.

"Toyota," Ueda observed, "operates exactly the way Drucker-*san* said a company ought to operate."

Tanaka replied: "Yes, when we have trouble explaining what we're doing, we can usually find a good explanation in one of his books."

Never, of course, has there been a more crucial time for Toyota to go back to the books. The company recently recalled 3.8 million cars and trucks, as regulators investigate hundreds of complaints that its vehicles are prone to accelerating without warning. At the same time, Toyota's finances have lurched into reverse: In May, the company reported a $4.3 billion deficit for the fiscal year—its first net loss since 1950. And with Toyota's luster fading, consumers appear to be turning their attention elsewhere.

A few weeks ago, a San Diego consulting firm called Strategic Vision released its annual Total Value Index, based on feedback about prices, expected fuel economy, innovation, and other factors from 48,000 car buyers who'd purchased 2009 models. For the first time since the index was launched in 1995, Toyota did not have a single winner in any of the 23 categories, which range from small cars to heavy-duty pickups. Instead, Ford, Volkswagen, and Honda dominated the list.

Turnaround in the Works

Toyota's struggles aren't new. Two years ago this column took note of the company's mounting quality problems and suggested that executives would be wise to slow down in their headlong rush to become the world's largest carmaker.

But what's called for now is not more piling on. Some seem to delight in knocking Toyota almost as much as they do in tearing down Tiger Woods. (One blogger has posted on the Web a song called *My Toyota*, sung to the tune of the old hit by The Knack, *My Sharona*: Are you gonna stop?/Speeding up/Such a scary ride, always speeding up.)

Rather, what's instructive is to focus on how Toyota President Akio Toyoda, Shoichiro's son, and his team are trying to engineer a turn-around. Not surprisingly, one can see some Drucker-like thinking in their approach.

Last October, Akio addressed the media in Tokyo. What captured most of the attention were his remarks that Toyota stood on the brink of "irrelevance or death" and was "grasping for salvation"—a public display of contrition extraordinary even by Japanese standards.

Waning Passion

But what Drucker would have zeroed in on, I think, was Toyoda's less hyperbolic comment that consumers have been demonstrating a decided lack of enthusiasm toward the company's products, even in its home market. "They say that young people are moving away from cars," Toyoda said. "But surely it is us—the automakers—who have abandoned our passion for cars."

To combat this, Toyoda—a self-described "car nut" who is qualified to race professionally—has been pushing his company to offer more autos that are "fun and exciting to drive." This might sound like pure fluff. But for Toyota, which has long made quality and reliability its only real hallmarks, it amounts to nothing less than a shift in what Drucker termed "the theory of the business."

"Every business, in fact every organization, operates on such a theory—that is, on a set of assumptions regarding the outside (customers, markets, distributive channels, competition) and a set of assumptions regarding the inside (core competencies, technology, products, processes)," Drucker wrote. "These assumptions are usually taken for holy writ by the company and its executives. It is on them that they base their decisions, their actions, their behavior. The longer such a business theory works, the more it pervades the organization.

A New Business Theory

"But, as an old proverb has it: 'Whom the gods want to destroy they send 40 years of success,'" Drucker added. "For a business theory is not a law of nature. Eventually it becomes inappropriate to the realities of the market and technology. Then long-successful companies—especially big ones—begin to deteriorate. They lose their bearings. And the only thing that can effect the needed turnaround is rethinking and reformulating the company's business theory and repositioning the business on a new set of assumptions."

This repositioning, Drucker advised, always starts with a few basic questions: Who are the company's customers and noncustomers, and what do they value? What are other players in the market doing and not doing? What assumptions are they making?

In the case of Toyota, the Total Value Index provides some answers, and it suggests the company is on the right track with its emphasis on "fun and exciting." The auto market, according to Strategic Vision, is undergoing "a revolution in buyer perceptions," with more and more manufacturers having greatly improved the quality of their cars over the years—inspired in part by Toyota's traditional excellence in this area. And that means Toyota is going to have to differentiate itself in other ways.

More Dazzle?

First and foremost, Toyota must overcome its production-line troubles. If it doesn't restore its own reputation for consistently high quality, nothing else will matter. But beyond that, it has to give customers more: a bit of dazzle along with the durability and dependability.

"Professor Drucker was long a believer . . . in always improving," Shoichiro Toyoda explained. "Asked which of his books was the best, he would reply, 'The next one.'" Similarly, he said, Toyota "is always better today than yesterday and better still tomorrow."

I'm not so sure about today. But if the company can manage to adjust its theory of the business, it may well be right about tomorrow.

December 18, 2009

A Lesson in Performance Metrics

In calling last week for wholesale changes to the way public school teachers are evaluated, American Federation of Teachers President Randi Weingarten noted that her union had developed its plan in conjunction with some of the nation's leading authorities in the field, including Harvard researchers Susan Moore Johnson and Thomas Kane. But it was hard not to feel in her bold remarks the spirit of another longtime educator: Peter Drucker.

For years, Drucker warned that, in a knowledge economy, there was no choice but to take the kinds of steps that Weingarten is now urging to measure the quality of classroom instruction and, where necessary, to remove bad teachers.

"Schools are . . . becoming much too important not to be held accountable—for thinking through what their results should be, as well as for their performance in attaining these results," Drucker wrote in his 1993 book, *Post-Capitalist Society*. "To be sure, different school systems will give different answers to these questions. But every school system and every school will soon be required to ask them, and to take them seriously."

Yet Drucker would have appreciated another truth reflected in Weingarten's National Press Club speech: the inherent complexity in devising a measurement framework that is fair and focused on the right things.

Indeed, one might broadly interpret Weingarten's push to make use of "good and meaningful data" as an imperative not just for our sick schools but also for any enterprise. The truth is, no matter what sector they're in, relatively few organizations define and measure results very well.

"A Tool of Control"

For starters, too many corporations, nonprofits, and government agencies fail to look at metrics as resources that employees should use to improve their performances. Instead, the boss mainly wields them to criticize and penalize. "As long as measurements are abused as a tool of control,"

Drucker asserted, "measuring will remain the weakest area" for most managers.

Even finding the right mix of measures is tricky. In his 1973 classic, *Management: Tasks, Responsibilities, Practices*, Drucker pointed out that many businesses use annual return on investment as a key determinant in judging success. He then went on to tell the story of a chemical company that failed to develop a much-anticipated new product for three years. When pressed on why there was such a delay, the executive in charge fessed up: "My entire management group gets its main income from a bonus geared to return on investment. The new product is the future of this business. But for five or eight years there will be only investment and no return. I know we are three years late. But do you really expect me to take the bread out of the mouths of my closest associates?"

Today, teachers are typically evaluated when an administrator makes a quick-and-dirty visit to the classroom once a year—a method that sheds little light on what's actually happening day to day and gives high marks to too many mediocre educators. In her address, Weingarten advocated a far more comprehensive approach: classroom observations, self-evaluations, appraisals of lesson plans, portfolio reviews, rigorous assessments of student work, and test scores that demonstrate real growth throughout the year.

Meeting the Mission

Drucker would have undoubtedly been impressed by Weingarten's instinct to collect both quantitative and qualitative data. "These two types of measures are interwoven—they shed light on one another," he wrote.

But there is also a danger here. Lots of executives get so caught up in counting this and analyzing that—often rolling out fancy IT systems to capture a whole host of numbers and other indicators—they forget that any measurement is at best meaningless and at worst counterproductive if it's not done in the service of helping the organization meet its mission.

Implicit in this notion, of course, is that the organization has a clearly articulated mission that it fully embraces—what Drucker described as its "purpose and very reason for being." Many do not.

"Finding the right metric has a lot less to do with technology than it does with the culture of the organization," says strategy consultant Howard Dresner. "The question is: What are the right metrics that will reinforce the right behavior?"

Teachers Teaching Managers

In his book *The Performance Management Revolution*, Dresner compares the data that most companies generate to what appears on a scoreboard at a sporting event: "It doesn't tell spectators anything about the play action that led to the teams achieving that score. It doesn't provide any information to the coach of the trailing team that would help it catch up and overtake its opponent. It doesn't tell individual players what they can do to play better for the remainder of the game." What's missing is context.

To her credit, Weingarten is envisioning an evaluation process that doesn't lose sight of the big picture. "We propose rigorous reviews by trained expert and peer evaluators and principals, based on professional teaching standards, best practices, and student achievement," she said. "The goal is to lift whole schools and systems: to help promising teachers improve, to enable good teachers to become great, and to identify those teachers who shouldn't be in the classroom at all."

If Weingarten and the teachers' union reach their aims—and given the depth of the challenge and the politics involved, it's far from certain that they can—they will do no less than lift the fortunes of millions and millions of young people. Nothing could be more crucial for the health of society. But there would be a pretty nifty side benefit, as well: By measuring results so skillfully, the teachers would provide a powerful lesson for managers everywhere.

January 22, 2010

Insourcing and Outsourcing: The Right Mix

Admittedly, it's not Cooperstown. But about a year ago, Peter Drucker received a major posthumous honor when he was inducted into the Outsourcing Hall of Fame—recognition of his having helped ignite the field with his 1989 article "Sell the Mailroom."

Yet ever since, it has been hard not to notice that the flip side of the equation—the insourcing of activities—seems to be getting renewed attention. And Drucker, his election to the Hall of Fame notwithstanding, would have been the first to praise the shift.

"In some areas we have outsourced too much," General Electric CEO Jeffrey Immelt acknowledged in a speech last summer as he announced plans to open a new manufacturing research center outside Detroit that will create more than 1,000 jobs. Shortly after Immelt made his remarks, Boeing acquired a South Carolina factory from one of its key suppliers, Vought Aircraft Industries. Bringing the facility in-house, Boeing said, would help "accelerate productivity and efficiency improvements" on its much-troubled 787 Dreamliner jet program.

An In-House Chip

Meanwhile, the latest high-profile example of doing things under one's own roof came last week when Apple unveiled its iPad touch-screen tablet computer. What many analysts quickly seized on was that Apple had designed the guts of the device, a semiconductor called the A4, instead of turning to a chip supplier such as Intel. During the product's introduction, Apple CEO Steve Jobs even crowed about the company's "custom silicon."

Notoriously tight-lipped, Apple hasn't said a whole lot else about the A4, and reviews of the technology have been mixed. But the company clearly believes that having its own chip provides an edge—an optimal balance between battery life and speed, perhaps—that will allow it, in Drucker's words, "to create a customer."

"Leadership" in any industry, Drucker wrote, "rests on being able to do something others cannot do at all or find difficult to do even poorly. It rests on core competencies that meld market or consumer value with a special ability" that the business possesses.

Avenues for Advancement

As Drucker saw it, the only areas a company should farm out are those in which it demonstrates no "special ability." And in these cases, it shouldn't hesitate to outsource at all. Drucker thought this made good economic sense and also considered contracting out an important social innovation—especially for service workers who are hungering to find pathways for advancement.

If "clerical, maintenance, and support work" are undertaken by an outside vendor, "it can offer opportunities, respect, and visibility," Drucker explained in his 1989 piece, which appeared in *The Wall Street Journal*. "As employees of a college, managers of student dining will never be anything but subordinates. In an independent catering company they can rise to be vice president in charge of feeding the students in a dozen schools; they might even become CEOs of their firms. If they have a problem, there is a knowledgeable person in their own firm to get help from. If they discover how to do the job better or how to improve the equipment, they are welcomed and listened to."

Notably, Drucker didn't call for outsourcing only the drudgery. He suggested that knowledge work—such as that performed by a quality-control specialist—was ripe for the same kind of treatment. In short, "you should outsource everything for which there is no career track that could lead into senior management," Drucker advised.

Not Just for Cutting Costs

But as keen as he was on the concept, Drucker also recognized that outsourcing was not without its pitfalls. Most serious of all, he warned, were the "substantial social repercussions" that would result "if large numbers of people cease to be employees of the organization for which they actually work."

Beyond that, Drucker anticipated dangers for the company itself. Many corporations, of course, have become quite sophisticated at managing their supply chains. But plenty of others still see outsourcing primarily as a blunt instrument to cut costs—a limited perspective that Drucker labeled "a delusion."

A company's real aim, Drucker said, should be to enhance effectiveness, not to try to lower expenses. (Drucker maintained that outsourcing, properly executed, might even increase costs.)

To that end, he added, the overriding question for executives is, "Where do activities belong?" Inside the company's walls? Or outside its doors? Or should they be reorganized as part of a joint venture or some other type of alliance?

The answer isn't always so obvious. To illustrate the point, Drucker cited a top manufacturer of consumer goods. For a time, the company assumed that the more it manufactured itself, the better. But on closer analysis, it decided to outsource its final assembly to a host of suppliers. At the same time, Drucker related, the company asserted greater control over other aspects of its operations, insourcing basic compounds to achieve higher quality.

The lesson in all this: Structure should follow strategy. Or, as Apple has shown, the last thing you want to do is outsource simply because it may save you a little money in the short run—and then just let the chips fall where they may.

February 5, 2010

Toyota's Management Challenge

To the dismay of its growing chorus of critics, Toyota Motor continued to insist this week that its electronic throttle control isn't to blame for any unintended acceleration in its cars. But what the company has readily conceded—and what Peter Drucker would have surely seen as the key to its hoped-for resurgence—is that it needs to get a much better handle on another type of control system: that by which the entire enterprise manages the reliability of its products.

"We are fundamentally overhauling Toyota's quality assurance process . . . from vehicle planning and design to manufacturing, sales, and service," Shinichi Sasaki, an executive vice president, told a Senate committee.

Given the pleasure that some lawmakers and news outlets seem to be taking in Toyota's fall, it would be easy to dismiss Sasaki's comments as empty rhetoric or to overlook them altogether. At the same time, Toyota hasn't done itself any favors with some of its behavior. The company's now-infamous "safety wins" presentation—in which it boasted of having saved $100 million by averting a full-blown recall of 50,000 sedans—has only helped fuel the tar-and-feather-them attitude that many have adopted.

Yet the steps that Sasaki outlined—and that have been echoed by others, including Toyota President Akio Toyoda—are anything but hollow or trivial. For they get right to the heart of a question that Drucker thought every company needs to rigorously address: What set of "controls" will provide the utmost "control"?

"The synonyms for controls are measurement and information," Drucker wrote in his 1973 book, *Management: Tasks, Responsibilities, Practices*. "The synonym for control is direction. . . . Controls deal with facts, that is, with events of the past. Control deals with expectations, that is, with the future. Controls are analytical, concerned with what was and is. Control is normative and concerned with what ought to be."

Manager Control

Drucker explained that to give a manager proper control, controls must satisfy a number of criteria, including several that Toyota seems to be zeroing in on. For example, the company has pledged to increase its collection of consumer complaints and to then respond to them more quickly than in the past by deploying "SWAT teams" of technicians. It has also vowed to give its executives in the U.S. and other regions across the globe a greater voice in safety-related decisions. Until now, such authority has resided largely in Japan.

Drucker, having stressed the need for controls "to be timely," would undoubtedly have favored these moves. But what may be most crucial here is the way that Toyota is positioning itself to meet another one of his specifications: "Controls," Drucker wrote, "must be operational. They must be focused on action."

In a day-to-day context, Drucker added, "this means that controls—whether reports, studies, or figures—must always reach the person who is capable of taking controlling action. Whether they should reach anyone else, and especially someone higher up, is debatable. But their prime addressee is the manager or professional who can take action by virtue of his position in the flow of work. . . . This further means that the measurement must be in a form that is suitable for the recipient and tailored to his needs."

More than Just Data-Tracking

There is more, as well. "Controls," Drucker wrote, "have to be appropriate to the character and nature of the phenomena measured." In other words, it's quite possible to track data on quality and safety—and yet completely miss "what the real structure of events is," as Drucker put it.

Toyota, for its part, seems to be cognizant of this danger. Rather than just paying attention to "technical and regulatory considerations" going forward, Sasaki said, "we need to do more to consider customer expectations and real-world usage of our vehicles, even irregular use."

Another Drucker insight: "Control is a principle of economy. The less effort needed to gain control, the better the control design." One imagines that Toyota had this very notion in mind when it committed to Congress that it would go beyond the use of Event Data Recorders—the so-called automotive black box—and "improve our vehicle diagnostic tools."

Finally, there is Akio Toyoda's promise to push senior managers to actually drive those cars in which troubles have surfaced. "I believe that only by examining the problems on-site can one make decisions from the customer perspective," he said. "One cannot rely on reports or data in a meeting room."

Such sentiments speak directly to a big concern that Drucker had about controls: their tendency to be inward-looking. "The central problem of the executive in the large organization is his . . . insulation from the outside," Drucker asserted. "This applies to the President of the United States as well as to the president of United States Steel. What today's organization therefore needs are synthetic sense organs for the outside."

Setting Values

In his testimony on Capitol Hill and in other recent remarks, Toyoda acknowledged that his company became preoccupied with precisely the wrong metrics: market share and short-term profitability. By enhancing its controls around safety and dependability, the automaker is sending a powerful message to all of its employees about what really matters.

Drucker, whose teachings have had a great influence on Toyota, noted that the mere act of measuring something is "neither objective nor neutral." For "no matter how 'scientific' we are," he wrote, "the fact that this or that set of phenomena is singled out for being controlled signals that it is . . . considered to be important." In this way, Drucker concluded, controls in any company are both "goal-setting and value-setting."

In the end, this is what's most significant about the overhaul that Toyota is undertaking: It recognizes that regaining control of the company's gas pedals and brakes cannot be achieved without also regaining control of its values.

March 5, 2010

Peter Drucker and the
Hon Hai Suicides

We will never really know why 10 workers at a Hon Hai Precision Industry plant in China have committed suicide this year and three others there have attempted to kill themselves. Yet their actions are a stark reminder for managers everywhere: The most complicated thing you will ever deal with, by far, is not some elaborate IT system or intricate financial model, but rather the people you must lead and inspire every day.

Work "is impersonal and objective," Peter Drucker wrote in his 1973 classic, *Management: Tasks, Responsibilities, Practices*. "But working is done by a human being. . . . As the old human relations tag has it, 'One cannot hire a hand; the whole man always comes with it.'"

Because of this, Drucker believed, working has five specific dimensions, each of which recognizes that what we do on the job is "an essential part" of our humanity.

First, there is a physiological dimension. "If confined to an individual motion or operation, the human being tires fast," Drucker pointed out. What's more, he added, people perform best if they're able to vary "both speed and rhythm fairly frequently" as they tackle a particular task. "What is good industrial engineering for work," Drucker concluded, "is exceedingly poor human engineering for the worker."

In China, some labor activists maintain that the shifts at Hon Hai, also known as Foxconn, are too long; the work is too repetitive; and the assembly line churning out products for Apple, HP, and others moves too fast. The company, based in Taiwan, has denied these charges. But there is no getting around the fact that all over the world, including in the U.S., Japan, and South Korea, a huge body of research has found that many people are overworked and their physical health is declining as a result.

Knowledge Workers Suffering, Too

This problem isn't confined to those in factory jobs; knowledge workers are suffering similarly. Late last month, a senior executive at Bank of New York Mellon in London sued the firm for, among other things, allegedly piling on too much work. He had previously complained to his employer that "we are all working . . . unbearably hard."

The second dimension of a person at work is psychological. "Work is an extension of personality," Drucker wrote. "It is achievement. It is one of the ways in which a person defines himself or herself."

Tellingly, perhaps, a 19-year-old Hon Hai worker who jumped to his death last week from a fifth-floor window of a training center left behind a note indicating that he had "lost confidence" in the future and had become convinced that what he once hoped to accomplish at work "far outweighed what could be achieved."

Although this young man's reaction to such feelings was obviously extreme, the struggle to find meaning and fulfillment on the job is hardly unusual. Earlier this year, the Conference Board reported that only 45 percent of the Americans it surveyed are happy with their jobs, down from 61 percent in 1987—a long-term slide that the research organization said "should be a red flag to employers."

The third dimension of working, according to Drucker, is that it provides a sense of community. Even in cases where people have outside activities, he wrote, the workplace is where they find much of their "companionship" and "group identification."

In the case of Hon Hai, some observers have suggested that the company has grown so quickly, with about 400,000 workers at its sprawling Longhua complex, it has been difficult to forge these social bonds. One news report from Beijing quoted a former employee as saying: The factory "is too big. When I was walking to and from work . . . I felt helplessly lonely."

How to Foster Community?

Those employing knowledge workers, meanwhile, face their own challenges on this front, as people have more and more choices about where they live and work and with whom they affiliate. For managers, this pattern leads to a tough question: How can you foster a close-knit community in an age of worker mobility?

Drucker's fourth dimension of working is that it's "a living"—"the foundation" of a person's "economic existence." In the U.S., Conference Board officials have made a direct link between people's low job satisfaction and the dual hardship of stagnant wages and high out-of-pocket health-care costs.

China, where income inequality is widening, is now dealing with its own economic strife. A Honda Motor transmission plant in Guangdong province resumed normal operations this week after the automaker offered to increase compensation by 24 percent to end a strike there. Also this week, Hon Hai announced that it would boost its workers' pay by 30 percent. The company stressed that the raise was a response to a labor shortage, not the suicides, but one representative acknowledged that the move could help lift morale.

The fifth and final dimension, Drucker explained, is that there "is always a power relationship implicit . . . in working within an organization." In any business, after all, "jobs have to be designed, structured, and assigned. Work has to be done on schedule and in a prearranged sequence. People are promoted or not promoted." The trick, said Drucker, is to balance this authority with employee participation—to make sure that workers are given an adequate amount of freedom and responsibility.

But this is far from the only trick. Indeed, the thorniest job for any manager is to simultaneously address all of these things: the physiological, the psychological, the social, the economic, and the power dimension of working. The interplay among them, Drucker cautioned, "may be far too complex ever to be truly understood."

Still, managers must try—with intelligence, sensitivity, and the constant realization that, while there is more to life than work, working is life.

June 4, 2010

A Bold Management Strategy: Keeping Quiet

Several weeks ago, I arrived at a meeting in Washington at the same time as Kathy Cloninger, chief executive officer of Girl Scouts of the USA. I hadn't seen her for a while, so I reached out to give her a hug and a big hello.

"Nice to see you," she said in a hushed tone. I strained to pick up her words. Obviously something was wrong.

Cloninger had mysteriously lost her voice a few months before. For some reason, which her doctors still haven't pinned down, one of her two vocal cords had become paralyzed. For a while, she couldn't talk above a whisper. A recent injection of medication had helped her to raise the volume slightly, but even such modest relief, she told me, would be only temporary.

My first reaction was to tell Cloninger how sorry I was that this had happened. But it wasn't long before my mind veered from sympathy to curiosity. What was it like, I asked, to run an organization with 10,000 employees and more than 3 million members—and suddenly have such a hard time being heard?

As Cloninger describes it, she has gleaned from her ordeal three vital lessons, all of which Peter Drucker—who was such a close adviser to the Girl Scouts that he was honored with a lifetime membership—surely would have advocated.

A Greater Understanding of Stigma

The first has to do with the customer. Cloninger has been widely praised for encouraging girls in the scouting movement to have empathy for others and embrace diversity. Her struggles with her voice have given her an even deeper appreciation of young people who find themselves set apart from the crowd.

"I've been thinking a lot about our work with girls who are different in some way," Cloninger explains. "This is the closest I've come to really understanding what that must be like," including how stigmatized some must feel.

The message for managers everywhere: There is no better way to conduct customer research than to actually experience what the customer does. While in Cloninger's case, the opportunity to do this stemmed from an unfortunate illness, others can be proactive about it. Drucker pointed out, for instance, that the nineteenth-century orchestra conductor Gustav Mahler used to require his musicians to sit in the audience so that they could hear what the music sounded like in front of the stage. Likewise, Drucker said: "The best hospital administrators I know have themselves admitted once a year as a patient."

Cloninger's second lesson pertains to empowering people. Because of her condition, she has had to rely more than ever on colleagues. This has caused her to discover strengths in some employees who previously lacked such opportunities to shine.

Giving the Spotlight to Subordinates

"I've too often let myself be the organization's spokesperson," says Cloninger, who has overseen the Girl Scouts since 2003. "Because I lead very well verbally, I haven't really given others the chance" to play this role.

For Drucker, one of the essential ingredients of exemplary leadership is finding a way to step out of the spotlight so as to bring out the best in others. "An effective leader wants strong associates; he encourages them, pushes them, indeed glories in them," Drucker wrote in his 1992 book, *Managing for the Future*. "Because he holds himself ultimately responsible for the mistakes of his associates and subordinates, he also sees the triumphs of his associates and subordinates as his triumphs, rather than as threats."

Drucker believed, moreover, that organizations must give knowledge workers in particular more and more responsibility if they are to remain satisfied and productive. This, he asserted, "will have to be done by turning them from subordinates into fellow executives, and from employees . . . into partners."

The third lesson Cloninger has absorbed is about the importance of listening. She has always prided herself on being an excellent listener. But her current circumstances—in which she participates in large conference calls by typing out e-mails that are then read aloud by one of her staffers—have made Cloninger pay attention more intently. "I have to listen for the spaces where I can get into the conversation in an efficient way," she says. "Your listening ear really has to be acute."

Drucker: "Listen First, Speak Last"

Above all, Cloninger now realizes that her long periods of silence are just fine. "I'm not going to be valued less if I don't speak up," she says. To be a leader, she adds, "you don't have to have an opinion on everything."

Drucker would have been pleased with this insight. One of his favorite bits of management advice—frequently quoted by Frances Hesselbein, the former Girl Scouts CEO who now runs the Leader to Leader Institute in New York—couldn't be more straightforward: "Listen first, speak last."

In the time since I met with Cloninger, her voice has improved about 60 percent. Nevertheless she continues to manage the Girl Scouts differently from the way she once did. "I still lean on others more than before," she says, "and I am much more conscious about giving others a chance . . . versus just jumping in and taking charge."

Learning from adversity is a hallmark of great leadership, and Kathy Cloninger is a great leader. It's a quality that, even when she's quiet, comes through loud and clear.

July 6, 2010

BP Needed an Andon Cord

Peter Drucker, who took to calling himself "a very old environmentalist" as far back as the early 1970s, would surely have felt saddened by the devastation resulting from the explosion of the Deepwater Horizon oil rig in the Gulf of Mexico. But I believe he would have been distressed, as well, by the damage done to one of his guiding management principles: the need for employers to hand workers a healthy mix of independence and responsibility.

During his infamous appearance on Capitol Hill last month, BP's Tony Hayward assured lawmakers that the British oil company's own workers and those from rig owner Transocean have "stop-order authority," meaning they can instantly shut down a drilling operation if something appears unsound. Once such an order is given, the chief executive explained, "it requires everyone to agree to continue. And if there is one person who does not agree, then they do not continue."

Exactly what triggered the massive spill is still being determined. But in the months since oil first gushed into the Gulf, a steady flow of media reports and congressional findings has made clear that there was no shortage of concern leading up to the tragedy. Less than a week before the explosion, for instance, a BP engineer called Deepwater Horizon a "nightmare well." Subcontractor Halliburton warned that a "SEVERE gas flow problem" could occur. Another worker has said he raised a red flag about leaks in a crucial device called a blowout preventer.

All this begs the question: Why didn't anybody on that rig step up and issue a stop order?

Line Workers Know Best

In a sense, a stop order is the utmost expression of something that Drucker advocated for many decades: pushing authority down through the organization to the lowest level possible. He thought this was particularly vital for knowledge work (and running an oil rig, with its myriad technical demands, certainly qualifies as that).

In highly specialized fields, Drucker asserted, "each worker should know more about his or her specific area than anyone else in the organization." In turn, he or she "should be expected to work out his or her own course and to take responsibility for it. . . . Knowledge work requires both autonomy and accountability."

For years, Toyota has touted its own version of the stop order, in which every factory worker at the automaker has the ability to signal for help and ultimately halt the assembly line by pulling a rope known as an *andon* cord.

John Shook, who in the early 1980s helped Toyota launch a joint venture with General Motors, knows firsthand that this concept invites great skepticism. "Some of our GM colleagues questioned the wisdom of trying to install *andon*," Shook recalled in a piece he wrote earlier this year for *MIT Sloan Management Review*. "'You intend to give these workers the right to stop the line?' they asked. Toyota's answer: 'No, we intend to give them the obligation to stop it—whenever they find a problem.'"

Too Much Control at the Top

Of course, a stop-the-line system is no cure-all, as Toyota has painfully discovered. But it is equally true that any organization with too much control concentrated at the top is likely to fail. As Drucker noted, "In the old days the 'boss' issued a proclamation or order 'to my workers.' After 1900, he increasingly addressed himself 'to our fellow employees.'" He added, "No one yet addresses workers as 'fellow managers.' . . . Yet this is the goal."

So if they really had stop-order authority, why didn't anyone on the Deepwater Horizon rig intervene before it was too late? Based on the evidence that has emerged so far, it appears that some may have tried to sound the alarm, but higher-ups disregarded them. In other cases, it seems that BP and Transocean workers felt themselves under tremendous pressure to save time and money, despite claims by the companies that safety always comes first. Some have even suggested that they were afraid they could lose their jobs for making a stink—a situation Drucker would have regarded as especially perilous.

Any business in which the flow of information is "circular from the bottom up and then down again" is capable of "fast decisions and quick response," Drucker wrote in his 1986 book, *The Frontiers of Management*. But "these advantages will be obtained only if there are understanding, shared values, and, above all, mutual respect. . . . There has to be a common language, a common core of unity" throughout the organization.

What's more, Drucker cautioned, any company in which "financial control is the only language is bound to collapse in the confusion of the Tower of Babel."

Robert Dudley, who is set to take over Hayward's job as CEO of BP, has a full agenda: soothing regulators, restoring investor confidence, and most important, cleaning up the Gulf. But if he's smart, he'll put another task at the head of the list: ensuring his workers have the power—and the responsibility—to stop a disaster before it happens, and not just on paper.

July 30, 2010

Facebook's Privacy Puzzle

In his book *The Facebook Effect: The Inside Story of the Company That Is Connecting the World*, David Kirkpatrick describes how when Mark Zuckerberg was beginning to build his social-networking business, he would sit around on weekends and read the works of Peter Drucker. Now, it seems, would be a pretty good time for Zuckerberg to make sure he and his entire team brush up on Drucker's teachings about the customer.

In particular, the folks at Facebook would do well to consider Drucker's notions about how to juggle the needs of primary customers (in Facebook's case, its 500 million users, who have certain expectations when it comes to privacy) and supporting customers (the company's advertisers, who are eager to access and exploit as much customer data as possible).

"The primary customer is never the *only* customer, and to satisfy one customer without satisfying others means there is no performance," Drucker asserted. "This makes it very tempting to say there is more than one primary customer, but effective organizations resist this temptation and keep to a focus—the primary customer."

Creating a Community

On a basic level, Facebook has clearly figured out how to give its primary customers what they're looking for: a way to share messages, photos, videos, and other information with groups of friends. Indeed, that one out of every 13 people on the planet is now on Facebook attests to the staggering power of the product.

It is an innovation that Drucker, even though he was computer-shy, would have greatly appreciated. "People do need a community," Drucker wrote in his 1993 book, *Post-Capitalist Society*. "They need it particularly in the sprawling huge cities and suburbs in which more and more of us live. One can no longer count . . . on neighbors who share the same interests, the same occupations, the same ignorance, and who live together in the same world. Even if the bond is close, one cannot count on family."

At the same time, Facebook also seems to be satisfying its other customers—the marketers hoping to target ads to those online. In an interview last week with Bloomberg, Facebook's chief operating officer, Sheryl Sandberg, crowed that some of the Palo Alto (Calif.) company's biggest advertisers have upped their spending at least tenfold in the past year.

A Clash with Advertisers

But increasingly, the needs of these two camps—users (who participate on Facebook for free) and advertisers (who pay the bills)—appear to be coming into conflict. Striking the proper balance can be tricky for all sorts of enterprises. A hospital, for instance, must decide "whether the patient or the physician is the primary customer," Drucker noted. And nonprofit organizations routinely run into a thicket of competing "customer" interests: those of funders, volunteers, and the people they serve.

At Facebook, tensions have been mounting steadily. In May, *The Wall Street Journal* reported that once someone clicked on an ad, data were being shared with the advertiser that could potentially reveal the user's name, age, hometown, and occupation, depending on how much public information the person had disclosed on his or her profile. After the story broke, Facebook said it was fixing the situation, while maintaining that its policy is never to share user information without the person's consent.

More generally, though, privacy advocates see a troubling pattern in Facebook's behavior. Kurt Opsahl, a senior staff attorney with the Electronic Frontier Foundation, has traced Facebook's privacy policy since the site's early days in 2005. And his analysis shows, without question, that Facebook has been transformed from a relatively safe space for communicating "with a group of your choice" to a platform where it has gotten harder and harder not to put pieces of your life on display. Along the way, Opsahl says, the company has "slowly but surely helped itself—and its advertising and business partners—to more and more of its users' information."

"The Stupidest Thing We Could Do"

Zuckerberg insists there is a line he won't cross. "We don't sell any information" to advertisers "and we never will," he told an interviewer earlier this year. In another forum, Zuckerberg declared that selling user data to advertisers is "the stupidest thing we could do. . . . People are only going to stay on there as long as they trust us."

Yet Zuckerberg has also suggested that people are growing more and more comfortable with being transparent and, in turn, having their online experience used for "personalized" marketing. Perhaps he is on to something, and if he has gleaned this insight by honestly probing and understanding what his primary customer values, then Facebook should by all means continue pushing in that direction.

"The question, What do customers value?—what satisfies their needs, wants, and aspirations—is so complicated that it can only be answered by customers themselves," Drucker wrote. "Leadership should not even try to guess at the answers but should always go to the customers in a sympathetic quest for those answers."

But there are reasons to be skeptical. The 2010 American Customer Satisfaction Index gave Facebook very low marks, in part because "privacy concerns . . . and commercialization and advertising adversely affect the consumer experience." Even young adults—the supposed exhibitionists of the Web—are "far from being nonchalant and unconcerned about privacy matters," according to a recent study by two researchers at Harvard's Berkman Center for Internet & Society.

The real impetus to make Facebook more of a glass house, I suspect, comes from Zuckerberg's supporting customers, who are tempting him to betray his primary customers. And that's something Drucker wouldn't have "Liked" one bit.

August 13, 2010

The Rules of Alliance

The news last week that Intel is buying security software maker McAfee for $7.68 billion has people buzzing from Silicon Valley to Wall Street. But another Intel deal, announced earlier this month, is what would have likely captured Peter Drucker's attention.

In that one, the Santa Clara (Calif.) chipmaker said it is forming a jointly owned company with General Electric to serve the home health-care market—the kind of arrangement that Drucker believed, even more than mergers and acquisitions, would increasingly become a recipe for "business growth and business expansion."

Drucker held that such partnerships are a smart vehicle for small and midsize businesses "to go international." As for bigger companies, he added, "they are the way to become multitechnological." Nevertheless, creating an alliance that will last for the long term is far from easy.

Tug-of-War Over the Child

"These are all dangerous liaisons," Drucker warned in his 1992 book, *Managing for the Future*. "While their failure rate in the early years is no higher than that of new ventures or acquisitions, they tend to get into serious—sometimes fatal—trouble when they succeed. Often when an alliance does well, it becomes apparent that the goals and objectives of the partners are not compatible. Each partner may want the 'child' to behave differently now that it is 'growing up.' . . . What makes it worse is there usually is no mechanism to resolve these disagreements. By that time it is usually too late to restore the joint enterprise to health."

The trick to making the marriage work is to abide by a handful of rules that Drucker spelled out. And by the early sound of things, Intel and GE are, consciously or not, closely following these principles. (This isn't surprising; both companies have Drucker in their blood. He advised Andy Grove, Intel's cofounder, and counseled a series of GE chief executives, beginning in the 1950s with Ralph Cordiner.)

The first two rules: "Before the alliance is completed," Drucker wrote, "all parties must think through their objectives and the objectives of the 'child.'" Just as important, he said, "is advance agreement on how the joint enterprise should be run."

Hormones in Command

These may seem like stunningly simple notions. But there is a powerful temptation for two companies that are strongly attracted to each other to rush things along, like teenagers with hormones raging. "You get impatient. You want to get moving. You're excited," says Louis Burns, vice president and general manager of Intel's Digital Health Group, who is set to become CEO of the as-yet-unnamed new venture, which will be owned fifty-fifty.

Often during negotiations, Burns notes, if two sides agree on nine points and are stuck on the tenth, they'll let the tenth one slide and agree to revisit it down the line, if need be. But for joint ventures, he warns, "the problem is that the tenth point will come and bite you in the backside later." According to Burns, the worst thing that Intel and GE could possibly have said to each other was, "Let's decide that after we form."

Instead, the two corporate giants hashed things out for the better part of a year to make sure everyone involved agreed on specific goals. "You don't want a Las Vegas wedding," Burns says. The companies, which had struck a looser alliance last year, even drafted a prenup of sorts—an accord that, in fewer than 20 pages, lays out the basic structure and governance of the new venture, provides a product road map, and identifies target markets. Even though it is not legally binding, the document has become a much-referred-to guide for both companies, helping the partners stay focused on what matters.

Only One Steering Wheel

Drucker's third rule: "There has to be careful thinking about who will manage the alliance." In particular, Drucker said, "it cannot be managed by committee." In the case of Intel and GE, there is no doubt that Burns is in charge. Everyone at both companies recognizes that "there are not two steering wheels in the front of the bus," he says. At the same time, Burns is unequivocal that his individual responsibility has to be, as Drucker put it, "to the joint enterprise, not to one of the parents."

Drucker's fourth rule is that "each partner needs to make provisions in its own structure for the relationship to the joint enterprise and the other partner." Most critical, he said, is for those in the alliance to "have access to someone in the parent organization who can say yes or no without having to go through channels." Burns stresses that both he and his GE counterpart, Omar Ishrak, have close ties to the highest levels of their respective corporations—but that, again, the two companies have also codified how these open lines will "survive past the personal relationships."

Drucker's final rule was that "there has to be prior agreement on how to resolve disagreements." At Intel and GE, "we weren't naïve enough to think" that occasional disputes won't erupt, Burns says. So the companies have been "crystal clear" on what happens "if there are deadlocks," with certain calls in Burns' hands as the CEO and others to be made by the joint venture's board, which will be composed of equal numbers of Intel and GE representatives and be chaired by Ishrak.

In the end, Intel and GE are confident that by coming together, they can speed along the delivery of innovations that will help the elderly and those with chronic diseases manage their medical conditions from home. Yet plenty of challenges remain. The companies are not the market leaders. And neither Medicare nor private insurers in the U.S. currently offer reimbursement for home health-monitoring systems, raising questions about revenue generation.

Still, should success be realized, Burns and his new colleagues will find themselves with a huge advantage: Through thoughtful up-front planning, they've taken the danger out of their liaison.

August 27, 2010

Burger King: Start Courting the Noncustomer

Peter Drucker wasn't one to eat much in fast-food joints, usually stopping but once a year for a quick meal at McDonald's on the way to his family's summer sojourn in Colorado. Still, he would have had a very clear idea of what Burger King needs to do to turn itself around, beginning with paying far more attention to its "noncustomers."

"Even the biggest enterprise (other than a government monopoly) has many more noncustomers than it has customers," Drucker wrote in *Management Challenges for the 21st Century*, noting that hardly any companies supply even 30 percent of a given market. "And yet very few institutions know anything about the noncustomers—very few of them even know that they exist, let alone know who they are. And even fewer know why they are not customers."

Burger King, which sealed a deal last week to sell itself to private equity firm 3G Capital for $3.26 billion, has seemed to do just about everything it can to ignore its noncustomers. The Miami company has focused almost exclusively on what it calls "superfans": males, 18 to 34 years old, who've tended to frequent its restaurants.

Certainly, Burger King knows what this testosterone-fueled group likes. It has geared its advertising accordingly (to the point, in fact, that some women have found the company's spots creepy and offensive). Product innovations, such as fire-grilled ribs, have also been aimed at the same carnivorous demographic.

Recession's Effect

But after a period of success for Burger King, the nation's economic woes have hit the company disproportionately hard. Sales and profits have flagged, as the unemployment line has apparently replaced the line queuing up at a BK counter for many an erstwhile superfan. Some analysts also suspect that a longer-term trend is at play: As people become more health conscious, scarfing down bacon double cheeseburgers isn't quite so appealing.

It is a trap that Drucker watched others tumble into. In his 1964 book, *Managing for Results*, Drucker told of a maker of do-it-yourself home-repair equipment that was happy with its base of customers: newly married couples who had just purchased a house. But after about five years, they'd invariably stop buying. "This seemed perfectly logical to the manufacturer," Drucker wrote. It was only when they were a bit younger, the company figured, that these people "had the energy to do manual work. And, having small children, they normally spent most of their evenings and weekends at home."

But when the company finally bothered to examine its noncustomers, it discovered it was overlooking a potentially vast market: people married longer than five years. "They were noncustomers primarily because the company had chosen a distributive channel, especially the neighborhood hardware store, which was not easily accessible to them except Saturday morning," Drucker wrote. And "Saturday morning is not a good shopping time for men" once their children get a little older and have various activities to get to. By moving its products into shopping centers, which stayed open into the evening, and adding mail-order sales directly to the home, the manufacturer doubled its revenue.

Ignoring 70 Percent of the Market

Another, later example: At their peak in the 1970s, Drucker pointed out, department stores accounted for more than a quarter of nonfood retail sales in the U.S. And, just like at Burger King, the managers of these businesses had a very sharp sense of who their dedicated shoppers were.

"They questioned their customers constantly, studied them, surveyed them," Drucker wrote. "But they paid no attention to the 70 percent of the market who were not their customers. They saw no reason why they should." After all, their assumption—which was then totally valid—was that "most people who could afford to shop in department stores did."

But eventually, behavior shifted. "For the dominant group among baby boomers—women in educated two-income families—it was not money that determined where to shop," Drucker explained. "Time was the primary factor, and this generation's women could not afford to spend their time shopping in department stores." Executives in the department store world failed to recognize this, however, because they had been concentrating solely on their customers, not their noncustomers. "After a time," Drucker said, "they knew more and more about less and less."

Examining the "Satisfaction Areas"

To prevent this from happening, Drucker advised managers to regularly pose a series of questions "that are not asked in the ordinary market survey or customer study." Among them: What do customers—and noncustomers—buy from others? What value do these purchases have for them? What satisfactions do they offer? Do they compete with the satisfactions presented by our products or services? Do they give satisfactions that our products or services could possibly fulfill, perhaps even better? Are there new products or services we could introduce to meet these satisfaction areas?

In sharp contrast to Burger King, rival McDonald's has in recent years addressed these very issues—and as a result, it has thrived during the recession. Specifically, McDonald's started serving fancy coffee drinks and smoothies, as well as providing free wireless Internet connections, with the intent of luring noncustomers through its doors.

At the same time, the company has been careful not to alienate existing customers by shaking things up too drastically. "We've learned not to mess with the core menu items—I personally would not change a single sesame seed," McDonald's executive chef and director of culinary innovation, Dan Coudreaut, has said. Yet "we're also excited about pushing the envelope . . . to stay relevant."

Burger King has a lot of hard work to do, including sprucing up its restaurants and improving its technology. But if it really hopes to get its sizzle back, it needs to remember that, as Drucker put it, "it is with the noncustomers that changes always start."

September 10, 2010

Bank of America's Self-Imposed Exam

L ike other large financial institutions, Bank of America was put through a "stress test" by U.S. officials last year. But it's a self-imposed procedure—one akin to Peter Drucker's "Business X-Ray"—that may ensure the company's long-term health.

Drucker, who was fond of medical analogies, thought every organization should regularly go through this kind of rigorous examination for all of its current lines: products, services, technologies, processes, and distribution channels. "The Business X-Ray is a tool for decision making," Drucker wrote. "It enables us, indeed forces us, to allocate resources to results in the existing business. But it also makes it possible for us to determine how much is needed to create the business of tomorrow. . . . It enables us to turn innovative intentions into innovative performance."

In the case of Charlotte (N.C.)–based Bank of America, the nation's biggest lender, figuring out how to drive innovative performance is crucial. Like other banks, it faces tough questions about how it's going to grow amid regulatory clampdowns on credit and debit cards, mortgages, reserve requirements, and derivatives.

Systematic Evaluation

The answer at which Bank of America appears to have arrived would surely please Drucker: Under Brian Moynihan, who became chief executive officer in January, the company has made clear that it isn't going to automatically leap at the next opportunity to make an acquisition or dive into a new market just because it's considered "hot." Rather, Moynihan and his colleagues have been systematically going through most every part of the business and diagnosing what to sell, what to revamp, and where to invest capital and resources to meet customer needs for the long haul.

"We continue to streamline our franchise, getting rid of things that customers just don't ask us for," Moynihan said last week at a financial-services conference in San Francisco.

For his part, Drucker advised placing each piece of the business into one of a number of categories. These include "today's breadwinners" as well as "tomorrow's breadwinners," or those products that already command a sizable market but whose best days still lie ahead. There are also the "productive specialties," which serve a decidedly narrow niche but maintain a leadership position within it. "Their net revenue contribution should be higher than their volume; their share in the cost burden, a good deal lower," Drucker explained.

Next come "development products," which are still being fine-tuned but where "hopes run high," Drucker wrote. "The number of people allocated to them should be small—though it will, of course, be larger than the revenue generated yet justifies."

Then there are the outright "failures." In a sense, things that fall into this group are the easiest to deal with. "They announce themselves and they liquidate themselves," Drucker wrote.

Tricky Categories

More complicated, by contrast, are those aspects of the enterprise that Drucker called "the problem children." Among these are "yesterday's breadwinners." "Everyone in the business loves yesterday's breadwinner," Drucker noted. "It is the 'product which built this company.'" But yesterday's breadwinners, he added, are on the verge of becoming obsolete, and in the meantime, "their gross revenue tends to be low in relation to their volume, while the number of transactions needed to keep them alive" is steadily increasing.

Equally tricky to deal with are "repair jobs." These, Drucker said, should "suffer from one—and only one—major defect," and this problem must be fairly simple to identify and correct. What's more, anything inserted into this category should have a "high probability of exceptional results" if the fix works.

The rest of Drucker's 11 categories include "unnecessary specialties," in which products are needlessly sliced into different segments instead of concentrated into one high-volume offering; "unjustified specialties," in which a product or service has been given a "meaningless differentiation for which the customer is not willing to pay"; "investments in managerial ego," where more resources get pumped into a product the poorer it performs; and "Cinderellas," or areas that might do well if only they were given a chance.

Growth Analysis

Once a company classifies all of its products and services in this manner, Drucker's X-Ray machine can be switched on. It is then that a company may anticipate when a critical change is likely to occur (such as today's breadwinner suddenly becoming yesterday's breadwinner). But this won't happen automatically. According to Drucker, the key is to make certain that every product is analyzed in terms of "the cost of further increments of growth," which will help reveal where it stands in terms of its life cycle. Is this a product on the rise? Or is it about to go into decline? And, if so, how fast is it destined to fall?

At Bank of America, its review of what's poised to grow and what doesn't really fit anymore has led to a string of significant decisions in the last nine months. Specifically, the company has shed, or is getting set to sell off, a substantial list of assets, including stakes in a couple of Latin American banks, an insurance operation, and a portfolio of private equity interests.

At the same time, it is investing in a new product line that will reduce onerous overdraft fees for its mass-market customers. It is also shifting more employees to spots where cultivating deep customer relationships is important—an integral part of Moynihan's overarching strategy to cross-sell products and services to Bank of America's retail, corporate, and wealth-management clients.

Moynihan pointed out last week, for example, that the bank's most affluent customers hold $7 trillion worth of investments at other financial institutions. This is a huge sum that, if played right, could start flowing to Merrill Lynch, which Bank of America bought last year.

Or, to put it another way, by having X-Ray vision, Moynihan might well be in the process of transforming a Cinderella into tomorrow's breadwinner.

September 24, 2010

Churchill and Drucker:
Perfect Together

A few weeks ago, Winston Churchill went digital. The former British Prime Minister's estate announced that it was launching its own iPhone app featuring Churchill's "wit and wisdom." A related website, along with Facebook and Twitter profiles, has also been set up. About the only thing missing, from what I can tell, is a link to the work of Peter Drucker.

Ties between the two men go way back. In May 1939, Churchill reviewed Drucker's first major book, *The End of Economic Man*, for *The Times Literary Supplement*, praising him as "one of those writers to whom almost anything can be forgiven because he not only has a mind of his own, but has a gift of starting other minds along a stimulating line of thought."

But even more than by pen, Churchill and Drucker seem to be connected by deed—at least in the eyes of one Churchill authority. Daniel Myers, chief operating officer of the Churchill Center in Chicago, has in recent years been delivering to business executives a lecture that examines the British leader's actions as "an executive success story." More specifically, Myers details how Churchill illustrated Drucker's eight rules for being an effective executive.

Myers came across these principles when Drucker laid them out in a 2004 *Harvard Business Review* article. "I read it and said 'Wow,'" recalls Myers, whose educational organization boasts 3,000 members worldwide. "It's pure Churchillian."

What Needs to Be Done?

The first practice of effective executives, Drucker wrote, is "to ask what needs to be done" as opposed to "What do I want to do?" This can't be a hollow gesture, either. "Taking the question seriously," Drucker advised, "is crucial for managerial success."

Myers recounts a number of stories that capture Churchill's embodiment of this trait, including his sending aid to Russia in 1941. Churchill had long been a bitter foe of the Communists, but the Germans had invaded Russia earlier that year and Churchill knew what the situation demanded. As Myers tells it: "When questioned by Jock Colville, his principal private secretary, on his apparent about-face, Churchill explained, 'If Hitler invaded hell, I would make at least a favorable reference to the devil in the House of Commons.'"

Drucker's second rule for effective executives is to ask, "What is right for the enterprise?" "They do not ask if it's right for the owners, the stock price, the employees, or the executives," Drucker added. That's because unless choices are made in the long-term interest of the organization, it will ultimately "not be right for any of the stakeholders."

Here, Myers cites a chapter from the eve of World War I, when Churchill served as head of the British Navy and the fleet was on maneuvers. Although his officers were clamoring to get back to their home port at Scapa Flow, Churchill kept them at sea and continued their training. "In everything Churchill did, he always asked, 'What is right for the country?'" Myers says. In this case, "even his staunchest opponents begrudgingly admitted that the fleet was ready for war, thanks to Churchill."

Action Plans

Drucker's third rule for effectiveness: Develop action plans. The best executives, he said, "think about desired results, probable restraints, future revisions, check-in points." For Myers, at no time have these qualities been put to the test more than when Churchill in May 1940 was pressed by his foreign secretary, Lord Halifax, and others in his cabinet to explore an armistice with Hitler.

Churchill rebuffed them all by laying out clear goals and expectations. "It was idle to think that if we tried to make peace now, we should get better terms from Germany than if we went on and fought it out," Churchill asserted. "Therefore, we shall go on and we shall fight it out, here or elsewhere, and if at last this long island story of ours is to end, let it end only when each of us lies choking in his own blood upon the ground."

The next two things that effective executives do, according to Drucker, are to take responsibility for decisions and take responsibility for communicating. Regarding the former, Myers points to what many believe was

Churchill's greatest blunder—his failed attempt during World War I, as Britain's First Lord of the Admiralty, to seize the Dardanelles in the eastern Mediterranean. "He never placed the blame on others," Myers says. As to the latter, Myers says that Churchill worked hard to ensure that he was being fully understood; even his quips were practiced and refined.

Drucker's sixth rule is to focus on opportunities rather than problems. "Above all," wrote Drucker, "effective executives treat change as an opportunity rather than a threat." Myers sees Churchill's early years, during which he had published five books and traveled the globe by the age of 26, as a wonderful example of this Drucker principle come to life.

Productive Meetings

The seventh rule is to run productive meetings—to make sure, as Drucker put it, that they "are work sessions rather than bull sessions." A big key to this, Drucker wrote, is good follow-up. Churchill was a master of this, Myers says, affixing to his most urgent memos bright red labels marked "Action This Day" to help drive his staff to results.

Finally, Drucker wrote, effective executives share one more characteristic: They think and say, "we" rather than "I." So it was, says Myers, that Churchill refused to be knighted after his party's electoral defeat in 1945. "How can I accept the Order of the Garter," Churchill is said to have asked, "when the people have just given me the Order of the Boot?"

Two decades after that dour comment, Drucker would remember Churchill most fondly. He wrote that when the world was coming apart in the 1930s, "what Churchill gave was precisely what Europe needed: moral authority, belief in values, and faith in the rightness of rational action."

That quote from Drucker, it might be noted, is 134 characters—just perfect for a Churchill tweet.

October 22, 2010

The Wall-Less Office

Last week my colleagues and I at the Drucker Institute moved back into our office, which earlier in the month had been redesigned, top to bottom, by Herman Miller. It's a beautiful facility, the perfect blend of form and function, featuring 140 new pieces of furniture that are flexible, mobile, multifunctional (with storage cabinets that double as benches, for example), and environmentally friendly.

Still, my favorite detail is this: There are no interior walls. Eight of us sit all together in one large, sunlit space, without any obstacles in between. We were configured pretty much this way before, but, as the boss, I'd had a work area enclosed by partitions. They've now been tossed away.

Far more than symbolism is at play here. With no walls, my team and I communicate in precisely the ways that Peter Drucker advocated. In fact, our 1,400 square feet of openness is, I'm convinced, a major driver of our results.

One of the most crucial things that any leader can do, Drucker wrote, "is to build the organization around information and communication instead of around hierarchy."

Knocking down walls is the perfect way to achieve this. Not a day goes by in my shop when an idea isn't honed as follows: One staffer is talking with another, wrestling with a particular challenge. Another overhears what they're saying and weighs in. A fourth person then becomes engaged and offers up an altogether different perspective. Out of this ferment, some of our best innovations have been born.

Free-Flowing Dialogue

Just this week, for instance, we decided to refine our efforts to attract readers to our blog, *the Drucker Exchange*, after a semispontaneous discussion broke out among three of us; a coworker's ears pricked up a bit later and he joined in, pushing our thinking even further. For me, as the supervisor, the best part was that two of my employees had initiated the conversation, and I was able to listen to them first—just as Drucker prescribed.

"Downward communications cannot work and do not work," Drucker declared in his 1973 classic, *Management: Tasks, Responsibilities, Practices.* Initiatives from the top, he added, have a shot only if "they come after upward communications have successfully been established." They must be "reaction rather than action; response rather than initiative."

At our small university-based think tank, brainstorming in this fashion is part and parcel of the trade. But even the largest corporations can benefit from being imaginative with their space. In the late 1990s, when Paul O'Neill was the chief executive of Alcoa, he constructed a new headquarters with a largely open floor plan. Traditional offices gave way to 81-square-foot work areas—complete with "pass-through portals"—for most employees, O'Neill included.

Typical office layouts, with their nods to status, "are a barrier to the notion of collaboration, and they 'put people in their place' every day," O'Neill says. A pecking order is "established by access to sunlight, square feet of space, proximity to 'important people.' I wanted to give physical expression to the idea that 'if you work here, you are important, but no more or less important than anyone else who works here.'"

Eschewing Formal Jurisdictions

For Drucker, the very essence of teamwork is "communications sideways," as "people of diverse knowledge and skills . . . work together voluntarily and according to the logic of the situation and the demands of the task, rather than according to a formal jurisdictional structure." The free-flowing dialogue that emerges naturally from physical proximity only increases the chances for this kind of cooperation.

Another who believes strongly in this approach is Carlos Brito, the chief executive of Anheuser-Busch InBev, who hasn't had his own office for more than 20 years. He shares a big table with his direct reports.

"We cherish informality and candor and encourage colleagues to bring ideas to the leadership team and to each other on the floor and even in the hallway," Brito told me. To facilitate that, the giant beermaker has "people of all levels sitting near each other so that we can all learn from each other and so that leaders and managers can stay close to the day-to-day work that their teams are doing.

"It's also more efficient to communicate more openly and on the fly," Brito says. "Meetings are a necessary . . . part of business, but I've found that oftentimes you can get more accomplished with a five-minute conversation in the hallway than an hour-long meeting. You cannot schedule a five-minute meeting in Outlook."

No Place to Hide

Brito perceives other advantages, too. Employees who work in a common area are apt to learn best practices from each other. What's more, an office without walls increases individual accountability. "There's no hiding in an open workspace," Brito explains. "Because everyone sits in the open, it's easier for people of all levels to recognize the high performers and the lower performers day to day, not just occasionally at big meetings or during performance reviews."

There are times when a little private space is required, of course. A few people in my organization put on headphones when they need quiet. It's also quite common for us to step outside onto the patio to take a phone call from a spouse or to speak confidentially with someone. But this minor inconvenience is greatly outweighed by the pluses of constant personal interaction—especially in an age when many organizations are drowning in data.

"Only direct contact . . . can communicate," Drucker noted. "The more we automate information-handling, the more we will have to create opportunities for effective communication."

Drucker once famously remarked, "The most important thing in communication is to hear what isn't being said."

Undoubtedly that's true. But we also shouldn't forget: There's a lot to be gained, as well, from hearing what is being said by the person right next to you.

November 5, 2010

As the Walkman Retires,
Sony Rewires

When the news hit late last month that Sony was discontinuing production of its original Walkman, the pioneering portable cassette-tape player, many in the media marked it as the passing of an era. Yet here's what most everyone is missing: Thanks in part to a student of Peter Drucker's, Sony may well be on the verge of creating a new slate of devices that have a shot at becoming as hot as the Walkman once was.

For Sony, that would certainly be a welcome development. For years now, competitors from South Korea, the U.S., and elsewhere have been clobbering the Japanese electronics company. The mojo that Sony had three decades ago, when the Walkman first hit the market, has long since faded away.

But now, Sony is being pushed in new directions. George Bailey, who was hired in 2009 from IBM and carries the title "chief transformation officer," has been steadily tackling Sony's cost, efficiency, and productivity problems. The company's year-over-year operating margin has improved for four consecutive quarters.

But perhaps even more important than these financial reforms is the philosophy that Bailey is helping to instill at Sony: The business must start on the outside with the customer, not on the inside at the engineer's workbench.

Customer Satisfaction

The message is pure Drucker, from whom Bailey took half a dozen classes at Claremont Graduate University in the early 1980s, when the Walkman was still the greatest gadget around. "The customer defines the business," Drucker wrote in his 1973 classic, *Management: Tasks, Responsibilities, Practices*. "A business is not defined by a company's name, statutes, or articles of incorporation. It is defined by the want the customer satisfies when he or she buys a product or a service."

As basic as that insight may seem, it's one that Sony has neglected. The company, Bailey says, has always been able to make superior products from an engineering standpoint. "A whole lot of what Sony did was make things smaller, faster, of higher quality," he explains. And for quite some time, that was good enough. The formula fueled Sony's incredible growth into the early 1990s.

But in more recent years, both technology and the marketplace have changed dramatically. For instance, the picture quality on televisions is generally so good these days that many new advances are "not even perceptible to the human eye," Bailey says. Rivals such as Vizio, which uses contract manufacturers in China for its relatively low-priced sets, are closing the gap with Sony in terms of what Bailey calls "specmanship."

Sony's edge in design—Bailey likens some of the company's offerings to works of art—has also slipped. "It's not that Sony got any worse at that," he says. "Others got a lot better," including Samsung and LG.

Drucker's Concept of Quality

At the same time, customers' desires have evolved. Having fantastic hardware isn't sufficient anymore. "All of a sudden, people have started to think differently about electronics," Bailey says. "They want software that's intuitive and makes things easy to use. They want applications, content, and services.

"What excites a Japanese engineer in Shinagawa," he adds, "may not be what makes a consumer happy in Helsinki or New York or Mumbai."

In this sense, the technician's traditional concept of "quality" isn't really relevant anymore, just as Drucker counseled. "Quality in a product or service is not what the supplier puts in," Drucker asserted in his 1985 book, *Innovation and Entrepreneurship*. "It is what the customer gets out and is willing to pay for. A product is not quality because it is hard to make and costs a lot of money, as manufacturers typically believe. This is incompetence. Customers pay only for what is of use to them and gives them value. Nothing else constitutes quality."

And so Bailey and other Sony leaders are forcing the engineering team to ask the kinds of questions it hasn't been asking: "It's great that you made this thing faster, lighter, smaller. But what's it going to do for the customers who buy it? Will it change their experience?"

Culture Shift

Bailey believes that the company's culture is starting to shift, pointing to Sony's new NEX-5 camera as one example. It is not only well-built but has managed, with its interchangeable lenses and a slew of other features, to provide "a vital difference" in "photography experience," in the words of one product review. Sales are soaring.

Changing the mind-set of Sony's engineers is only one part of the equation for success, of course. In addition, Bailey has introduced a program called FAST, for "focus, accountability, speed, and teamwork." All of these are principles that also echo back to Drucker, whose "thoughts," says Bailey, "are as valuable today as when he wrote them."

But in the end, it is likely to be Sony's renewed attention to the customer that proves most crucial. Bailey acknowledges that in some ways he, as well as Chief Executive Officer Howard Stringer and others, are attempting to nudge the company "back to the future." The Walkman, after all, sold more than 200 million units not merely because it was small and lightweight but because it revolutionized the way people consumed music.

For Sony, the battle cry is clear: The Walkman is dead. Long live the Walkman.

November 19, 2010

A Different Steve Jobs
Departs This Time

In 1985, when Steve Jobs left Apple in the wake of an ugly boardroom struggle, Peter Drucker wasn't the least bit surprised—or sympathetic. The problem, he suggested, was that Jobs didn't adequately understand the discipline of management.

Jobs and Apple cofounder Stephen Wozniak "never got their noses rubbed in the dirt," Drucker said. "Success made them arrogant. They don't know the simple elements. They're like an architect who doesn't know how one drives a nail or what a stud is.

"If you look at the successful companies," Drucker added, "they are the ones who either learn management or they bring it in. In the really successful high-tech companies, usually the originator isn't there five years later. He may be on the board; he may be honorary chairman. But he is out, and usually with bitterness. . . . Jobs lacked the discipline. I don't mean the self-discipline. I mean the basic knowledges and the willingness to apply them."

The Difference This Time

More than two decades later—with Jobs again departing Apple, this time for his second medical leave since 2009—it's a good bet that Drucker wouldn't say such disparaging things anymore. Jobs, after all, has more than mastered the fundamentals that Drucker thought he failed to grasp in his younger days.

Jobs, who returned to Apple in 1997 after several more-seasoned chief executives had nearly run the company into the ground, has emerged as particularly adept at implementing one of Drucker's core principles: creating a customer.

"Markets are not created by God, nature, or economic forces, but by executives," Drucker wrote. "The want a business satisfies may have been felt by the customer before he was offered the means of satisfying it. Like food in a famine, it may have dominated the customer's life and filled all his waking moments, but it remained a potential want until the action of businessmen converted it into effective demand. Only then is there a customer and a market."

Or perhaps, Drucker continued, "the want may have been unfelt by the potential customer; no one knew that he wanted a photocopier or a computer until these became available." To this list, of course, we would now add the iPod, iPhone, and iPad.

A Deep Bench

But Jobs has apparently grown into a terrific manager in another respect: He has surrounded himself with a highly talented group of senior executives, including Chief Operating Officer Tim Cook, who will serve as chief executive during Jobs' absence; Phil Schiller, Apple's worldwide marketing chief; and Jonathan Ive, the senior vice president for industrial design, who is widely credited with giving many of Apple's products their sexy look and feel. Without question, the bench is much deeper than conventional wisdom would have it.

"At its inception, a company is often the 'lengthened shadow of one man,'" Drucker wrote in his 1954 landmark, *The Practice of Management*. "But it will not grow and survive unless the one-man top is converted into a team."

Drucker pointed out that even if only one person carries the CEO title, he must have a coterie of equally—if not more—talented colleagues "who are on his level and who do not therefore want anything from him; people with whom he can 'let down his hair' and speak freely, with whom he does not have to watch every one of his steps or words, with whom he can 'think aloud' without committing himself."

Getting to this stage takes diligence. "Teams cannot be formed overnight," Drucker cautioned in his 1985 book, *Innovation and Entrepreneurship*. "They require long periods before they can function. Teams are based on mutual trust and mutual understanding, and this takes years to build up"—three at a minimum.

To be sure, many people—especially among those who aren't ardent Apple watchers—view Jobs as strictly a solo act. And that's for good reason: He qualifies as what Drucker called "a CEO superman." The trouble is, Drucker noted, "organizations cannot rely on supermen to run them; the supply is both unpredictable and far too limited." Ultimately, he explained, "organizations survive only if they can be run by competent people who take their job seriously."

More About Elves

For Apple, that's precisely the point: The company clearly boasts an impressive slate of competent people. And though no single one of them may make a perfect replacement for Steve Jobs, as a team they might very well remain highly successful.

In the meantime, it would benefit Apple to showcase the contributions of some of these other, extremely capable leaders better. As Yale School of Management Professor Jeffrey Sonnenfeld remarked this week: "You only hear about Santa, but it's time that we hear more about the elves."

The No. 1 elf, at least for now, is Cook, who by all accounts did a splendid job overseeing Apple during Jobs' previous hiatus. This week, with many wondering whether Jobs will ever actually come back, Cook tried to mollify people's concerns. "The team here has an unparalleled breadth and depth of talent and a culture of innovation that Steve has driven in the company," he said. "Excellence has become a habit."

If that turns out to be true in the long run, Jobs will have proven himself more than a great visionary; he will have proven himself a great manager.

January 21, 2011

For Nokia, One Good Call, One Bad

Investors and technology watchers are trying to figure out whether Nokia has markedly improved, or furthered damaged, its position in the cutthroat mobile communications business. But it's the company's internal communications that Peter Drucker would have wondered most about.

Nokia announced last week that it planned to form an alliance under which it will use a Microsoft product as its primary operating system for smartphones. In going with Windows Phone 7, the Finnish company will largely leave behind its own Symbian operating system. By joining with Microsoft, Nokia also has elected to bypass other options, such as tapping Google's Android software.

The partnership with Microsoft represents a dramatic shift for Nokia— and for good reason. The company's share of the smartphone market has deteriorated rapidly in the face of Android and Apple's iPhone. In some crucial parts of the world, such as the U.S., Nokia is all but invisible.

Making a Splash

Nokia Chief Executive Stephen Elop, in what has turned into an instant shoo-in for the Corporate Memo Hall of Fame, went so far as to liken the company's situation to a man who finds himself standing on a burning oil rig. To save himself, the man jumps into the North Sea.

"In ordinary circumstances, the man would never consider plunging into icy waters," Elop wrote employees in a missive issued shortly ahead of the Microsoft announcement. "But these were not ordinary times—his platform was on fire. The man survived the fall and the waters. After he was rescued, he noted that a 'burning platform' caused a radical change in his behavior.

"We too, are standing on a 'burning platform,' and we must decide how we are going to change our behavior."

Drucker would have appreciated the candor and sense of vision in Elop's comments, especially given the hotly competitive environment in which Nokia finds itself. During the most challenging times, Drucker wrote, management's most important task is to make sure of the institution's "structural strength and soundness, of its capacity to survive a blow, to adapt to sudden change, and to avail itself of new opportunities."

Selling the Decision

The tougher question, though, is this: How effectively did Elop communicate his thinking in advance of unveiling the Microsoft deal?

Drucker believed that a key step in any decision is to achieve sufficient buy-in throughout the company before going forward. It's a lesson, he added, that he learned from the Japanese. "As soon as the decision-making process starts, and long before the final decision is made, Japanese management sells the decision," Drucker explained. "Japanese decisions are not being made by consensus; that's a mistranslation of the Japanese term. The correct translation would be something like 'common understanding.'"

There are, of course, practical and legal limits to how much any leader can say to the troops on the front end of a transaction. That holds particularly true at a huge corporation such as Nokia, which has more than 130,000 people on the payroll. But the general notion—that leadership is, in Drucker's words, largely "a marketing job" and organizations need to view employees as a kind of customer—is one that more managers need to pay attention to.

In the case of the Japanese, "everyone who is likely to be affected by a decision—say, to go into a joint venture with a Western company or to acquire a minority stake in a potential U.S. distributor—is asked to write down how such a decision would affect his work, job, and unit," Drucker noted. "He is expressly forbidden to have an opinion or to recommend or to object to the possible move. But he is expected to think it through. Top management, in turn, knows where each of these people stands. Then top management makes the decision from the top down."

At that point, everyone already has a stake in the company's new direction. Each employee is thoroughly prepared for what's coming. "There is no need to sell it—it's been sold," Drucker concluded.

Sharing the Journey

At Nokia, by contrast, employees seemed taken aback by the Microsoft news. The day it came down, more than 1,000 workers walked out of the company's offices in protest. Many are concerned about layoffs. Meanwhile, rivals are busy poaching talent. "Any Nokia software engineers need a job? We're hiring," read the tweet from a Google recruiter.

Elop, who left Microsoft to join Nokia last September, has taken his lumps for hooking up with his old company. A group of small shareholders is calling for his ouster, and plenty of analysts are questioning the wisdom of the alliance.

But in the end, even if Elop persuades these outsiders that his strategy makes sense, it's the insiders who will have to deliver the results. As Drucker said, "Unless the organization has 'bought' the decision, it will remain ineffectual."

Asked about the negative reaction from so many his workers, Elop remarked: "Every employee goes through an emotional journey, and the emotional journey is difficult, because this is such a big change. I've had four and a half months to go through my emotional journey, ending up in a very different position from what I had assumed when I first joined."

Had more Nokia workers gone through at least some of the journey with him, and not been handed the road map after the fact, the company would be in a stronger place now.

February 18, 2011

3

Management Challenges for the Twenty-First Century

The Problem with GM's UAW Deal

In 1946, Peter Drucker's intimate, multiyear examination of General Motors, *Concept of the Corporation*, was published. GM hated it. Drucker's take—that the then-wildly-successful automaker might want to reexamine a host of long-standing policies on customer relations, dealer relations, employee relations, and more—was viewed from inside the corporation as hypercritical. GM's revered chairman, Alfred Sloan, was so upset about the book that he "simply treated it as if it did not exist," Drucker later recalled, "never mentioning it and never allowing it to be mentioned in his presence."

The United Auto Workers didn't exactly embrace Drucker's thinking either. Among his specific recommendations was for GM's hourly workers to assume more direct responsibility for what they did, adopting a "managerial aptitude" and operating within a "self-governing plant community." The UAW's powerful president, Walter Reuther, greeted that notion this way: "Managers manage and workers work, and to demand of workers that they take responsibility for what is management's job imposes an intolerable burden on the working man."

Six decades later, were Drucker alive to set down the latest chapter in the GM saga, my guess is that, once again, neither the company nor the union would care much for what he'd have to say. At the least, Drucker would surely be skeptical of how transformational the four-year contract reached last week between GM and the UAW really is.

Obsolete Industrial Model

Yes, the restructuring of GM's massive obligations for UAW retiree health care, along with wage and benefit concessions made by the union, promise to bring the company's cost structure more in line with that of its Asian rivals. That may well allow GM to become consistently profitable, which is no small thing.

Yet on some level, the agreement clings to an industrial model that is already obsolete. And it runs counter to GM Chief Executive Rick Wagoner's previously articulated strategy of designing new vehicles so they can be put together anywhere across the globe.

In particular, according to news reports, GM has pledged to invest billions of dollars to keep making certain cars, trucks, and engines in the U.S., providing a boost to facilities in Wisconsin, Michigan, and Indiana and, the UAW hopes, a measure of job security for its 74,000 unionized workers. As the company characterized the contract, it "paves the way for GM to significantly improve its manufacturing competitiveness" while simultaneously "strengthening its core manufacturing base in the U.S."

Shifting Away from Manufacturing

But these two principles—preparing for the future while locking into a made-in-America mind-set—are fundamentally at odds.

As Drucker saw it, huge economic and demographic forces have set the U.S. and other developed nations on a course in which manufacturing jobs are destined to play a lesser and lesser role. Much of this work, he said, will invariably keep moving offshore.

To try to thwart this change through what amounts to bargaining-table protectionism is folly. The twenty-first-century shift from traditional lines of manufacturing to what Drucker called "knowledge work"—laboratory analysis, software design, and so on—is as inexorable as the twentieth-century transition from agriculture to manufacturing.

After World War II, about one in three U.S. workers was employed in manufacturing. Today that figure stands at about 1 in 10 (although manufacturing output, as a share of total economic output, has remained steady, thanks largely to rising productivity).

Education Over Apprenticeship

"Most people continue to believe that when manufacturing jobs decline, the country's manufacturing base is threatened and has to be protected," Drucker wrote in 2001, four years before he died. "They have great difficulty in accepting that, for the first time in history, society and economy are no longer dominated by manual work, and a country can feed, house, and clothe itself with only a small minority of its population engaged in such work."

Drucker didn't mean that people would cease using their hands altogether; in fact, in many cases, they might use them more. But their work will be "based on theoretical knowledge that can be acquired only through formal education," he explained, "not through apprenticeship."

All of this suggests that whatever investment GM is making in solidifying its manufacturing presence in the U.S. would be better spent on launching programs to retrain and redeploy its younger workers for a fate that, ultimately, many of them won't be able to escape.

The End of the Assembly Line

This must not be some halfway initiative, either. Indeed, imagine a major corporation creating a lifelong learning curriculum that had as much energy and talent and financial strength behind it as the building of a battery of new factories. Imagine a retraining effort so robust and pathbreaking that the union could never dismiss it as some corporate sop.

In 1983, in a new epilogue to *Concept of the Corporation*, Drucker wrote: "GM may, within a decade, develop into a true transnational company that integrates markets of the developed world and their purchasing power with the labor resources of the Third World.

"And while it is much too early even to guess what GM's labor relations will look like," he added, "the assembly line, that symbol of industry during the first half of the century, will, by the year 1990 or the year 2000, probably have faded into history."

Drucker was, obviously, a little off in terms of timing. But there's no denying the trend—even for those who'd like to pretend, as Alfred Sloan once did, that it just isn't there.

September 30, 2007

Drucker and the Complexities of Race

L ong before so much of the nation became fixated on what was being preached inside black churches on Sunday mornings, Peter Drucker would go on occasion and listen for himself.

It was the late 1930s, and Drucker had just landed in New York, having fled the Nazis. Whenever he happened to spend the weekend in Washington, Drucker recalled years later, he would sneak into Rankin Chapel to be "shaken and moved" by Howard Thurman, the chaplain at Howard University. His was the kind of voice, said Drucker, that "reached the inner core of one's being."

Thurman's soul-stirring oratory, as well as relationships Drucker forged with other black intellectuals of the era, left quite an impression on him. After all, he always viewed the importance of management as transcending the corporate arena to reach into all segments of society.

Indeed, Drucker found the racial discrimination that permeated his adopted country so disturbing, he once turned down "the most attractive academic job" that ever came his way—a deanship at Emory University in Atlanta. "It was offered to me in the late 1940s, when the South was still fully segregated, and I had to say no," Drucker recounted in his autobiography, *Adventures of a Bystander.*

Obama Resonates

It is impossible to know which candidate, if any, Drucker would have supported in the 2008 Presidential race; he was tough to pin down politically. Not long before he died in 2005 at age 95, he praised a Democrat (Harry Truman) and a Republican (Ronald Reagan) as the two most effective Presidents of the previous 100 years.

But I imagine Drucker would have felt a strong connection with Senator Barack Obama's (D-Ill.) speech this month on "the complexities of race in this country that we've never really worked through." Drucker would have understood Obama's take, that the incendiary language used by his former pastor, the Rev. Jeremiah Wright—while, on some level, "simply inexcusable"—was fueled by a real and powerful anger with roots that run deep.

"Slavery was not a mistake, but a sin—and the fruits of the father's sins are borne by the sons for seven generations," Drucker said in a 1991 speech at the Economic Club of Washington. "We are now in the fourth generation," he added, alluding to the need for at least another six decades to overcome this shameful legacy.

Knowledge and Work

At the same time, Drucker would have surely admired Obama's frankness in asserting that, too often, African Americans have failed to face up to "our own complicity in our condition." As Drucker saw things, this failure was particularly severe in terms of the most sweeping economic development of the last half-century: the move from manual, blue-collar jobs to "knowledge work," in which people are called upon to use their heads more than their hands.

By the early 1990s, Drucker declared, this transition to knowledge work was well on its way to completion in the U.S.—and, with it, there had emerged the realization that education is "the center of the knowledge society, and schooling its key institution." This new reality, said Drucker, has "largely been accepted (except in the black community) as appropriate or, at least, as inevitable."

Needless to say, a lot of thinking went into that parenthetical clause.

"In the 50 years since the Second World War, the economic position of African Americans in America has improved faster than that of any other group in American social history—or in the social history of any country," Drucker wrote in a 1994 article for the *Atlantic Monthly*. "Three-fifths of America's blacks rose into middle-class incomes; before the Second World War the figure was one-twentieth.

"But half that group rose into middle-class incomes and not into middle-class jobs," Drucker continued. "Since the Second World War more and more blacks have moved into blue-collar, unionized, mass-production industry—that is, into jobs paying middle-class and upper-middle-class wages while requiring neither education nor skill. These are precisely the jobs, however, that are disappearing the fastest."

Shifting Economic Status

This path—so tempting but, ultimately, so tenuous—helps explain why the overall economic status of blacks today measures just 56 percent of that of whites, according to the National Urban League.

"The economically rational thing for a young black in postwar America was not to stay in school and learn; it was to leave school as early as possible and get one of the plentiful mass-production jobs," Drucker concluded. "As a result, the fall of the industrial worker has hit America's blacks disproportionately hard—quantitatively, but qualitatively even more. It has blunted what was the most potent role model in the black community in America: the well-paid industrial worker with job security, health insurance, and a guaranteed retirement pension—yet possessing neither skill nor much education."

The obvious remedy is to improve high-quality educational opportunities for black children and adults alike. But, again, the past has complicated the present. In the 1950s and 1960s, schools were integrated—an act that Drucker appreciated deeply. "Racial discrimination had to be corrected, had to be expiated," he said. But in doing so, many schools wound up "putting social ends ahead of the goal of learning," Drucker wrote in 1993's *Post-Capitalist Society*. The upshot was that the education system actually undermined many of the very children it had set out to help.

The way forward, Drucker implored, is to create a new culture "in which the most disadvantaged children learn because it is expected of them and demanded of them"—an audacious cry for hope, if there ever was one.

March 27, 2008

Leveraging the Strengths
of the Disabled

When the House passed legislation in late June that expanded protections for disabled people, it marked an important step forward on an important issue. But what the workplace needs, even more than a new law, is an old insight—one first offered by Peter Drucker more than 40 years ago.

"To make strength productive is the unique purpose of organization," Drucker wrote in his 1967 classic, *The Effective Executive*. "It cannot, of course, overcome the weaknesses with which each of us is abundantly endowed. But it can make them irrelevant."

This holds true for everyone, of course. As Drucker noted, "Strong people always have strong weaknesses too. Where there are peaks, there are valleys. And no one is strong in many areas. Measured against the universe of human knowledge, experience, and abilities, even the greatest genius would have to be rated a total failure. There is no such thing as a 'good man.' Good for what? is the question."

The Barrier of Workplace Attitudes

But this perspective has particular resonance for the disabled—a substantial and growing population. Across the globe, the U.N. estimates, some 650 million people live with disabilities. In the U.S., the Census Bureau counts more than 50 million people with some level of disability.

And many of these folks find themselves struggling to land a job, even though they have skills to offer and are hungry to work. The Disability Funders Network, a nonprofit group, reports the unemployment rate for people with disabilities is 10 times higher than for the nation as a whole. A 2003 study by researchers at Cornell University leaves little doubt as to why that is: "Workplace attitudes," it concluded, "are a continuing barrier to the hiring and retention of people with disabilities."

The bill that just passed the House, after months of negotiations between business lobbyists and advocates for the disabled, should help. Upset that the Supreme Court had eroded the original intent of the 1990 landmark Americans with Disabilities Act, lawmakers made plain that people with epilepsy, diabetes, cancer, multiple sclerosis, cerebral palsy, and other ailments should be afforded antidiscrimination protection under the ADA, even if they control their conditions with medication or are in remission. The Senate is expected to pass a similar measure.

Channeling Unique Talents

But what's required most of all is a fundamental shift in thinking among employers. Too often they are preoccupied with what they see as a disabled person's limitations. Instead, the focus should be "How do you leverage the person's strengths?" says Jonathan Kaufman, president of Disability-Works, a New York consulting firm that counsels public- and private-sector clients. "Drucker's concept," he adds, "is critical."

Kaufman, who was born with cerebral palsy, says he knows of disabled people who possess all sorts of amazing talents that would be a boon to the right company—individuals with Asperger's syndrome, for example, who are capable of "multiplying 12 or 15 digits in their head, faster than a calculator. The question is how you channel this, how you manage it."

In his autobiography, *Copy This!*, Kinko's founder Paul Orfalea recounts how being dyslexic made certain things difficult for him, including reading and writing. But he also discovered he had a natural advantage over his copy-shop rivals.

Human Diversity

"Dyslexics are extraordinarily empathic," he explained. "Perhaps dyslexics are so empathetic because, as kids, so many of us became accustomed to not being listened to. They suffer and pick up on the suffering of others. That was the case with me. I became a good listener to cope." Years later, Orfalea realized that this made him unusually attuned to "understanding and attending to our customers' and workers' emotional needs."

Kaufman believes companies can reap other benefits from signing up, retaining, and advancing the careers of the disabled. For one thing, such an approach can help provide "the human diversity" that Drucker believed was vital to the well-being of every organization.

What's more, hiring the disabled can engender customer loyalty among the employee's friends and relatives—a potentially huge market when you consider that of the 70 million families in the U.S., more than 20 million have at least one member with a disability. The ranks of the disabled constitute an enormous market in their own right, boasting more than $1 trillion in aggregate annual income.

The end result, says Kaufman, is that if a company learns to value the disabled, it can "affect the bottom line" in a positive way, while at the same time, "it can have a real social impact"—Drucker's favorite one-two punch.

Viewed this way, the disabled aren't a liability; they're an opportunity.

Stubbornly Unconvinced

Some businesses get it. Virginia Commonwealth University has developed 20 case studies, including sketches of Alaska Airlines, Bank of America, and Hyatt, that highlight "corporate models of success" for dealing with the disabled. Of the 485 workers at a Walgreens' distribution center in South Carolina, more than 35 percent are disabled. And the drugstore chain is now recruiting disabled workers for a new distribution facility in Connecticut.

"In fact," the company says in its outreach material, "we are actively seeking qualified people including those with cognitive and intellectual disabilities. Why make an extra effort to hire workers with cognitive and intellectual disabilities? Because this is a group that is seldom offered real jobs. We want to change that. We think we can."

Still, many businesses remain obstinate. They say they worry about the possibility of increased costs, safety issues, the specter of legal liability, and how colleagues and customers will react.

But all of these things are simply excuses for shoddy management. Drawing on the parable of the Talents from the Bible, Drucker points out that the manager's task couldn't be clearer: It's to "multiply performance capacity of the whole by putting to use whatever strength, whatever health, whatever aspiration there is in individuals."

July 3, 2008

When 2008 Feels Like 1968

It's been a bummer of a summer, hasn't it? At the gas station the other night, I found myself staring in disbelief—as I have for weeks—while the numbers on the pump kept spiraling higher and higher. The total: $67.83 to fill my Passat. I hopped back in my car and flipped on the radio, figuring a little music might take my mind off the lightness of my wallet, but the news came on instead: Fannie Mae and Freddie Mac were reeling. Nervous depositors had stormed IndyMac Bancorp, looking to pull their money. General Motors was poised for another round of cuts.

Sigh. You don't have to be much of a sourpuss to feel like things are falling apart these days—much of it the result of terrible management across a wide range of institutions. We've been undermined by corrupt mortgage brokers and bankers, lax financial regulators, myopic auto executives, and visionless politicians. Lord knows, there is plenty of blame to go around.

Yet it's worth considering that these problems—the mortgage crisis, $4-plus gasoline, the ongoing struggles of an American icon like GM—reflect more than deep failure. They also say a lot about our future: "the future," as Peter Drucker put it, "that has already happened."

Looked at this way, we may be mired less in the Summer of Our Discontent than we are still coming to grips with what Drucker called The Age of Discontinuity.

It was 40 years ago when Drucker used that phrase as the title of his tenth book. It foretold an era, then just dawning, that promised to bring "a period of change—in technology and in economic policy, in industry structures and in economic theory, in the knowledge needed to govern and to manage."

Shifting Foundations

This time of transformation—which we remain in the middle of—stands in stark contrast to the one that came before it. During the previous period, which Drucker marked from the end of World War I to the mid-

1960s, trends in production and income across the globe had been altered so slightly that a "Rip Van Winkle economist" who fell asleep in 1914 and woke up 50 years later would have been stunned to discover how much had stayed on track. Fewer major modifications in the economic landscape occurred during this span, Drucker said, than at any time in the preceding 300 years.

"Every single area that is today a major industrial power was already well along the road to industrial leadership in 1913," he explained. "No major new industrial country has joined the club since." Similarly, "most industrial technology" in the 1960s was merely "an extension and modification of the inventions and technologies" that had blossomed during the half-century after the Civil War.

But all this calm, all this stability, Drucker knew, was about to end. "The foundations," he wrote, "have shifted under our feet."

Among the most profound changes Drucker saw unfolding was the move away from a traditional "international economy"—one characterized by individual nations acting as disparate units, each with "its own economic values and preferences, its own markets, and its own largely self-contained information." What had suddenly emerged in its place, he said, was a true "world economy" in which "the differences no longer lie in what people have or want, but in how much of the same things they have and can afford to buy."

We see aspects of this playing out now at the gasoline pump. Although speculation and manipulation may have had some hand in the recent run-up in prices, it's escalating petroleum demand by developing countries that will keep them high. The International Energy Agency tells us that China and India are on pace to import a combined 19 million barrels of oil a day by 2030, up from about 5 million in 2006. Nevertheless, we have no concrete national energy policy to deal with the pressure this will invariably put on supplies.

Season of Gloom?

Meanwhile, the mortgage meltdown—which continues to be felt not only in the U.S. but also in Europe and Asia—underscores the world's interconnectedness, as well as our failure to adequately manage the system. "There is greater need . . . to regulate the global international financial markets," Joseph Stiglitz, a Columbia University professor and former chief economist of the World Bank, told a conference in Frankfurt earlier this year. "But we have neither the institutions, nor the mind-sets, with which to do this effectively and democratically." We are still acting as if this were 1968, not 2008.

As for GM, its plans to accelerate the closure of some truck and SUV factories and shed thousands more blue-collar jobs is, in the largest sense, a sign of another monumental change that Drucker explored in *The Age of Discontinuity*: "On the eve of World War II," he wrote, "semiskilled machine operators, the men on the assembly line, were the center of the American workforce. Today the center is the knowledge worker, the man or woman who applies to productive work ideas, concepts, and information rather than manual skill or brawn."

This is all the more true now, of course. Once again, though, we're not behaving accordingly. Between 1940 and 2000, the proportion of those 25 years and older in the U.S. with at least a college diploma swelled from less than 5 percent to more than 25 percent. But in the last few years, the Peter G. Peterson Institute for International Economics has shown, this growth has stagnated. What's more, the U.S. is set to experience a decline in the number of workers holding master's, professional, and doctoral degrees. Is this really how we want to prepare ourselves to succeed in a knowledge-based economy?

It has been a full four decades since *The Age of Discontinuity* appeared. We better start absorbing its lessons, lest the summer turn into a season of gloom that never ends.

July 17, 2008

No Magic Bullet
for the Economic Crisis

With the economy sputtering and the future unclear, managers everywhere are looking for answers. Or, more precisely, many are bent on finding *the* answer—the single strategy that will allow them to weather these turbulent times.

Is this the moment to scale back? Or is this an opportunity to swallow up assets on the cheap? Should the organization stay the course? Or should it tack in a new direction? To Peter Drucker, the answer to such questions could always be summed up in three words: It all depends.

That may sound dreadfully wishy-washy, especially during a period when so many are groping for a bit of certainty that they can hang on to. But for Drucker, determining what a business should do next was something that only the business itself could figure out through a continuous, "systematic analysis of all existing products, services, processes, markets, end uses, and distribution channels."

When scrutinizing all these dimensions of the operation, one has to ask, "Are they still viable?" Drucker wrote in his 1973 masterpiece, *Management: Tasks, Responsibilities, Practices.* "Are they likely to remain viable? Do they still give value to the customer? And are they likely to do so tomorrow? Do they still fit the realities of population and markets, of technology and economy? And if not, how can we best abandon them—or at least stop pouring in further resources and efforts?"

Think Carefully

With things so shaky in the world today, companies should be working methodically through these complex issues. The tendency, however, is to do just the opposite. As Drucker remarked in a 1997 interview, whenever people are "caught in a period of very rapid change . . . the feeling is that there must be a right answer" that everyone can easily turn to.

This feeling stems in part from peer pressure. "If a fellow CEO on the golf course says, 'We are using this, and we wouldn't do without it,' you have to do it too," Drucker observed.

Drucker hastened to add that it isn't only executives who fall victim to this sort of lazy thinking. "When I was growing up in Vienna, everybody felt the need to be psychoanalyzed," he recalled. "And there was a time when every child older than four years had to have his tonsils out. . . . The search for the one quick fix is a universal human failing."

In the realm of business, it is a failing that manifests itself in a ceaseless succession of management fads and fashions offered up by a parade of self-styled gurus. "Each evangelist," Drucker asserted, "is quite sure that his own patent medicine cures everything. And it's very hard to get management to ask, 'Is this for us?'"

"Bandwagon Psychology"

But in truth, there is no panacea. "The stuff that is good for my arthritis," Drucker said, "would not help me at all with a broken leg, even though it's in the same general area."

Notably, it's this "bandwagon psychology," as Drucker called it, which contributed to the crisis in which we're now mired. Rather than diligently tackle the tough questions Drucker suggested—Is what we're doing viable? Does it fit reality?—far too many banking executives were happy to ignore the risks and plunge into the subprime cesspool. The reason for this was obvious: It seemed like a way to get rich fast. And, besides, everybody else was doing it.

Well, not quite everybody. William Taylor, coauthor of the book *Mavericks at Work*, pointed out recently that online banker ING Direct "managed to avoid the march of folly in its industry" by sticking to "plainvanilla mortgages rather than exotic instruments that sounded too good to be true (and were)." According to Taylor, ING has generated 100,000 mortgages worth $26 billion, while suffering a mere 15 foreclosures.

ING Direct's Chairman and CEO Arkadi Kuhlmann takes pride in being a recusant, building his business on inexpensive, no-frills services and high interest rates. Still, he conceded to Taylor that following the crowd has a definite appeal sometimes. "Every person who tries to do real innovation is going to be tempted by money, greed, acceptance, being in the middle of the action," Kuhlmann said. "But at the core," he explained, "there is one fundamental difference: I know why I'm here. I want to make a difference."

As Taylor sees it—and surely Drucker would have agreed—this is one of the most important and courageous things a manager can do: "resisting an innovation that takes hold in your field when that innovation, no matter how popular with your rivals, is at odds with your long-term point of view."

So what's a manager to do amid such a fragile economy? Take a hard look at your business and in the context of your mission—and nobody else's—decide what is ripe to pursue and what makes sense to give up. In the end, maybe you'll zig. Maybe you'll zag. Or maybe you'll just stand pat.

"Nine times out of 10," said Drucker, "when you make the diagnosis, you don't operate. You just wait"—and let the bandwagon roll by.

October 24, 2008

Auto Bailout: What Drucker Would Have Said

In the mid-1970s, Peter Drucker stood before a group of executives at New York University and listened to one of them gripe about his struggles in a difficult economy. Drucker offered a bit of advice, but the executive evidently was not persuaded.

"I don't think that will work for me," the man said in an exchange recounted in John Tarrant's book *Drucker: The Man Who Invented the Corporate Society.*

"Then you had better go out of business," Drucker replied. "There is no law that says a company must last forever."

I imagine Drucker would have said pretty much the same thing had he been able to spend a few minutes with the CEOs of the Big Three automakers as they trekked to Capitol Hill this week to plead for $25 billion in federal relief.

He wouldn't have done this cavalierly, mind you. For Drucker understood all too well the personal pain and social dislocation that can result when an industry implodes.

Six decades ago, he watched the mechanical cotton picker begin to sweep across the South, obviating the need for labor in the fields. "No doubt," he wrote, "the replacement of the economically most inefficient sharecropper by the efficient machine should eventually result in a higher income for all, including the displaced sharecroppers or their descendants."

Lessons from Cotton

"But where will the 5 or 8 million sharecroppers go, and what will they do?" Drucker went on. "And what about the social and economic fabric of the South of which they have been the warp? Surely a sudden displacement of sharecroppers would be a social and political catastrophe not only for the South but for the whole country."

And yet Drucker also recognized that trying to stand in the way of the machine—in the way of the future—by implementing some sort of industrial policy would "result eventually in even worse catastrophe; with every year, the adjustment will become more difficult, the status quo less tenable."

The analogy between cotton and cars is far from perfect. But the painful conclusion is inescapably the same: Giving a crutch to a group of companies that can't compete on their own will only delay the inevitable and make it tougher to adjust down the road.

Drucker's relationship with the auto industry was long and at times quite strained. His words of warning about the Cotton South, in fact, were penned as part of his 1946 book *Concept of the Corporation*, which was first and foremost a study of the most troubled of the automakers today, General Motors.

Advice Anathema to GM Brass

At the time GM sat atop the world, and *Concept of the Corporation* was more than respectful. "Most reviewers," Drucker would later remember, "considered the book to be strongly pro-GM." But among the company's senior managers, it became anathema immediately upon publication.

Drucker's work was reviled, he explained, because he'd had the temerity to say that GM might want to review some of its core policies and strategies, especially those that had been in place for 20 years or more. The fact that these approaches had been so successful, he added, made it all the more urgent that they be reevaluated.

"It was not so much my specific suggestions for changes that upset the GM executives, but my suggesting that policies must be considered as temporary and subject to obsolescence," said Drucker. "To the GM executives, policies were 'principles' and were valid forever, or at least for very long periods."

By the 1990s, Drucker took another look at GM and concluded that, on some level, not much had really changed—although now, instead of being highly profitable and widely admired, the company was faltering badly (especially against its Japanese rival, Toyota, which had welcomed many of Drucker's ideas, particularly in the area of human relations). The Detroit giant, as Drucker saw it, was as slow-footed and resistant to fresh thinking as ever.

The reasons for GM's "inability to pull itself out of the mire," Drucker wrote in a new introduction to *Concept of the Corporation*, "are largely the problems . . . pointed out 50 years ago."

The question today is: Why would anybody think anything's suddenly going to be different because of a $25 billion infusion?

Invest in Job Training

Still, just saying no to the automakers' bailout bid isn't responsible, either. Behind every Hummer, after all, stand the humans who've built it. So instead of $25 billion in aid for the companies, why not a $25 billion investment in those autoworkers and others who may be displaced as abruptly as the sharecroppers of the old South?

The federal government currently spends about $20 billion on all its various job-training programs combined, according to the Workforce Strategy Center, a New York–based think tank. It's the right time for a big boost in that budget, especially with millions of green jobs expected to be created over the next 30 years.

"Protecting aging industries does not work," Drucker asserted in his 2002 book, *Managing in the Next Society*. "That is the clear lesson of 70 years of farm subsidies." Whatever is being spent on propping up failing enterprises, he wrote, "should instead go to subsidizing the incomes of older laid-off workers and to retraining and redeploying younger ones."

Money won't solve everything: Many workforce development initiatives are poorly managed and need to be overhauled. But there are some promising models out there, and the general thrust is pure Drucker: providing access to increased knowledge while putting the past in the rearview mirror.

November 21, 2008

The Old College Buy

Hundreds of students rallied at the University of Washington last week in opposition of a proposed tuition increase. Had he been around, you can bet that Peter Drucker would have grabbed a megaphone and joined in.

For decades, Drucker decried the escalating cost of going to college in this country. "The financing of higher education affects everybody's pocketbook," he wrote in *Harper's Magazine* in 1956. "It is the central problem of American education."

Some 40 years later, Drucker was voicing the very same concern. "Such totally uncontrollable expenditures," he told *Forbes* in 1997, "means that the system is rapidly becoming untenable. Higher education is in deep crisis."

By all rights, most universities should have priced themselves out of existence long ago. That they haven't points to something else that Drucker recognized and also worried about: the unparalleled clout they wield as "gatekeepers" to people's futures. It is a role that has allowed many a school to get away with the kinds of sins that would sink almost any other organization.

The cost of a college diploma has been soaring at about twice the rate of inflation for years; that's a faster pace than what we're shelling out for medical care. Middle-income families now pay 25 percent of their earnings to send a kid to a four-year state school, according to the National Center for Public Policy & Higher Education. And that's after taking into account any financial aid the student receives.

Education Quality Not Climbing Like Tuition

Meanwhile, it's hard to argue that the customer is getting a lot of additional benefit for the extra dough. There are, to be sure, many wonderful programs and professors out there. But "all in all, it is difficult to say if, in any meaningful sense, the quality of the undergraduate experience has improved all that much" as prices have skyrocketed, economist Richard Vedder asserts in his book *Going Broke by Degree*. It "certainly has not done so any more than goods and services generally."

Drucker, who started teaching at Sarah Lawrence College in the 1930s and commanded a classroom at Claremont Graduate University as late as 2002, suggested that, if anything, today's colleges were slipping badly by turning out "highly schooled and very poorly educated" young adults.

Toward the end of the nineteenth century, "when my father graduated . . . he was as nontechnical, nonscientific a person as you could imagine," Drucker recalled. "And yet he and educated people of his generation were expected not to understand the contents of physics, but what physics is, what physics deals with. . . . It didn't mean being able to do surgery, but it meant being able to understand medicine. It didn't mean to be able to do linguistics, but it meant to be able to understand what linguists are up to. And in the last 100 years we have lost that faculty.

"It isn't only that our kids don't learn to read and write," Drucker added. "It is that our engineers know designing and machine tools, but they don't know anything about the world in which they live. They don't know anything about the areas of information outside of their own."

Innovative University Model Awaits

But despite these huge flaws—break-the-bank pricing and a questionable-at-best value proposition—it's hard to get past two facts: Most universities continue to deliver their product pretty much the same way that they have for centuries, on sprawling campuses with students sitting in lecture halls. And despite all the grumbling about the cost and the real hardships faced by a growing number of families, there is no shortage of people clamoring for what's being sold.

"The old model persists not only because it's time-tested but because there's little relationship between price and demand," says Zach First, my colleague at the Drucker Institute, who is serving as the principal investigator for a study of innovation in higher education funded by the Spencer Foundation.

A handful of entrepreneurial ventures, such as Capella University with its online curriculum, have burst on the scene. But these efforts remain, in the scheme of things, largely at the fringes.

One can imagine, First says, that should a major research university figure out how to "deliver high quality with half the faculty or through some other big breakthrough—so that it can shed costs and reduce tuition—it's going to be in a very strong position." But for now, he explains, there is little incentive to even try. This year, despite the deep recession, school after school will spurn two-thirds or more of their applicants. How many other businesses get to do that?

Knowledge Economy

The reason for this, of course, is that we're living in the very age that Drucker, beginning in the late 1950s, foresaw and helped define: one built on knowledge. It isn't news that a college degree is absolutely essential now for advancement in the workplace—no matter the failings of the system that produces the sheepskin.

All of this has left our institutions of higher education with what Drucker described as a "social monopoly." "Few organizations in history have been granted the amount of power that today's university has," he wrote in his 1993 book, *Post-Capitalist Society*. "Refusal to admit or grant the diploma is tantamount to debarring a person from access to a career."

As long as this is the case—and I say this as the weary parent of an eleventh-grader who has just started looking at colleges—it's tough to see anything changing. We'll keep on complaining and arguing, as we have for 50 years, that the mounting cost of an education is unsustainable. And those of us who are lucky enough to find a way will keep on paying regardless.

April 17, 2009

Brand Velocity's
Knowledge-Worker Innovation

Brand Velocity may well be the smartest company you've never heard of. Jack Bergstrand, who used to oversee information technology at Coca-Cola, launched the consulting firm five years ago with a goal of more than just making money. He wanted to take on what Peter Drucker identified as the single greatest business challenge of our day: enhancing knowledge-worker productivity.

"The most important, and indeed the truly unique, contribution of management in the twentieth century was the fiftyfold increase in the productivity of the manual worker in manufacturing," Drucker declared in 1999. "The most important contribution management needs to make in the twenty-first century is similarly to increase the productivity of knowledge work and the knowledge worker."

But figuring out how to lift the output of those who use their brains more than their brawn—a group that now accounts for at least one-quarter, and perhaps as much as half, of all employees in the U.S. and other developed nations—is no easy feat. Most organizations, even as they engage in knowledge work, continue to rely on processes that come straight out of Frederick Taylor's "scientific management" principles of the early 1900s.

It's an awful fit. "The underlying system that made manual work successful is the very same system that constrains our ability to move forward faster in the Knowledge Age," Bergstrand writes in his newly published book, *Reinvent Your Enterprise*. (Full disclosure: Bergstrand is donating a portion of book sales to the Drucker Institute, the nonprofit think tank that I run.) In fact, the differences between old-line manufacturing and knowledge work are stark: Manual work is highly visible; knowledge work is largely invisible—it happens between people's ears. Manual work is highly specialized; knowledge work is, as Bergstrand points out, much more "holistic."

Manual work tends to be stable; knowledge work is ever-changing. Manual work focuses on the right answers; knowledge work must zero in on the right questions. Manual work involves a lot of structure with relatively few decisions; knowledge work emphasizes less structure with more decisions.

But this isn't to say there's no structure at a firm like Brand Velocity. Far from it. Bergstrand and his colleagues have taken "a clean sheet of paper," as he describes it, and methodically thought through everything they do: how and where and under what conditions they hold meetings; how they buy equipment, from PCs to paper clips; how they compensate employees; and much more.

Brand Velocity is based in Atlanta, but in some sense that's an illusion. It has no fixed assets. Headquarters is little more than a mailing address and a secure 64-square-foot space it leases to store sensitive documents.

When someone from Brand Velocity gets together with a client—the firm provides counsel on giant IT projects—they rent out a conference room for a couple of hours from Regus, which operates a string of posh business centers around the world. Many of those who are ushered into the appointed meeting place by a receptionist never realize that they're not actually at a Brand Velocity facility. Bergstrand calls this setup "traditionally virtual."

The underlying idea here—and the same holds true for functions such as payroll and legal affairs and data storage, all of which are outsourced—is that rather than own and manage buildings, Brand Velocity is left to concentrate on what it does well. Having no central office also gives knowledge workers the mobility and flexibility they crave. Many at Brand Velocity plug in from home.

Supplies are also handled in an unusual fashion. Every quarter, the 10 Brand Velocity employees are each given $6,000 to buy what they need, from new computers to pens. If they spend more, it comes out of their pocket. If they spend less, they keep the difference as part of their income. (One can't help but wonder whether Merrill Lynch's John Thain would have purchased a $1,400 trash can under such circumstances.) Besides reducing paperwork—at Brand Velocity, you file only four expense reports a year—the point is to give workers exactly the tools they need to do their jobs. You perform best on a PC, but I prefer a Mac? No problem. We each get what we want, and the company doesn't find itself struggling (and paying a fortune) to standardize everything.

Brand Velocity offers employees a base salary. But much of their remuneration is determined by a points system, with points awarded for three —and only three—things: selling great work, delivering great work, and recruiting and developing great talent. Under this arrangement, says Bergstrand, "highly productive knowledge workers don't need to be a partner to be compensated like one. At the same time, the most senior people aren't guaranteed the highest compensation." This is more than a theory. Though he's the CEO, Bergstrand himself often doesn't make the most dough.

If this all seems a little freewheeling, it's not. Bergstrand and his team are rigorous in the way they do most everything, including reaching decisions. On any given project, they solicit lots of input throughout the organization but leave no doubt who the final decision maker is. That person then acts—and acts quickly.

"The pursuit of consensus becomes the Anaconda snake of large enterprises," Bergstrand maintains. "The Anaconda doesn't bite. It kills its prey through suffocation."

The bottom line: Brand Velocity is profitable and growing. It claims that its costs run 20 percent less than the industry average. And most notably, it says it delivers to clients the same high-quality results they would get from much larger consulting firms—but in half the time and with less than half the manpower, resulting in huge customer savings.

The real question is how big Brand Velocity can get. It's one thing to do this at the firm's current size and quite another to pull this off with a staff of thousands.

Bergstrand says that, having generated about $15 million in business to this point, Brand Velocity is ready now to move beyond the "prototype" stage. He has hired top executives from major corporations—Kimberly-Clark and Ernst & Young, among them—so that as Brand Velocity has tested various knowledge-worker productivity concepts, "we could factor in the need for scalability."

The effort certainly bears watching. If Brand Velocity thrives—and teaches others along the way—the implications could be nothing short of revolutionary.

May 1, 2009

Japan: Rethinking Lifetime Employment

The Democratic Party of Japan rode to victory in a landmark election last week by advancing an ambitious agenda, which includes reassessing Tokyo's relationship with Washington and playing a greater role in international climate talks. But there is one particular plank in its platform that managers—and not just those in Japan—would be wise to reflect upon, just as Peter Drucker did.

Among the DPJ's aims is banning the hiring of temporary workers on factory floors—a nod to the unease that many people in Japan are feeling as the country's decades-old model of "lifetime employment" continues to dissolve (and its labor practices look more and more like those of the U.S.).

Exactly how many Japanese ever really enjoyed the reliability and comfort of lifetime employment is difficult to say. Slicing the statistics and interpreting a series of changes to Japanese employment law in different ways, scholars have come up with figures as low as 20 percent of the workforce and as high as 80 percent. What is indisputable, though, is that the long-term employment security enjoyed by many in Japan (many men, that is) has been a cornerstone of the country's corporate culture and a symbol of its cohesion as a society.

"Japan's success—and there is no precedent for it in history—very largely rested on organized immobility—the immobility of 'lifetime employment,'" asserted Drucker, who first visited Japan in 1959 and was among the earliest observers to predict the nation's rise as a world economic power.

Promoting Teamwork

Indeed, the old approach certainly has its virtues, including the fostering of allegiance among employees—not a bad thing when you're trying to promote teamwork throughout the organization. Edward Lincoln, a professor at New York University and director of its Center for Japan–U.S. Business & Economic Studies, believes that Japanese workers may also have eagerly embraced technological change over the years because they didn't worry about a machine casting them to the streets. "They knew they'd get moved into another job elsewhere in the company," he says.

Drucker, too, thought that there was much to learn from the Japanese. In a seminal 1971 piece in *Harvard Business Review*, he praised the country's managers for the deliberate manner in which they puzzled through decisions, lauded their commitment to continuous worker training, and found lessons in the way they mentored younger employees.

Drucker also touted the concept of lifetime employment, which he deemed far less rigid than many assumed. That was in part, he pointed out, because Japanese workers faced mandatory retirement (then at age 55), making "lifetime" something of a misnomer.

What's more, Drucker wrote, companies in Japan never hesitated to lay off people when business got bad. "Yet they can do so in such a fashion that the employees who need incomes the most are fully protected," he explained. "The burden of adjustment is taken by those who can afford it and who have alternate incomes to fall back on."

Looking Beyond Tradition

Still, despite all this, Drucker over time reached the same conclusion that many Japanese executives have: Thriving in today's global economy requires more flexibility in hiring people and letting them go than the traditional system has allowed.

And so it is that, since the late 1990s, most big Japanese corporations have restructured themselves, moving from "unwieldy goliaths to nimble competitors," in the words of the University of California at San Diego's Ulrike Schaede. Among the steps they've taken has been to increase the use of low-cost part-timers, contract workers, and temporary staff. This group now makes up more than a third of Japan's labor force.

The trend isn't being driven by industry alone. As more people shift from manual work to knowledge work, some employees have come to relish the ability to bounce from job to job (presumably snatching ever better offers along the way). In the U.S., author Bruce Tulgan has dubbed this phenomenon "just-in-time loyalty."

But what worried Drucker—and what the Japanese election under-scores—is that the flip side of mobility is instability, especially for those workers lacking the skills and education to be in high demand. In these cases, Drucker suggested, employers have a special obligation to help those they dismiss find their way through the dislocation and land new positions.

Helping "Redundant" Workers

This "requires active and energetic attempts at retraining for specific new job opportunities," Drucker wrote. "It requires that the employer takes responsibility for placing redundant employees in new jobs." This was advice, Drucker noted, that he dispensed both in Japan and in the U.S.

"I very much hope," he added, "that Japan will find a solution that pre-serves the social stability, the community—and the social harmony—that lifetime employment provided, and yet creates the mobility that knowl-edge work and knowledge workers must have."

It's far from clear that the DPJ has found the right answer. But it has touched on a subject—the proper shape of the social contract between employer and employee in the twenty-first century—that merits consider-ably more attention, regardless of which side of the Pacific we happen to be on.

September 4, 2009

Women and the
Knowledge-Work Trend

The news this month that women now outnumber men on the nation's payrolls generated less heat than a burning bra. Relatively few major media outlets took note of the milestone, which was tucked amid the Labor Department's employment report for January. And some of the analysts who did bother to pay attention pointed out that it wasn't based on the government's most reliable or robust set of statistics. Others focused on the fact that women reached this mark only because men have been losing jobs faster than their female counterparts during the economic downturn.

But Peter Drucker, I believe, would have viewed the figure—that women held 50.3 percent of the nation's nonfarm payroll jobs last month, according to seasonally unadjusted data—with a strong appreciation for both its historic import and for the kinds of changes it portends across the corporate world.

Indeed, in Drucker's eyes, the number would surely serve as the latest evidence of the momentous movement to the kinds of jobs—ones in which brains beat brawn—that have dramatically altered the traditional relationship between the sexes.

"Equally Accessible" Jobs

For centuries, Drucker explained in his 1995 book, *Managing in a Time of Great Change*, "men and women did the same work only when it was menial. Men and women both dug ditches. . . . Men and women both picked cotton in the fields.

"But any work involving skill, and any work conferring social status or providing income above minimum subsistence, was segregated by sex," Drucker continued. Telephone operators were almost universally women, for example, while telephone installers were practically all men.

Knowledge work, however, is different. Such occupations—which Drucker first identified in the late 1950s and now, according to various estimates, account for anywhere from a quarter to a half of all jobs in this country—are "equally accessible to both sexes," as Drucker put it.

"The higher up the ladder we go in knowledge work, the more likely it is that men and women are doing the same work," Drucker wrote. "Being a secretary in an American bank still means being a woman, but a vice president in the same bank may be a man or a woman."

This unprecedented flow of women into the same lines of work as men shows no signs of abating, either. If anything, it is poised to accelerate, given that women now earn about 60 percent of the university degrees awarded in the U.S.

Manager Material

For companies—more and more of which are finding that knowledge has replaced land, labor, and capital as "the one critical factor of production," in Drucker's words—this trend represents a tremendous opportunity.

Generalizing about any group of people is boneheaded and bound to get you into trouble; and when you're talking about half the human species, you're certain to find countless exceptions to any rule you come up with.

Nonetheless, a host of compelling studies—by researchers at INSEAD, McKinsey & Co., and elsewhere—suggest that women outshine men when it comes to team building, displaying emotional intelligence, setting clear expectations, and exhibiting other traits often associated with effective knowledge work. Having cited some of these findings at a conference last year, Avivah Wittenberg-Cox, CEO of the Paris-based consultancy 20-First, couldn't help but ask: "Are women the managers Drucker was waiting for?"

Drucker himself seemed to think so. Many of today's jobs, he told an audience in 1986, depend on a person's "willingness to work with other people." Then Drucker added, "Let's face it, women are usually better at that than men."

Corporate Attitude Shift

Yet to fully capitalize, many corporations have to overhaul the way they approach women as workers. This goes beyond simply promoting more women to top corporate jobs and board positions, or closing the still-yawning wage gap between male and female employees, or offering a more flexible, family-friendly environment—though all of these things are terribly necessary.

For many organizations, taking advantage of this rich talent pool will depend on a fundamental shift in attitude—the realization that men and women tend to have different strengths and that the smartest strategy is to achieve a balance among them.

"Many employers have long believed that the best way to integrate women is to treat everyone in the same way," Wittenberg-Cox writes in her book *Why Women Mean Business*, coauthored with Alison Maitland. "This approach was reinforced over decades by equal-opportunity legislation and by women themselves demanding equal treatment. The only problem was that in pursuing fairness and equality, companies resolutely ignored differences between women and the male employees on whom they had previously relied. They dealt with the arrival of women en masse by requiring them to fit in—and to adapt to male career models and leadership styles."

Wittenberg-Cox counsels executives to become "gender-bilingual"—that is, "fluent in the language and culture of both men and women" so that they can get the best out of both.

A final point (for the record): Feminists didn't actually burn their bras in the 1960s; that's a myth. But the need for companies to recognize, as Drucker did, that "knowledge is gender-neutral" without homogenizing men and women in the workplace couldn't be more real.

February 19, 2010

The Service Sector Snag

Whenever I am in Seoul, as I was earlier this week, I find myself marveling at the place: its top-flight airport, its shimmering skyscrapers, its ubiquitous high-tech gadgetry—all of these outward signs of an economic transformation achieved largely in a single generation. It's no wonder that Peter Drucker called South Korea "undoubtedly" the most entrepreneurial nation on earth.

And yet if there is a weak spot to be found in Korea—and in many other countries around the world—it is one that Drucker also understood well: a huge service sector that is struggling to be productive.

Earlier this month, the South Korean government announced that it would invest 300 billion won (or $260 million) in research and development aimed at enhancing service-provider productivity. "Korean industries took it for granted to invest in R&D for products but questioned the same necessity in services," one official explained. Now the plan is to promote technology that can spur advances in health-care delivery, advertising, design, business services, and more.

The Koreans are being driven, in part, by statistics showing that the nation's service sector is only half as productive as that of the U.S. But some wonder whether the strides the U.S. has made in this area over the last 15 years are more illusion than reality. Economist Paul Krugman, for one, has pointed out that much of the U.S.'s productivity prowess has supposedly been in financial services. "Given recent events," he asks, "are we even sure that the expansion of the financial system was doing anything productive at all?"

Wage Gap

In any case, what we do know for sure is that wages for many service workers continue to lag badly—and this is what most concerned Drucker. In fact, with the ranks of service firms growing rapidly, he warned of "the prospect of social tensions unmatched since the early decades of the Industrial Revolution."

The service sector is varied and vast. In the U.S. today, more than 80 percent of jobs are to be found in services; in Korea, that number stands at about 70 percent. Drucker, for his part, tended to divide this giant universe into two different categories: knowledge work and unskilled or semiskilled positions.

The former group is, of course, in relatively good shape—especially those who have been able to obtain high levels of education. In the U.S., for instance, those with a college degree earn on average two-thirds more than those who've finished high school, according to the Goldman Sachs Global Markets Institute. And those with professional degrees boast incomes nearly twice as large as those with just a college diploma.

But the unskilled or semiskilled—janitors and waitresses, retail clerks and nursing-home attendants—are in a much tougher spot. "In their social position," Drucker wrote in a 1991 piece in *Harvard Business Review*, "such people are comparable to the proletarians of years ago: the poorly educated . . . masses who thronged the exploding industrial cities and streamed into their factories."

Targeting Productivity

For these workers to get ahead, Drucker believed that there was only one remedy: increasing their productivity (or output per hour of work). "The less productive an economy," Drucker asserted, "the greater the inequality of incomes. The more productive, the less the inequality."

Over the years, some experts have maintained that by its very nature, service work is labor-intensive and not conducive to productivity gains—a phenomenon known as "Baumol's disease" (so named for William Baumol, the economist who first described it).

But Drucker was convinced that it's possible to make significant leaps in service-sector productivity—though they won't typically come through the adaptation of new technologies, as the Koreans are hoping. Rather, Drucker said, the way to get there is to hark back to what Frederick Taylor, the "scientific management" pioneer, prescribed long ago: "working smarter."

Specifically, Drucker maintained that companies with proven success in this arena:

- "have defined the task" at hand;
- made certain that work is focused on that particular task, instead of running off in different directions;
- "defined performance";
- engaged every employee as "a partner in productivity improvement and the first source of ideas for it"; and
- "built continuous learning" into each job.

"As a result," Drucker added, these enterprises "have raised productivity substantially—in some cases even doubled it—which has allowed them to raise wages. Equally important, this process has also greatly raised the workers' self-respect and pride."

How Soon?

The question is how soon any of this may actually happen on a scale big enough to narrow the wage gap between knowledge workers and their unschooled, unskilled service-worker cousins.

"Even in the most settled and stable societies, people will be left behind in the shift to knowledge work," Drucker acknowledged. "It takes a generation or two before a society and its population catch up with radical changes in the composition of the workforce and in the demands for skills and knowledge. It takes some time—the best part of a generation, judging by historical experience—before the productivity of service workers can be raised sufficiently to provide them with a 'middle-class' standard of living."

All of which suggests that, in addition to the sort of investment the Koreans are attempting or the kinds of management techniques that Drucker advocated, nations may need something else if they hope to lift the fortunes of those with service jobs: a little patience.

March 19, 2010

When Retirement Is Not an Option

In 2001, in a series of essays for *The Economist*, Peter Drucker pointed to a demographic transformation unfolding across the developed world while, poetically, he found himself at the leading edge of the trend.

"The dominant factor in the Next Society will be something to which most people are only just beginning to pay attention: the rapid growth of the older population and the rapid shrinking of the younger generation," Drucker asserted. "Politicians still promise to save the existing pensions system, but they—and their constituents—know perfectly well that in another 25 years people will have to keep working until their mid-70s, health permitting."

At the time, Drucker was fast approaching his ninety-second birthday and still writing, teaching, and consulting. Only the most blessed among us can hope to be going so strong at that age. But there's no denying the general phenomenon that Drucker identified as well as the important implications it holds for those leading corporations and nonprofits alike.

"Tectonic Shift"

Indeed, just last month, RAND, a nonprofit research institution in Santa Monica, Calif., issued a study showing that more and more Americans are delaying retirement. The study also predicted that this "tectonic shift" in the workplace is bound "to continue and even accelerate over the next two decades."

After declining for more than a century, according to RAND, the number of older men and women in the workforce began to rise modestly during the 1990s. While about 17 percent of Americans aged 65 to 75 were employed in 1990, that figure is expected to rise to 25 percent this year. RAND believes the pattern will persist until at least 2030—longer than other experts have forecast.

For government policymakers trying to ensure the health of Social Security and Medicare, the ramifications of this swing are quite substantial. But individual enterprises need to pay close attention, too.

"Employing organizations—and by no means only businesses—should start as soon as possible to experiment with new work relationships with older people and especially with older knowledge workers," Drucker wrote in his 1999 book, *Management Challenges for the 21st Century.* "The organization that first succeeds in attracting and holding knowledge workers past traditional retirement age, and makes them fully productive, will have a tremendous competitive advantage."

"New Ways of Working"

To get there, Drucker said, employers must learn to be more flexible. As baby boomers hit their 50s and 60s, he suggested, many of them are likely to want to serve as part-timers and consultants or to take on special assignments. "New ways of working with people at arm's length will increasingly become the central management issue" at many different organizations, Drucker wrote.

Compared with their younger colleagues, he added, older workers with sufficient education and talent "will have much more choice and will be able to combine traditional jobs, nonconventional jobs, and leisure in whatever proportion suits them best."

Part of the reason this group now finds itself in such a strong position boils down to supply and demand. Another recent study, released by the MetLife Foundation and the San Francisco think tank Civic Ventures, predicts that over the next eight years there could be as many as 5 million job vacancies in the U.S.—and workers 55 and older will be crucial to closing the gap.

"Not only will there be jobs for . . . experienced workers to fill," says Northeastern University economist Barry Bluestone, the study's author, "but the nation will absolutely need older workers to step up and take them."

Achieving Social Purpose

Bluestone projects that nearly half the labor shortages (2.4 million jobs) will be in four fields: education, health care, government, and the nonprofit arena. All of these stand to provide what many baby boomers, in particular, are looking for: a chance not only to stay active but also to make a meaningful contribution.

More than a decade ago, Drucker spotted this growing desire among knowledge workers to achieve some social purpose during the second half of their lives. "These people have substantial skills," Drucker wrote. "They know how to work. They need a community. . . . They need the income, too. But above all, they need the challenge."

To help them along, Civic Ventures launched a program last year in which Silicon Valley executives are given fellowships at area nonprofits. The idea is not only to bring these organizations much-needed expertise in marketing, finance, and human resources, but also to have the executives prepare for their eventual transition to an "encore career" in the social sector.

The irony, of course, is that all this activity and insight by Civic Ventures and RAND comes amid a brutally weak job market, especially for those 55 and older. Last month, the Pew Fiscal Analysis Initiative reported that about 30 percent of those in this age bracket have been unemployed for a year or more. "Another generation of U.S. workers, at least significant numbers of them, [is] being forced into retirement sooner than expected and without ceremony, by the bust," economics writer David Warsh noted earlier this week.

But smart organizations are aware that every bust is invariably followed by a boom. And the next one could well be a boom driven, in large part, by a bunch of aging boomers.

May 21, 2010

Wal-Mart's Blended Learning Plan

In his provocative book, *The Retail Revolution: How Wal-Mart Created a Brave New World of Business,* Nelson Lichtenstein invokes Peter Drucker's pioneering exploration of General Motors in describing how every era has its "industry of industries."

When Drucker published *Concept of the Corporation* in 1946, Lichtenstein notes, automobile makers were dominant, and GM was the king of kings. Today, he explains, it's "the retailers, Wal-Mart above all," that have "set the standard for a new stage in the history of corporate capitalism."

It is precisely because Wal-Mart occupies this prominent, if not preeminent, place that its announcement this month about providing assistance for its workers to receive college degrees struck me—and surely would have struck Drucker—as potentially of great significance. Just how great remains to be seen.

On-the-Job Learning

At a glance, it's actually tempting to dismiss this effort, for which Wal-Mart says it will spend $50 million in tuition assistance and other related items over the next three years, as less than ideal. Under the arrangements the Bentonville (Ark.) company has made with American Public University, employees can receive course credit, equivalent to as much as 45 percent of what it takes to earn a degree, for Wal-Mart training and "on-the-job learning." By 2012, 70 percent of Wal-Mart's 1.4 million U.S. workers will have had their jobs reviewed for "college credit eligibility."

Some will certainly see this as a strange way to promote learning. Why, after all, give credit for training and tasks that a Wal-Mart worker was going to be doing anyway?

Others are bound to attack this aspect of the Wal-Mart program as an attempt by the company to make a huge PR splash with relatively little investment. Although Wal-Mart embraced health-care reform and has

become widely praised for its environmental practices, the low-price pur-
veyor remains a polarizing force.

"Over the last few years, we've built a model for making a big difference on big issues," Wal-Mart's chief executive, Mike Duke, said recently.
"We are well into this journey now. No one can doubt our sincerity."
Actually, many do doubt the company's sincerity, continuing to see it,
in Lichtenstein's words, as the leading example of a group of corporations that "churn their workforce, whipsaw their vendors, and have turned
retirement pay and health provision into a financial lottery for millions of
workers."

Promise of the Internet

But at least in terms of this latest educational initiative, I think Drucker
would have been open to Wal-Mart's approach. For starters, he probably
would have liked Wal-Mart's decision to link up with American Public,
an online education company in West Virginia, instead of a better-known
academic partner.

Drucker never much cared for the hauteur exhibited by elite colleges
and universities, and he saw tremendous promise in teaching over the
Internet. "The college won't survive as a residential institution," Drucker
predicted in the late 1990s. "Today's buildings are . . . totally unneeded."
In Wal-Mart's own survey of employees, more than two-thirds told the
company they preferred an online university to a traditional campus.

Yet most intriguing to Drucker, I believe, would have been this notion
of marrying corporate training and people's regular work routines with
more formal instruction from American Public.

Wal-Mart says that the advantage to employees of racking up credits
in such subjects as retail inventory management and customer relations
while on the job is that it will put them "on a faster track to earning a
college degree, reducing their length of time in school, and making the
overall cost more affordable."

But that is missing the larger opportunity here. If coursework and regular work are integrated in a smart and thoughtful manner, each stands to
reinforce the other, helping Wal-Mart's employees learn from both in new
ways.

The Intellectual vs. the Manager

Too often, we consider learning to be something done stiffly, in a classroom. But that's silly. "Learning is a continuing biological process," Drucker said. "It begins at conception and ends only at death. We further know that learning is not an activity of one specific learning organ—the mind or the intellect. It is a process in which the whole person is engaged: the hand, the eye, the nervous system, the brain."

Being able to use all of these assets, Drucker suggested, will increasingly come to define "the educated person." More and more, he wrote in his 1993 book, *Post-Capitalist Society*, we are going to "have to be prepared to live and work simultaneously in two cultures—that of 'the intellectual,' who focuses on words and ideas, and that of the 'manager,' who focuses on people and work.

"The intellectual's world, unless counterbalanced by the manager, becomes one in which everybody 'does his own thing' but nobody achieves anything. The manager's world, unless counterbalanced by the intellectual, becomes the stultifying bureaucracy of the 'Organization Man.' But if the two balance each other, there can be creativity and order, fulfillment and mission."

Whether Wal-Mart succeeds will depend not simply on how many of its workers become college graduates, but on whether it has found a way to blend education for a new age—one in which doers must also be thinkers, and vice versa.

June 18, 2010

Cloud Computing and Peter Drucker

O ne of the most amusing photographs I've ever seen of Peter Drucker shows him sitting in front of a boxy Compaq computer. He awkwardly holds a mouse in his right hand, while his left hand stretches stiffly to the keyboard. The quizzical look on his face says, "Get me out of here."

None of this is terribly surprising for a man who was so ill at ease on a PC that, while ruminating on how the Web was changing the world at the start of the twenty-first century, he chose to write the last of his books on a Brother typewriter. As for the computer, Drucker once remarked, "I treat it just like a big adding machine."

Beyond his personal discomfort, Drucker worried that managers have a tendency to become overly enamored of the latest gizmo. As a result, they forget that technology is not an end in itself and that for certain decisions—those requiring intuition, for example—humans will always have an advantage over machines. "All a computer can handle are abstractions," Drucker wrote. "And abstractions can be relied on only if they are constantly checked against the concrete."

Like Electricity Through the Grid

Still, for all his wariness, even Drucker would have been taken with an essay written by a young economist named Florian Ramseger, who asserts that "we are at the doorstep of a new era" due to the advent of "cloud computing." This is the Internet-based system in which shared resources, software, and information are provided to devices on demand, much the way that electricity moves across the grid. Indeed, as Ramseger sees things, it is an era that Drucker himself helped define.

"Cloud computing has the great potential to put in place the three main elements of Drucker's knowledge society," writes Ramseger, 29, a German native who just joined the World Economic Forum in Geneva as a research analyst. His composition on the topic was recently picked as the winner of the Peter Drucker Challenge, a contest that drew more than

200 entries from around the globe; participants could be no older than 35. (The competition was sponsored by the Drucker Society of Austria, an affiliate of the Drucker Institute, which I run.)

The first element, according to Ramseger, is enhanced connectivity. This is crucial because in a knowledge society, workers tend to take on highly specialized tasks. But "by itself," Drucker explained in his 1995 book, *Managing in a Time of Great Change*, this "specialized knowledge yields no performance." To produce meaningful results, groups of people boasting different areas of expertise must often come together and contribute to a common goal. Cloud computing promises to make this increasingly easy, Ramseger writes, because it will "create many new platforms of exchange for knowledge workers to engage in."

Leverage for Workers

The second element, he says, is a shift in "the balance in employer-employee relations." In his 2002 book, *Managing in the Next Society*, Drucker advised corporations to recognize that they need knowledge workers more than knowledge workers need them. Unlike laborers of the past, Drucker wrote, "they know they can leave" most any time for other opportunities. Ramseger suggests that with cloud computing, this trend toward mobility will only accelerate. "Workers will no longer need to be deskbound," he says. "Instead, by being able to plug into the cloud anytime and anywhere, they will finally be able to own their work tools: a netbook and some server space."

The third element, Ramseger writes, is "flatter hierarchies." Drucker believed that knowledge workers respond only to sound objectives, not the whims of their bosses. "They require a performance-oriented organization rather than an authority-oriented organization," he wrote. Cloud computing, Ramseger says, should help further "liberate the workforce" by encouraging "constant coordination" among all sorts of people, with no reference to their corporate rank or social standing. All that matters is the quality of the knowledge.

Others see the same trend unfolding. A couple of weeks ago, at the second annual Drucker Forum in Vienna, where Ramseger was honored for his winning essay, the London Business School's Lynda Gratton mused about what the planet might be like in 2020 if, as some predict, 5 billion people are then connected through their handheld devices. "The cloud has huge implications for work," Gratton said, because "anyone anywhere will be able to download anything at a cost that's near nil."

Missing the Point

Not everyone is so enthusiastic. Some say the cloud is overhyped, or they dismiss it as a mere fad. Others are focused on security or technical challenges. For his part, Ramseger acknowledges that "there remain many countries with poor Internet infrastructure," which may keep their residents from accessing the cloud. Still others have reduced all discussion of cloud computing to a high-tech horse race, as they handicap which company will emerge as the long-term leader in the field: Amazon, Salesforce .com, Google, Microsoft, or IBM. Or they characterize it simply as a way to ramp up IT outsourcing and thereby save money.

But all of this misses the point. Perhaps more than any technology out there, the cloud stands, in Ramseger's words, to "revolutionize the way we work," if not the way we live. It is a vision so tantalizing, it's hard to imagine that Peter Drucker, if he were still alive today, wouldn't be writing about it himself, mulling the possibilities on his Brother Correctronic.

December 3, 2010

Accelerating UAW's Buy-In at GM

In the mid-1940s, with Peter Drucker serving as a consultant on employee relations, General Motors President Charlie Wilson became convinced that the automaker needed a new approach to dealing with its workers. He designed an early version of "quality circles" in which the rank and file could, as Drucker put it, "identify themselves with product and company," as well as "be held responsible for quality and performance."

The initiative never even got into first gear. To most of GM's executives, the plan "represented the abdication of management's responsibility," Drucker later recalled. The United Auto Workers, Drucker said, also stood "in violent opposition" to the concept—for much the same reason. Walter Reuther, the union's president, didn't want his members performing what he perceived as a manager's job. In fact, Drucker added, Reuther was leery of anything that created a "common center of interest between employer and employee."

I couldn't help but remember Reuther's adamancy this week when I read of the far-more-collaborative spirit advanced by Bob King, the current UAW president. King—who this year faces negotiations with GM, Ford, and Chrysler and is also determined to organize workers at the U.S. factories of foreign companies, including Toyota and Volkswagen—sounds almost like Reuther in reverse.

"We're really committed to the success of companies where we represent workers," King declared in an interview with Bloomberg News. At another point he advocated having his members sit on corporate boards, saying: "The more meaningful voice workers have in all aspects of their employment, the more successful the employer will be."

Partnership in the Employer's Mission

Meanwhile, a set of 11 negotiating principles issued by the union explicitly calls for "partnership in the mission of the employer." It states: "The UAW embraces a performance-based and participatory culture where the union contributes to continual improvement of processes and shared responsibility for quality, innovation, flexibility, and value."

In some respects, we've heard this before. Beginning in the 1970s, unions and companies entered into a range of labor-management participation programs with all sorts of labels: "Total Quality Management," "Employee Involvement," "Quality of Work Life," and so on. The automakers and UAW engaged in more than their fair share of these efforts while experimenting with other forms of teamwork, such as those undertaken at GM's Saturn operation.

But King's vision seems to extend far beyond anything tried before. Earlier attempts at cooperation "were circumscribed by an overall relationship that was more adversarial," says Harley Shaiken, a professor at the University of California–Berkeley who has closely followed the labor scene for many years. King's willingness to have his members weigh in on matters related to productivity—a subject the union has traditionally ignored—is especially noteworthy, according to Shaiken. "We're in new waters going forward," he says.

King is no pushover. He has made clear that the prosperity enjoyed recently by Detroit's automakers needs to flow to those in the UAW, which granted deep concessions to the Big Three to help them cheat their own colossal mismanagement and survive. "We want our membership to share in a very meaningful way in the upside of these companies," asserted King, who was elected union boss last June.

Wealth of Worker Skill and Experience

Still, right alongside this issue of "social justice," Shaiken says, is a companion view that "the UAW in the twenty-first century means working with the automakers to have successful, competitive firms globally." He notes that Detroit's aging workforce, often seen as a negative, offers a wealth of skill and experience for the companies to draw on.

There are lots of reasons to doubt that King's stance will make any real difference. Many smart people believe that the UAW, whose membership has plunged from a high of 1.5 million in 1979 to about 355,000 today, is ultimately headed for extinction.

Richard Block, a professor at the School of Human Resources and Labor Relations at Michigan State University, sees King's platform as merely the latest in a long line of overtures from the UAW. And he suggests that the best thing to come from any of these labor-management alliances is the union's ability to help coordinate the industry's massive downsizing and "cushion the blow" by ensuring that its members aren't involuntarily laid off and receive buyouts instead. When a business is in serious decline, he says, a kind of "industrial-relations hospice may be the best its workers can hope for."

Yet perhaps—just perhaps—King can beat the odds. In his 1989 book, *The New Realities*, Drucker again urged the UAW and car manufacturers to join forces in a way they never had. "The union would still have a role as the representative of the employees against management stupidity, management arbitrariness, and management abuse of power," he wrote. Yet things wouldn't get too contentious, for the UAW would also "work with management on productivity and quality, on keeping the enterprise competitive, and thus maintaining the members' jobs and their incomes."

One can only imagine what the situation might look like now had the UAW and the automakers banded together more than a half-century ago, when Peter Drucker and Charlie Wilson first contemplated going down this road.

January 7, 2011

Uncertainty? Get Over It

If there is one thing you can be certain about, it's that Peter Drucker wouldn't countenance all the complaining by businesspeople about uncertainty.

They're directing their grousing primarily at the federal government, as illustrated by an interview I caught last week on National Public Radio with Andrew Liveris, the chief executive of Dow Chemical. Commenting just before President Barack Obama's State of the Union address, Liveris reeled off a litany of concerns that many American chief executive officers have expressed in recent months.

"Well, I not only have high taxes; I have uncertain taxes," he said. "Right now, I have more regulations coming at me that are not fact-based, not science-based, not data-based. I actually don't even know what my costs are going to be in the next five years. And so I'm sitting back waiting for regulatory reform, and the government, of course, is now engaged on that—health care and the uncertainty around the health-care bill and what's going to end up happening there. Energy policy—we've got lots of uncertainty in the energy policy regimen. I mean, I can keep going, but that's half a dozen."

It's not that Drucker would have felt entirely unsympathetic. "Modern government has become ungovernable," Drucker asserted in his 1968 book, *The Age of Discontinuity*, hitting on a theme that he never backed away from as the decades wore on. "There is no government today that can still claim control of its bureaucracy and of its various agencies."

But Drucker also believed that in the grand scheme of things, government's influence tends to be relatively minor. (Unless, I suppose, you're a federal contractor and your primary customer is Uncle Sam.) Forces outside the public arena act as the main drivers of the most profound changes shaping our world, including the continuing transition to a knowledge age.

"The Futility of Politics"

"If this century proves one thing, it is the futility of politics," Drucker wrote in 1994. "It is the social transformations, like ocean currents deep below the hurricane-tormented surface of the sea, that have had the lasting, indeed the permanent, effect. They, rather than all the violence of the political surface, have transformed not only the society but also the economy, the community, and the polity we live in." Drucker added that "headline-making political events" would remain in this lesser role well into the twenty-first century.

Yet beyond all that there exists another, more fundamental reason to stop griping: Uncertainty is simply part of doing business. Executives need to manage uncertainty, not whine about it.

In fact, ever since the economy shifted from agriculture to manufacturing, uncertainty has been part of the equation. "The farmer knew that if he did not have a corn crop by the time the frost came, he would not have a corn crop at all that year," Drucker wrote in his 1950 book, *The New Society*. "The husbandman knew that if the ewes failed to lamb in the spring, he would not be able to restock his herd. But in industrial production it cannot be predicted with any certainty when a product or service will be successful. Whether it will be successful . . . we call 'risk proper'; but whether it will be successful in one year, five years, or in 20 years is 'uncertainty.'"

More than 50 years later, with the bulk of the nation's blue-collar manufacturing jobs supplanted by knowledge and service work, the amount of haziness managers face has only increased.

"Uncertainty—in the economy, society, politics—has become so great as to render futile, if not counterproductive, the kind of planning most companies still practice: forecasting based on probabilities," Drucker wrote in his 1995 book, *Managing in a Time of Great Change*.

So what then, is a bewildered executive to do?

"Planning for Uncertainty"

To begin, Drucker advised, it's essential to frame things in a new way. "Traditional planning asks, 'What is most likely to happen?'" Drucker noted. "Planning for uncertainty asks instead: 'What has already happened that will create the future?'"

One place to spot these developments, Drucker suggested, is in demographics, particularly the rapidly aging population ballooning across the U.S., Europe, Japan, and elsewhere. Another area to look at is changes in science and technology or in our basic values (think about the environmental movement) that have, as Drucker put it, "already occurred but have yet to have full impact."

"It is commonly believed that innovations create changes, but very few do," Drucker wrote. "Successful innovations exploit changes that have already happened. They exploit the time lag—in science, often 25 or 30 years—between the change itself and its perception and acceptance."

Drucker also called for analyzing structural changes to an industry: fluctuations in productivity, the way consumers' disposable income is distributed, and so forth.

"Over any short-term period their effects are slight," Drucker pointed out. "But in the not-so-long run these structural trends are of far greater importance than the short-term fluctuations to which economists, politicians, and executives give all their attention."

Especially around the time of the State of the Union address.

February 4, 2011

4

On Wall Street and Finance

The Countrywide Conundrum

It's more than a little difficult to imagine Angelo Mozilo, the embattled chief executive of mortgage lending giant Countrywide Financial, being a Drucker disciple. But just last year he didn't hesitate to paint himself that way and, in at least one sense, he was right.

"As the late Peter Drucker once said, the entrepreneur always searches for change, responds to it, and exploits it as an opportunity," Mozilo told an audience of bond holders, bankers, and others. "This is the essence of Countrywide's culture."

Countrywide, lashed like many other companies by the subprime storm, isn't crowing as much anymore. A few weeks ago, it reported a loss of $1.2 billion for the third quarter. Included in that were charges related to plans to cut as many as 12,000 jobs, or about 20 percent of Countrywide's workforce.

The First Responsibility

Meanwhile, Mozilo—long a target of critics for his king-size compensation—is under heavy fire from shareholder activists. (Drucker, too, abhorred excessive CEO pay.) And the Securities & Exchange Commission has reportedly been poking around in Mozilo's prearranged sales of company stock.

More broadly, the mortgage mess brings to mind everything Drucker taught businesses not to do. By peddling complex financial instruments to legions of borrowers who couldn't understand what they were getting into and were unequipped to handle the debt they were taking on, unscrupulous mortgage brokers violated what Drucker termed "the first responsibility" of any professional: to "not knowingly do harm."

By devising ever-more-exotic mortgage-backed securities, Wall Street firms made it tough for most investors to properly assess risk and helped fuel a bubble—precisely the kind of unsustainable, short-term-profit-driven model that Drucker loathed. "Pigs gorging themselves at the trough are always a disgusting spectacle, and you know it won't last long," Drucker said during an earlier market shakeout in the late 1980s.

Regulation Is Key

And by taking advantage of lax regulatory oversight, subprime lenders sidestepped one of their main obligations: to make sure that sufficient standards and oversight are in place, even if it pushes up their costs. In most cases, Drucker wrote in his 1973 magnum opus, *Management: Tasks, Responsibilities, Practices*, "regulation is in the interest of business, and especially in the interest of responsible business."

Without it, Drucker added, there is inevitably crisis and scandal. And that "leads to governmental inquisition, to angry editorials, and eventually to loss of confidence in an entire industry, its management, and its products by broad sectors of the public." Which is, of course, where we are today.

But before totally giving up on subprime mortgages, it's worth remembering they also represent something Drucker applauded (and to which Mozilo referred): a genuine social innovation.

During the 1990s the U.S. saw its homeownership rate rise more than at any time since the '50s; it now stands at about 68 percent. Minorities, who'd been systematically locked out of the system for generations, have made strides. The number of blacks owning homes has climbed from about 42 percent in 1994 to nearly 47 percent. The rate of Latino homeownership has jumped from 41 percent to 50 percent. One big reason for these gains is subprime loans.

Obviously Risky

Yet as the subprime contagion continues to spread—and the ousters of Stan O'Neal at Merrill Lynch and Charles Prince at Citigroup indicate it's going to for some time—the pressure will only increase to tighten mortgage lending to where it was 20 years ago.

Indeed, many commentators "have suggested that we throw out the whole market and go back to the constricted situation of the early 1990s," Edward Gramlich, a senior fellow at the Urban Institute and the author of *Subprime Mortgages: America's Latest Boom and Bust*, told those gathered at a Federal Reserve conference last summer. But "that seems exactly the wrong message to take from the experience," Gramlich said. "The subprime mortgage market was a valid innovation, and it did enable 12 million households to become homeowners."

Lending large sums to people with scant or shaky credit histories is, obviously, risky. Then again, Drucker noted in his 1985 book, *Innovation and Entrepreneurship*, "All economic activity is by definition 'high risk.'"

Simple Greed

The problem with subprime lending was not the nature of the innovation itself. It was the way it was carried out. Correctly executed, "innovation is both conceptual and perceptual," Drucker wrote. "Successful innovators use both the right side and the left side of their brains. They look at figures and they look at people. They work out analytically what the innovation has to be to satisfy an opportunity. And then they go out and look at the customers, the users, to see what their expectations, their values, their needs are. Otherwise one runs the risk of having the right innovation in the wrong form."

In a way, that's just what happened here. Because of simple greed, all sorts of subprime loans were sold with reckless disregard for whether these particular products were appropriate for the consumers snapping them up.

The end result, as Drucker might say, is that the crisis has put all the focus on what shops such as Countrywide have done to society. Largely forgotten is what they've done for it.

November 9, 2007

The Financial Crisis:
What Drucker Would Have Said

Peter Drucker didn't have a whole lot of nice things to say about those on Wall Street, at one point likening them to "Balkan peasants stealing each other's sheep."

Given the magnitude of the latest crisis to grip Fannie Mae, Freddie Mac, American International Group, Lehman Brothers, and their friends, one can only imagine what kind of acid analogy he might have used today.

Or perhaps he would have simply said, "I told you so."

After all, so much of the trouble that has befallen these giants of the investment banking, mortgage, and insurance sectors—and that threatens to "undermine the financial security of all," as President George W. Bush put it—comes from a foolish disregard for the kinds of fundamental lessons that Drucker taught about risk, reach, and responsibility.

Some prefer to complicate things, particularly now that the Bush administration has announced a $700 billion rescue package. Indeed, there is a temptation, in certain quarters, to fuzzy up what has happened here—to mask the basic management failures that are at the root of this disaster by pointing to the intricacies of credit-default swaps, "naked shorts," and other arcana.

Luck Doesn't Last

But as Drucker knew so well, none of this is really very complex: If you make enough dangerous bets—and amassing your fortune on a foundation of laughably loose lending standards and mountains of debt is nothing if not dangerous—you're eventually going to run out of luck.

"No matter how clever the gambler," Drucker asserted, "the laws of probability guarantee that he will lose all that he has gained, and then a good deal more." He wrote these words in the 1990s, as a different group of once-illustrious institutions—Barings, Bankers Trust, Yamaichi Securities—were felled by their recklessness.

Drucker noted that top management professed to be shocked by some of the activities that had taken place at these firms, and it won't be surprising if we hear similar talk this time around—especially if people wind up going to jail. It was reported that the FBI has opened more than two dozen probes into possible fraud connected to the financial meltdown, including investigations at Fannie Mae, Freddie Mac, AIG, and Lehman.

But Drucker didn't buy that senior executives were blind to their employees' egregious behavior a decade ago, and he wouldn't buy it now. "In the first place," he wrote, "there is a limit to coincidences. Such widespread breakdowns cannot be blamed on 'exceptions.' They denote systems failure."

Too Big to Hide

Besides, Drucker added, "in every single one of these 'scandals,' top management seems to have carefully looked the other way as long as trading produced profits (or at least pretended to produce them). Until the losses had become so big that they could no longer be hidden, the gambling trader was a hero and showered with money."

Of course, the pressure to produce these profits—and, in turn, prop up a company's share price—has become unrelenting. It used to be, veteran financial journalist Bob Reed remarked recently, "the stock price was an important component of something more grand: how well the company was managed, product quality, innovations, customer satisfaction—you know, the business." But over time, those pursuits have become largely overshadowed by just one: maximizing shareholder value.

To Drucker, this mentality was anachronistic. "One thing is clear to anyone with the slightest knowledge of political or economic history: The present-day assertion of 'absolute shareholder sovereignty' . . . is the last hurrah of nineteenth century, basically preindustrial capitalism," he wrote in a 1988 article. "It violates many people's sense of justice."

Perhaps even more important, Drucker said, this lack of balance is unsettling in a world in which large institutions have such an enormous effect on so much—on the portfolios of shareholders, yes, but also on the lives of millions of other people, as we're seeing right now.

Long-Term Thinking

In this day and age, "modern enterprise, especially large enterprise, can do its economic job—including making profits for the shareholders—only if it is being managed for the long run," Drucker wrote. "Altogether far too much in society—jobs, careers, communities—depends on the economic fortunes of large enterprises to subordinate them completely to the interests of any one group, including shareholders."

All of which leads, in the end, to the biggest thing missing today on Wall Street and in much of Corporate America: an ethic of responsibility.

Drucker believed strongly that every business must contribute to the general health of society. This means doing "good works" where appropriate. But above all, it means ensuring that the business itself is well-managed and built to last.

"The institution's performance of its specific mission is . . . society's first need and interest," Drucker wrote in his 1973 book, *Management: Tasks, Responsibilities, Practices*. "A bankrupt business is not a desirable employer and is unlikely to be a good neighbor in a community. Nor will it create the capital for tomorrow's jobs and the opportunities for tomorrow's workers."

I often tell people that there are a million reasons to read and reread what Peter Drucker had to say. This week, it's more like 700 billion.

September 26, 2008

Financial Leadership, the Missing Ingredient

As the financial crisis went from bad to worse last week, policymakers and business executives fussed and fretted over the drying up of credit around the world. The bigger problem, though, is a severe shortage of something else entirely: leadership.

Peter Drucker—who began writing on the topic in the 1940s, long before it became fashionable—considered true leaders those who bring accountability, consistency, and a sharp sense of what must be accomplished to all they do. When it comes to the current mess, those in charge on Wall Street and in Washington have failed to deliver on all three fronts.

Most appalling, perhaps, were the performances on Capitol Hill by the former heads of Lehman Brothers and American International Group, who blamed devious short-sellers, unpredictable regulators, and careless colleagues for their firms' woes—just about everybody, that is, but themselves. "Looking back on my time as CEO," Robert Willumstad, AIG's former chief, told a House oversight committee, "I don't believe AIG could have done anything differently."

The Height of Prudence?

Richard Fuld, who presided over the downfall of Lehman, told the panel that all of his decisions "were both prudent and appropriate" given the information he had at the time. Yet if this is true, it indicates that his organization was ill-equipped to get him the information he required—a horrendous management breakdown in and of itself.

"Harry Truman's folksy 'The buck stops here' is still as good a definition as any" of leadership, Drucker wrote in his 1967 classic, *The Effective Executive*. Willumstad and Fuld made a mockery of the buck-stops-here standard.

Meantime, public officials haven't displayed many exemplary leadership qualities, either. "The leader's first task is to be the trumpet that sounds a clear sound," Drucker wrote. "Effective leadership—and again this is very old wisdom—is not based on being clever; it is based primarily on being consistent."

But clarity and consistency have been largely absent from the government's response to the crisis. At first, the Bush Administration had an awful time explaining why its $700-billion rescue plan wasn't simply a taxpayer-funded bailout for the companies responsible for the disaster. And all along, the Administration's efforts have seemed haphazard and uncertain, as if it isn't exactly sure what notes on the trumpet it should try to play. At one point, for example, Treasury officials belittled the idea of the government taking an ownership stake in the nation's banks. Then they reversed course and announced Tuesday that they'd invest $250 billion in the sector.

Their action helped spur a stock-market rally after shares were completely battered last week. But it remains to be seen whether the government's plan is even focused on the right things. It's quite possible, after all, that it could succeed in shoring up the banking system in the short term while neglecting to ensure that another financial meltdown doesn't materialize down the line.

One of the most serious issues that hasn't been adequately addressed, for instance, is mandating that financial institutions divulge precisely what kinds of risks they face today and going forward.

"There have been lots of halfhearted attempts at improving this over the years, most of them driven by big credit or trading losses, concerns about systemic stability or damage to clients," Merrill Lynch veteran Erik Banks wrote in his disturbingly prescient 2004 book, *The Failure of Wall Street*. "Something bad happens, regulators ask for more risk information, banks produce it for a while, no one finds it particularly useful because it is couched in such oblique terms that nothing is actually conveyed, and then it gets buried in unreadable form in the financial statement footnotes; regulators, clients, and investors forget about it, and it's back to the status quo till the next blowup."

This time, we must do better—but that calls for leaders who have the courage to treat not only the current calamity but also its underlying causes, including a lack of transparency.

Expanding the Boundaries

Indeed, the way Drucker saw it, one of a leader's most important jobs is to frame carefully what he or she hopes to accomplish with every major decision. "What are the objectives the decision has to reach?" Drucker wrote. "What are the minimum goals it has to attain? What are the conditions it has to satisfy?"

Drucker pointed out that in science, these are known as "boundary conditions." And falling short of them can be dire. "A decision that does not satisfy the boundary conditions," Drucker asserted, "is worse than one which wrongly defines the problem."

He recounted that President Roosevelt expanded his own boundary conditions after the "sudden economic collapse" between the summer of 1932 and the spring of 1933. Earlier, Roosevelt had pursued a relatively conservative policy of economic recovery. But when the situation deteriorated, his goal necessarily became not just recovery but comprehensive reform.

It is a path we'd be wise to walk again. The question is, will anyone provide the leadership to take us there?

October 14, 2008

10 Management Lessons from Lehman's Demise

Former Lehman Brothers Vice President Lawrence McDonald has titled his insider account of the firm's demise *A Colossal Failure of Common Sense*. Peter Drucker, meanwhile, was once said by the London Business School's Sumantra Ghoshal to "practice the scholarship of common sense."

With this sharp contrast in mind, here are 10 management lessons derived from Drucker's insights, a year after Lehman went bust:

1. Executives who are preoccupied with their company's daily stock price or consumed with quarterly earnings targets don't make very good stewards of the enterprise. "The most critical management job is to balance short term and long term," Drucker declared in a 1999 interview, adding that a "one-sided emphasis" on the former is "deleterious and dangerous."

Ultimately, said Drucker, deciding "whether a business should be run for short-term results or with a focus on the long term is . . . a question of values. Financial analysts believe that businesses can be run for both simultaneously. Successful businesspeople know better."

2. Tying individual compensation to short-term gains only exacerbates the problem. It rewards the executive "for doing the wrong thing," Drucker said. "Instead of asking, 'Are we making the right decision?' the temptation is to ask, 'How did we close today?' It is encouragement to loot the corporation."

The Aspen Institute recently urged companies to "define firm-specific metrics of long-term value," and then use these measures "both to communicate with investors" and to "better align executive compensation" with what truly matters. The Federal Reserve is also considering forcing financial institutions to adopt policies that tie pay to long-term performance. Drucker would have lauded this initiative.

3. People don't like it when those who've exhibited the worst cases of managerial myopia get filthy rich in the process. Inevitably, said Drucker, there is "an outbreak of bitterness and contempt for the super-corporate chieftains who pay themselves millions." Former Lehman Chief Executive Richard Fuld, who enjoyed $40 million in pay and benefits in 2007, recently complained that he has "been pummeled. They're looking for someone to dump on right now, and that's me," Fuld said.

Drucker, it's plain, wouldn't feel sorry for him. "Few top executives," he once remarked, "can even imagine the hatred . . . and fury that has been created" because of their unjustified pay. "I don't know what form it will take, but the envy developing from their enormous wealth will cause trouble."

4. High profits don't necessarily mean that you're producing anything of genuine value. Lehman, in fact, reported record earnings in 2005, 2006, and 2007. That may have impressed the investment community. But that's not what counts in the end. "Securities analysts believe that companies make money," said Drucker. "Companies make shoes."

5. Moving money around isn't the same thing as producing actual goods and services. To be sure, financial instruments have a vital role to play in spreading risk and ensuring the smooth functioning of the global economy. But when Wall Street is generating 40 percent of U.S. corporate profits, something has gotten way out of whack.

Drucker called this worldwide flow of capital and credit the "symbol economy," as distinct from "the real economy." "Americans," he said, "cannot live in a symbol economy where businessmen play only with numbers."

6. When you buy and sell lots of assets at prices that are considerably higher than the underlying value of what's being traded, the run-up can't possibly last. "The average duration of a soap bubble is known—it's about 26 seconds," said Drucker. "Then the surface tension becomes too great and it begins to burst. For speculative crazes, it's about 18 months."

7. Even professional bankers, who ostensibly are experts in "risk management," aren't immune from the soap-bubble syndrome. Of course, this doesn't mean that they don't try to outsmart the system. The tendency is for firms to resort to "'trading for their own accounts,' that is, to outright speculation," Drucker noted. "This, however, as centuries of financial history teach (beginning with the Medici in fifteenth-century Europe) has only one—but an absolutely certain—outcome: catastrophic losses."

8. It's especially hard to avoid those losses when you don't want to hear any bad news. Lehman and most other investment banks refused to even contemplate the "potential danger" of becoming overly leveraged, McDonald recounts in his book. "Wall Street was listening for calm seas, record profits, best-ever growth, joy, wealth, prosperity, and b-o-o-o-o-n-u-u-s. Anything less was essentially out of the culture." When Lehman's fixed-income chief warned Fuld about the unsustainable bets that the firm was making, McDonald adds, Fuld "decided to bully him, to belittle him publicly."

Other former Lehman bankers paint a similar picture, saying that Fuld and his top lieutenant weren't interested in dissenting views. But "dissent . . . is essential for effective decision making," Drucker said. Without it, those at the top simply can't take on what Drucker described as "the most important task" they're responsible for: "to anticipate crisis."

9. As long as human beings are in charge of our major institutions, this won't be the last crisis we see. "Scandals are a normal feature of the landscape," said Drucker, who wouldn't be shocked that companies are once again taking on substantial risk and selling the kinds of exotic financial products that triggered the Great Recession. "They very typically begin with something that goes wrong, and you . . . brush it under the rug. And you end up by trying to brush elephants under the rug. And then it doesn't work any more, and it collapses."

10. "Stupid people make stupid mistakes. Brilliant people make brilliant mistakes."

September 18, 2009

Goldman Sachs: Failure of Innovation

Whether Goldman Sachs Group broke the law remains to be seen. But one thing is for sure: The firm violated one of Peter Drucker's core principles of innovation.

"Innovation is an effect in economy and society, a change in the behavior of customers . . . of people in general," Drucker wrote. "Or it is a change in a process—that is, in how people work and produce something. Innovation therefore always has to be close to the market, focused on the market, indeed market-driven."

By sharp contrast, so-called innovations exploited by Goldman—mortgage-related securities the firm was betting would decline in value—weren't geared to the broader market at all; they were inwardly focused and traded by Goldman for its own profit.

As Carl Levin, the Michigan Democrat who chairs the Senate Permanent Subcommittee on Investigations, has observed: "The nature of Wall Street's function has changed. They still argue that they're providing capital and stimulating innovation, and to some extent they are. But there's been a significant shift here to the model where they're out for themselves. Their client is themselves."

Serving the In-House Trader

Drucker saw this mess coming a long time ago. In a piece he penned in 1999, "Financial Services: Innovate or Die," he frowned on the kind of transactions that have done such terrible damage to Goldman's reputation and, more important, to the world economy. Since the 1970s, he wrote, "the only innovations" among banks "have been any number of allegedly 'scientific' derivatives.

"But these financial instruments are not designed to provide a service to customers," Drucker continued. "They are designed to make the trader's speculations more profitable and at the same time less risky—surely a violation of the basic laws of risk and unlikely to work. In fact, they are unlikely to work better than the inveterate gambler's equally scientific system for beating the odds at Monte Carlo or Las Vegas."

The tendency to inflate one's bottom line without actually creating anything of real value (a good, a service, a job, a gain in productivity) hasn't infected only Wall Street, of course. Across countless industries, many executives now spend more time and energy on financial engineering than they do on product engineering.

Drucker, for his part, was hardly naïve about high finance. He understood full well that businesses must engage in hedging and option trading to deal with volatile fuel prices or fluctuating currencies. "Foreign exchange risks," Drucker noted, "make speculators out of the most conservative managements."

True Innovation: ATMs

But that is not the same as a bank actively trading for its own account, a practice that can quickly turn those who traditionally have been the institution's primary customers into secondary considerations. "I believe banks should be banks serving clients," Citigroup Chief Executive Vikram Pandit recently wrote to President Obama, in a statement that, in a different day and age, would have seemed as laughably obvious as the color of George Washington's white horse.

Former Federal Reserve Chairman Paul Volcker, who has been trying to erect a wall between banks that stick to taking deposits and those that want to make risky wagers for their own advantage, commented not long ago that only one financial innovation has been worth much of anything in the past 20 years. And it isn't the collateralized debt obligations (CDOs) at the center of the Goldman scandal. Rather, it's the automated teller machine. "That really helps people . . . and is a real convenience," Volcker said. "How many other innovations can you tell me that have been as important to the individual?"

Volcker's remark was made half in jest, but Drucker certainly would have appreciated the sentiment. In his 1999 essay, he explained that in the two or three decades following World War II, a steady stream of innovations flowed from the banking sector, including the Eurodollar, the Eurobond, the first modern pension fund, and the credit card.

He also highlighted the pioneering work of Citibank's Walter Wriston, who, as Drucker described it, "immediately changed his company from being an American bank with foreign branches into a global bank with multiple headquarters." Wriston's subsequent insight, "that 'banking is not about money; it is about information,'" Drucker said, "created what I would call the 'theory of the business' for the financial services industry."

The Middle-Class Market

But ever since Wriston's day, Drucker asserted, bankers have done little to innovate, at least for the benefit of their patrons. Drucker did, though, see a possible sweet spot for the industry: servicing individual middle-class investors around the globe.

Drucker pointed out that one of his consulting clients, the St. Louis–based brokerage Edward Jones, was the first to see the potential in this market about 40 years ago. Most of the people that Edward Jones serves aren't particularly wealthy, Drucker wrote, but "the sums they collectively pour into investments dwarf by several orders of magnitude everything all the world's 'superrich' together have available, including oil sheikhs, Indonesian rajas, and software billionaires."

Today, Drucker added, the kind of customer to which Edward Jones caters "constitutes the fastest-growing population group in every developed and emerging country," including Latin America, Japan, South Korea, and the cities of mainland China. "This market," Drucker suggested, "might become the twenty-first century's successor to the world's first financial 'mass market': life insurance."

I can't say whether Drucker's forecast will come true. But I do know this: We'd all be better off with innovations that look more like ATMs and less like CDOs.

May 7, 2010

5

On Values and Responsibility

Why Manners Matter at Work

For those of you who never bothered to pay attention to your mother, perhaps you'll listen to Peter Drucker, the father of modern management, instead.

This cheeky thought has crept into my head a couple of times in the last few weeks as I've read a run of stories about etiquette (or lack thereof) in the workplace. Most recently, there was the case study posted on the *BusinessWeek* website about a worker who had to deal with a boorish boss.

And just a couple of weeks ago, I saw that officials in Anaheim, Calif.—home to Disneyland—were set to hold classes for cabbies, hotel employees, and other service workers in town to ensure they act as knowledgeable and enthusiastic hosts for tourists, while also minding their p's and q's.

The hope is that the lessons they learn—to be professional and gracious—will be noticed not only by visitors but by their colleagues, too. "We teach them that they're part of a team, and that what they do rubs off on the team," says Mickey Schaefer, president of Mickey Schaefer & Associates, the Tucson, Ariz., firm overseeing the training. "We've become such an informal society that we all tend to slip. We want to get back to the basics. . . . Your attitude, your cleanliness, your friendliness all matter."

Drucker, who recalled watching his grandmother confront a young thug on a Vienna streetcar in the early 1930s and lecture him about the virtue of good manners, would certainly agree. "Manners are the lubricating oil of an organization," Drucker wrote. "It is a law of nature that two moving bodies in contact with each other create friction. This is as true for human beings as it is for inanimate objects. Manners—simple things like saying 'please' and 'thank you' and knowing a person's name or asking after her family—enable two people to work together whether they like each other or not."

Day In and Day Out

As the last part of his comment makes clear, Drucker was never particularly sentimental about all this. He wasn't interested in fostering friendships; he was, as usual, trying to enhance performance.

"Warm feelings and pleasant words are meaningless, are indeed a false front for wretched attitudes, if there is no achievement in what is, after all, a work-focused and task-focused relationship," Drucker cautioned in *The Effective Executive*, his 1967 classic. "On the other hand, an occasional rough word will not disturb a relationship that produces results and accomplishments for all concerned."

Yet Drucker knew that, day in and day out, maintaining a sense of decorum is an important ingredient in any well-managed enterprise. "Bad manners," he said, "rub people raw; they do leave permanent scars."

Maybe even literally. Last month, the Joint Commission, an accreditation body for the U.S. health-care industry, ordered 15,000 hospitals, nursing homes, laboratories, and other facilities to implement standards that spell out what is considered "acceptable and unacceptable" personal conduct and to establish "a formal process" to manage things when the rules get broken.

"Health-care leaders and caregivers have known for years that intimidating and disruptive behaviors are a serious problem," the commission said. "Verbal outbursts, condescending attitudes, refusing to take part in assigned duties, and physical threats all create breakdowns in the teamwork, communication, and collaboration necessary to deliver patient care."

Civility Is Crucial

It isn't just medical personnel who could stand a reminder of this. A study released last year, based on a survey of more than 54,000 employees from 179 organizations across Australia and New Zealand, found that one in five employees experiences an incident of bad manners at work once a month.

People who exclude coworkers from situations, interrupt them when they're speaking, make derogatory remarks, withhold information, and disparage others' ideas can have "a large impact on employee engagement," Barbara Griffin, an organizational psychologist from the University of

Western Sydney and the coauthor of the study, said at the time it was released. In fact, she noted, this kind of atmosphere may well determine "whether you stay in an organization, speak positively about your job, or go that extra mile. It can also cause psychological distress and poor physical health."

As commonsensical as this may seem, many managers fail to grasp just how crucial civility is. "Bright people, especially young bright people, often do not understand this," Drucker wrote. "If analysis shows that someone's brilliant work fails again and again as soon as cooperation from others is required, it probably indicates a lack of courtesy—that is, a lack of manners."

People Skills Trump Talent

This, of course, undermines not only the organization but the individual. In his acclaimed book *What Got You Here Won't Get You There: How Successful People Become Even More Successful,* executive coach (and fellow BusinessWeek.com columnist) Marshall Goldsmith points out that "people skills," more than smarts or technical talents, frequently "make the difference in how high you go" in your career.

Among the challenges in interpersonal behavior Goldsmith says many of us must strive to overcome: speaking when angry, being overly negative, making excuses, claiming undeserved credit, not listening well, and "failing to express gratitude—the most basic form of bad manners."

And with that, there is but one thing left to say: Thank you for reading.

August 14, 2008

Put a Cap on CEO Pay

For a guy whose astute counsel helped to make so many CEOs rich, Peter Drucker had an intense loathing of exorbitant executive salaries. He hated high CEO pay on every level: what it said about the individual as a leader, how it undermined the smooth functioning of the organization, and the way it tore at the fabric of society as a whole.

Drucker's strong feelings on the subject—he once termed sky-high CEO compensation "a serious disaster"—are well worth revisiting in light of the news that the men who sat atop Fannie Mae and Freddie Mac could be eligible for as much as $24 million in severance and other benefits after being ousted from their positions.

Last week the federal government was forced to step in and rescue the faltering mortgage giants in a move that could cost taxpayers billions.

Although it wasn't immediately clear whether the two departing CEOs, Fannie's Daniel Mudd and Freddie's Richard Syron, would actually walk away with all that dough, the prospect of such a windfall has resonated on the Presidential campaign trail and helped to stoke a national debate about executive pay.

Drucker's stance on the issue, articulated consistently over many years, was controversial. But it was rooted in his belief that the best leaders are those who understand that what comes with their authority is the weight of responsibility, not "the mantle of privilege," as writer and editor Thomas Stewart described Drucker's view. It's their job "to do what is right for the enterprise—not for shareholders alone, and certainly not for themselves alone."

Last year, according to a report just issued by the Institute for Policy Studies and United for a Fair Economy, S&P 500 CEOs received pay packages worth, on average, $10.5 million. That was 344 times the earnings of the average American worker.

What Drucker thought was more appropriate was a ratio around 25-to-1 (as he suggested in a 1977 article) or 20-to-1 (as he expressed in a 1984 essay and several times thereafter). Widen the pay gap much beyond that, Drucker asserted, and it makes it difficult to foster the kind of team-work that most businesses require to succeed.

"I'm not talking about the bitter feelings of the people on the plant floor," Drucker told a reporter in 2004. "They're convinced that their bosses are crooks anyway. It's the midlevel management that is incredibly disillusioned" by CEO compensation that seems to have no bounds.

This is especially true, Drucker explained in an earlier interview, when CEOs pocket huge sums while laying off workers. That kind of action, he said, is "morally unforgivable."

Notably, Drucker wasn't opposed to rewarding some people like kings. "There should, indeed there must, be exceptions," he wrote. "A 'star,' whether the supersalesman in the insurance company or the scientist in the lab who comes up with a half-dozen highly profitable research break-throughs, should be paid without any income limitation."

But the chief executive has a special duty to show that he or she is "just a hired hand," Drucker said, invoking the words of J.P. Morgan. "That's what today's CEOs have forgotten."

Not all of them, of course. Last year, Costco Wholesale CEO Jim Sinegal made $3.2 million, including a $350,000 salary, an $80,000 bonus, and stock grants and options valued at $2.6 million. While hardly chump change, that was far less than what his peers raked in—and far less than what Costco's compensation committee wanted to give him. But the panel said in a regulatory filing that it was willing to respect his "wishes to receive modest compensation, in part because it believes that higher amounts would not change Mr. Sinegal's motivation and performance."

Setting pay for top executives can be tricky, even for those whose instinct is to nip their remuneration. In the mid-1980s, after consulting with Drucker, furniture maker Herman Miller agreed that its CEO's pay would be restricted to 20 times the average of all its employees. "The subtle part of this limit was the message to the CEO: If you want to get more pay, you need to do it by raising the average pay" of everyone at the company, the man who used to hold the post, Dick Ruch, recalled in his book *Leaders & Followers*.

But in 1997, Herman Miller ditched Drucker's model. "From a com-petitive standpoint," Ruch said, "we needed to eliminate the cap to attract and retain the right people."

Drucker himself conceded that compensation formulas are inherently difficult to develop. "I would be the last person to claim that a 'fair,' let alone a 'scientific,' system can be devised," he wrote. Yet at the same time, he never gave up on the 20-to-1 rule for CEOs, touting it as the right thing for the good of the organization, as well as for the general health of society.

Allowing an enormous disparity in income to exist "corrodes," Drucker warned. "It destroys mutual trust between groups that have to live together and work together."

And, on occasion, bail each other out.

September 12, 2008

A Time for Ethical Self-Assessment

This may be the season of giving, but it sure feels like everybody is suddenly on the take. Siemens, the German engineering giant, agreed this month to pay a record $1.6 billion to U.S. and European authorities to settle charges that it routinely used bribes and kickbacks to secure public works contracts across the globe. Prominent New York attorney Marc Dreier—called by one U.S. prosecutor a "Houdini of impersonation and false documents"—has been accused by the feds of defrauding hedge funds and other investors out of $380 million.

And then, of course, there's financier Bernard L. Madoff, who is said to have confessed to a Ponzi scheme of truly epic proportions: a swindle of $50 billion, an amount roughly equal to the GPD of Luxembourg.

All told, it begs the question that Peter Drucker first raised in a provocative 1981 essay in the journal *The Public Interest* and that later became the title of a chapter in his book *The Ecological Vision*: "Can there be 'business ethics'"?

Drucker didn't pose this to suggest that business was inherently incapable of demonstrating ethical behavior. Nor was he positing that the workplace should somehow be exempt from moral concerns. Rather, his worry was that to speak of "business ethics" as a distinct concept was to twist it into something that "is not compatible with what ethics always was supposed to be."

What Drucker feared, specifically, was that executives could say they were meeting their social responsibilities as business leaders—protecting jobs and generating wealth—while engaging in practices that were plainly abhorrent. "Ethics for them," Drucker wrote, "is a cost-benefit calculation . . . and that means that the rulers are exempt from the demands of ethics, if only their behavior can be argued to confer benefits on other people."

It's hard to imagine that a Madoff or a Dreier would even attempt to get away with such tortured logic: an ends-justify-the-means attitude that Drucker labeled "casuistry." But we all know managers who've tried to rationalize an unscrupulous act by claiming that it served some greater good.

The Mirror Test

In his book *Resisting Corporate Corruption*, Stephen Arbogast notes that when Enron higher-ups sought an exemption from the company's ethics policy so that they could move forward with certain dubious financial dealings, the arrangement was made to "seem a sacrifice for the benefit of Enron." Reinhard Siekaczek, a former Siemens executive, told *The New York Times* that the company's showering of foreign officials with bribes "was about keeping the business unit alive and not jeopardizing thousands of jobs overnight."

For Drucker, the best way for a business—indeed, for any organization—to create an ethical environment is for its people to partake in what he came to call in a 1999 article "the mirror test." In his 1981 piece, Drucker had a fancier name for this idea: He termed it "The Ethics of Prudence." But either way, it boils down to the same thing: When you look in the mirror in the morning, what kind of person do you want to see?

The Ethics of Prudence, Drucker wrote, "does not spell out what 'right' behavior is." It assumes, instead, "that what is wrong behavior is clear enough—and if there is any doubt, it is 'questionable' and to be avoided." Drucker added that "by following prudence, everyone regardless of status becomes a leader" and remains so by "avoiding any act which would make one the kind of person one does not want to be, does not respect."

Drucker went on: "If you don't want to see a pimp when you look in the shaving mirror in the morning, don't hire call girls the night before to entertain congressmen, customers, or salesmen. On any other basis, hiring call girls may be condemned as vulgar and tasteless, and may be shunned as something fastidious people do not do. It may be frowned upon as uncouth. It may even be illegal. But only in prudence is it ethically relevant. This is what Kierkegaard, the sternest moralist of the nineteenth century, meant when he said that aesthetics is the true ethics."

Time to Reflect

Drucker cautioned that the Ethics of Prudence "can easily degener-ate" into hollow appearances and "the hypocrisy of public relations." Yet despite this danger, Drucker believed that "the Ethics of Prudence is surely appropriate to a society of organizations" in which "an extraordinarily large number of people are in positions of high visibility, if only within one organization. They enjoy this visibility not, like the Christian Prince, by virtue of birth, nor by virtue of wealth—that is, not because they are personages. They are functionaries and important only through their responsibility to take right action. But this is exactly what the Ethics of Prudence is all about."

Now is the time of year when many of us find ourselves sitting in church or in synagogue, or, if we're not religious, simply taking stock of who we are and where we want to be as the calendar turns. But what's even more critical is that we continue this sort of honest self-assessment when we return to our jobs in early 2009.

"I have learned more theology as a practicing management consultant than when I taught religion," Drucker once said. This, he explained, is because "management always deals with the nature of Man and (as all of us with any practical experience have learned) with Good and Evil as well."

So take the mirror test now—and then keep taking it well after the Christmas ornaments have been packed away and the Hanukkah candles have burned down to the nub. In the meantime, happy holidays to all.

December 23, 2008

Obama's Call to Duty Echoes Drucker on Ethical Organizations

When Peter Drucker was asked toward the end of his long life to list his greatest contributions, he pointed to his pioneering insight that management had extended beyond the realm of business to become "the governing organ of all institutions of modern society." He also noted, without embellishment or false modesty, that "I established the study of management as a discipline in its own right."

And then he added this: "I focused this discipline on people and power; on values, structure, and constitution; and above all on responsibilities." For extra emphasis, he typed the last part of the sentence in capital letters.

I thought about Drucker's list this week, as President Barack Obama summoned the R-word in an inaugural address that was by turns soaring and sober. "What is required of us now," he declared, "is a new era of responsibility."

Ethical Leadership

But what are these "duties to ourselves, our nation, and the world" that Obama has asked us to "seize gladly"? What, really, can we be expected to do at a time when as the President himself put it, "our economy is badly weakened. . . . Homes have been lost, jobs shed, businesses shuttered." How can each of us, in our own way, help provide for the common good?

Part of the answer lies in Obama's call for service and volunteering—a force that Drucker also viewed as "a powerful countercurrent" to the "decay and dissolution of family and community and . . . loss of values" in America.

But for Drucker, there was something even more fundamental to the notion of responsibility. It begins with the recognition that over the last 150 years we've become a society of big organizations. And when these organizations aren't effectively managed and ethically led, society as a whole stands to suffer.

Foresight Matters

Who could doubt that these days? What's good for General Motors may be good for the country, but the corollary is surely true: When things go bad at GM (or Citigroup or Fannie Mae), it's lousy for us all.

"Economic performance is the first responsibility of a business," Drucker wrote. "Indeed, a business that does not show a profit at least equal to its cost of capital is irresponsible; it wastes society's resources. Economic performance is the base without which a business cannot discharge any other responsibilities, cannot be a good employer, a good citizen, a good neighbor. But economic performance is not the only responsibility of a business. . . . Every organization must assume full responsibility for its impact on employees, the environment, customers, and whomever and whatever it touches. This is its social responsibility."

What's more, it can't do this after the fact. "It is the job of the organization," Drucker explained, "to look ahead and to think through which of its impacts are likely to become social problems. And then it is the duty of the organization to try to prevent these undesirable side results."

What's Socially Responsible?

And yet organizations must do more than simply keep the negative from happening; to be truly responsible, they must leave a mark on the positive side of society's ledger sheet.

The best way to accomplish this, Drucker advised, is for the organization to convert "into opportunities for its own performance the satisfaction of social needs and wants." This approach, Drucker noted in the late 1960s, another time of intense anxiety for the nation, "may be particularly important in a period of discontinuity."

If there is a danger in satisfying social needs, Drucker recognized, it occurs when organizations fall prey to the temptation to overreach—to try to take on tasks for which they're not properly equipped. "Organizations . . . do not act 'socially responsible' when they concern themselves with 'social problems' outside of their own sphere of competence and action," he said. "They act 'socially responsible' when they satisfy society's needs through concentration on their own specific job. They act most responsibly when they convert public need into their own achievement."

So what does this come down to for you and me?

Although Drucker wrote about "social responsibility" in the context of the organization, he was quick to remind that "the organization itself, like every collective, is a legal fiction. It is individuals in the organization who make the decisions and take the actions which are then ascribed to the institution, whether it be the 'United States,' the 'General Electric Company,' or 'Misericordia Hospital.'"

Mindful Managing

It is up to us, then, to be mindful of our impact, no matter what kind of work we're engaged in, to do no harm, and to actively look for ways to solve social ills whenever it makes sound business sense to do so.

Finally, it's up to us to perform. Otherwise, the organizations in Drucker's "society of organizations" will never be healthy and stable.

This holds true for both managers and other workers, especially the knowledge workers whose ranks continue to swell. "The well-being of our entire society," said Drucker, "depends increasingly on the ability of these large numbers of knowledge workers to be effective."

Being responsible not only means doing the right things. It means doing the right things well.

January 23, 2009

Trust: Effective Managers
Make It a Priority

L ast week, in describing how she has turned around Kraft Foods, Chief Executive Irene Rosenfeld highlighted the way the company has stepped up its marketing and spurred product development. But there's an additional ingredient that Rosenfeld mentioned, which far too many managers miss: inspiring trust throughout the enterprise.

As Kraft's restructuring has played out over the past few years, executives have made a real effort to be "straightforward, open, and honest"—even in the midst of plant closings and job cuts, Rosenfeld told the World Business Forum in New York. The strong sense of trust that this has fostered, she said, has "been a critical part of our ability to get things done."

Peter Drucker had a similar recipe for success. "Organizations are no longer built on force," he wrote in his book *Management Challenges for the 21st Century*. "They are increasingly built on trust."

No company, nonprofit, or government agency can "prevent a major catastrophe," Drucker added, "but you can build an organization that is battle-ready, that has high morale, that knows how to behave, that trusts itself and where people trust one another. In military training, the first rule is to instill soldiers with trust in their officers, because without trust they won't fight."

Plenty of businesses understand this, of course. Each year, the Great Place to Work Institute surveys tens of thousands of employees through its "Trust Index" and then extols those companies that offer extraordinary environments of "credibility, respect, fairness, pride, and camaraderie." Topping its latest roster are NetApp, Edward Jones, Boston Consulting Group, Google, and Wegmans Food Markets.

Lack of Trust Leads to Dysfunction

The stunning thing, though, is how many companies clearly don't get it. Polls in recent years by Watson Wyatt, BlessingWhite, and others have found that fewer than half of all workers trust what senior management is telling them. Too many executives try to hide things or spin them.

And once trust is undermined, everything else is prone to unravel. Patrick Lencioni, the author of *The Five Dysfunctions of a Team*, points out that for any organization to be effective—with results driven by employees who feel truly engaged in, and committed to, their work—there must exist an atmosphere where people can air opposing views, even passionately.

But without trust—without people willing to be vulnerable to one another and admit their weaknesses and mistakes—that's impossible. "Conflict without trust is politics," Lencioni remarked during his own World Business Forum presentation.

Drucker, who warned against reaching quick consensus when tough decisions have to be made, would certainly agree. "There is a very old saying—it goes all the way back to Aristotle and later on became an axiom of the early Catholic Church: In essentials unity, in action freedom, and in all things trust," Drucker wrote. "And trust requires that dissent come out into the open, and that it be seen as honest disagreement."

How Managers Can Establish Trust

As important as trust is, it's not easy to establish. It takes a while, which is why Drucker counseled companies not to thrust a brand-new hire into a major assignment. Even if this person is highly skilled, he or she won't yet have earned the trust of coworkers.

Wrote Drucker: "As Winston Churchill's ancestor the great Duke of Marlborough observed some three centuries ago, 'The basic trouble in coalition warfare is that one has to entrust victory, if not one's life, to a fellow commander whom one knows by reputation rather than by performance.' In the corporation as in the military, without personal knowledge built up over a period of time there can be neither trust nor effective communication."

But how does one win trust as a manager?

In Drucker's view, it's crucial to be able to set ego aside and do what's best for the organization. "The leaders who work most effectively . . .

never say 'I,'" he noted. "And that's not because they have trained themselves not to say 'I.' They don't think 'I.' They think 'we'; they think 'team.' . . . There is an identification (very often, quite unconscious) with the task and with the group. This is what creates trust, what enables you to get the task done."

Still, by far the biggest way to gain trust is simply to be consistent—to do what you say you're going to do, to act in ways that are in step with what you profess to believe in, to advance projects that are in harmony with the organization's mission and values. "Trust means that you know what to expect of people," Drucker declared. "Trust is mutual understanding. Not mutual love, not even mutual respect. Predictability."

Hypocrisy probably wouldn't rank very high on most managers' lists of the biggest missteps they could make. But it should. Your colleagues are watching closely. Trust me.

October 16, 2009

Executives Are Wrong
to Devalue Values

M cKinsey & Co. released a survey this week on "leadership through the crisis and after." Had Peter Drucker parsed the poll, however, I think he would have found it most revealing in terms of how we got into such a mess in the first place.

When asked what are the most important organizational capabilities for managing corporate performance, the 763 executives who responded—representing a range of regions, industries, and functions—picked two more often than any other. The first was "leadership," which was described as the facility to "shape and inspire the actions of others." The second was "direction," or the "capacity to articulate where the company is heading and how to get there" in an aligned manner.

Stuck at the very bottom of the list, meanwhile, was the ability to "foster a shared understanding of values." A mere 8 percent of respondents cited this factor as crucial, compared with 49 percent for leadership and 46 percent for direction. What's more, those taking the survey indicated that ensuring shared values has become less vital since the economic crisis began, while the other two qualities have become more significant.

For Drucker, these numbers surely would have been troubling. The way he saw things, any organization needs to demonstrate achievement in three major areas if it's to be successful: generating "direct results," "developing people for tomorrow," and the "building of values." If a business is "deprived of performance in any one of these areas, it will decay and die," Drucker warned in *The Effective Executive*, his 1967 classic. "All three therefore have to be built into the contribution of every executive."

Leadership and Values: Bound Together

Of course, it is tempting to dismiss any discussion of values as pure pablum—the mushy stuff written into corporate social responsibility reports and uttered at the company's annual awards banquet. But that's a misreading of what values are all about. Every employee knows, deep down, what his or her organization stands for. And unless it stands for the right things, it is terribly easy for its people to go astray.

"We hear a great deal of talk these days about the 'culture' of an organization," Drucker noted in a 1988 *Harvard Business Review* piece. "But what we really mean by this is the commitment throughout an enterprise to some common objectives and common values. Without such commitment, there is no enterprise; there is only a mob. Management's job is to think through, set, and exemplify those objectives, values, and goals."

Perhaps the oddest aspect of the McKinsey findings is the suggestion that providing leadership is somehow separate from promoting values. In fact, the two are bound together—the double helix of any corporation's DNA.

As Drucker wrote: "Leadership is . . . example. The leader is visible; he stands for the organization. He may be totally anonymous the moment he leaves that office and steps into his car to drive home. But inside the organization, he or she is very visible, and this isn't just true of the small and local one; it is just as true of the big, national, or worldwide one. . . . No matter that the rest of the organization doesn't do it; the leader not only represents what we are, but, above all, what we know we should be."

Which goes a long way to explain why so many banks exhibited such a high degree of recklessness in the run-up to the financial meltdown. In a report this year on lessons about corporate governance gleaned from the crisis, the Organisation for Economic Co-operation and Development cited "tone at the top" as a big part of the problem. In looking at remedies, the OECD highlighted standards calling for directors not only to approve a bank's strategic objectives but also its "corporate values," and to ensure that they "are communicated throughout" the firm.

For Every Business, a Choice

The same analysis concluded that in addition to lacking sufficient systems and procedures for properly evaluating certain types of securities, "soft factors were also at work" at some institutions. At French bank Société Générale, the study said, "an imbalance . . . emerged between the front office, focused on expanding its activities, and the control functions which were unable to develop the critical scrutiny necessary for their role."

In other words, like many others, Société Générale became so intent on ringing up "value," it forgot about its values. Now, according to the OECD, the bank is trying to "move towards a culture of shared responsibility and mutual respect"—one in which risk managers are as prized as traders.

Richard Ellsworth, a longtime colleague of Peter Drucker's at Claremont Graduate University, makes clear that, on some level, every business faces a similar choice. "The company can be viewed either as a money-making machine or as a vehicle for satisfying human needs," Ellsworth writes in a new book, coauthored with a group of Claremont faculty members, called (just like this column) *The Drucker Difference*. "By definition, if the central end value is not shared—if employees do not believe in its intrinsic worth—then this foundation and the resulting corporate culture are weakened, and corporate values lose much of their power to influence and direct actions."

Never mind the survey. Without setting values, offering leadership and supplying direction are hollow gestures at best.

October 30, 2009

Authentic Engagement, Truly

Whenever something is labeled "authentic," it's a good bet that it's anything but. Nevertheless, every manager would be wise to consider what FSG Social Impact Advisors, a Boston organization cofounded by Harvard Business School's Michael Porter, is calling "Authentic Engagement." The idea is for companies to take on social problems but in a competitive context—to look for ways to contribute to the larger community while tackling key business objectives.

"Many progressive companies . . . are seeing social issues through this new lens," FSG reported in its latest newsletter, citing a number of examples, including Toyota's targeting "zero emissions mobility," Unilever's promoting good health practices through its Lifebuoy soap, and the fragrance and flavor giant Firmenich's working with poor vanilla farmers on sustainable growing techniques.

One can easily imagine what Peter Drucker's response to this flash would have been: It's about time.

In his 1973 book, *Management: Tasks, Responsibilities, Practices,* Drucker urged companies to see social ills "as major sources of opportunity." What's more, he counseled them to make sure these opportunities were "built into the strategy" of the enterprise, not viewed as some philanthropic afterthought.

The Ultimate Responsibility

Yet it was even earlier, in 1954's *The Practice of Management,* when Drucker began to argue that meeting a corporation's mission and helping to transform society positively are not only compatible but also mutually reinforcing. "It is management's . . . responsibility to make whatever is genuinely in the public good become the enterprise's own self-interest," he wrote.

Drucker didn't view this as some quixotic exercise. Indeed, he believed it essential that a seamless blending of public and private gain become a common feature of corporate life. "In this lies the real meaning of the 'American Revolution' of the twentieth century," Drucker declared. "That more and more of our managements claim it to be their responsibility to realize this new principle in their daily actions is our best hope for the future of our country and society, and perhaps for the future of Western society altogether.

"To make certain that this assertion does not remain lip service but becomes hard fact," he continued, "is the most important, the ultimate responsibility of management: to itself, to the enterprise, to our heritage, to our society, and to our way of life."

Ersatz Engagement

A half century later, we can only shake our heads and wonder what went wrong. That we now feel compelled to use a term such as "Authentic Engagement" is a measure of just how far from Drucker's original vision we have strayed.

To start with, there is an awful lot of ersatz engagement out there. For many companies, invoking "corporate social responsibility" has become a halfhearted statement of noble intentions or, worse, a PR stunt.

Tellingly, the marketing firm TerraChoice announced last April that companies were guilty of some form of "greenwashing," or misleading the public about their environmental qualities, in 98 percent of the 2,219 products it had examined.

In addition, too many executives have become focused on doing well, with little regard for doing good—a mind-set that helped trigger the global financial crisis that continues to hurt so many people.

Some theoreticians and practitioners contend that the persistent pursuit of maximum profit will, in the end, accrue to everyone's advantage. But Drucker held this Gordon Gekko–like logic to be nonsense, dangerous even. "A society based on the assertion that private vices become public benefits cannot endure," he warned. "For in a good, a moral, a lasting society, the public good must always rest on private virtue."

Customer Creation

Still, discovering ways to satisfy corporate goals and society's needs simultaneously—what FSG describes as "shared values"—isn't necessarily easy. A survey released last summer by IBM found that only 30 percent of executives receive adequate data on carbon emissions, labor standards, product composition, and the like to figure out how to make a societal contribution in these areas, even if they want to.

Companies, meanwhile, must also guard against being pushed or pulled into projects that don't make sound financial sense. "Whenever a business has . . . assumed social responsibilities that it could not support economically, it has soon gotten into trouble," Drucker wrote.

Yet Drucker, as well as others who share his philosophy, would also encourage companies to recognize that, as globalization accelerates and technology spreads, there is an ever-increasing chance—if not an obligation—to both further economic performance and make the world a better place.

"Business, as the most powerful institution in society, must be the instrument of social justice," management scholar C.K. Prahalad, author of *The Fortune at the Bottom of the Pyramid*, proclaimed a couple of weeks ago in Vienna, at a forum marking what would have been Drucker's 100th birthday. At the same time, he stressed "the practical value" of this approach—namely, how 5 billion underserved and unserved people across the globe present an extraordinary opening to carry out what Peter Drucker said was the primary purpose of any business: creating a customer.

Opportunities Everywhere

For many, looking at things this way requires an adjustment in thinking—a lesson David Cooperrider, a professor at Case Western Reserve University, learned when he visited Drucker in 2003, two years before Drucker died at age 95. "Can social responsibility also be profitable?" Cooperrider asked.

Drucker smiled and told his guest that he had it backward: The question is not whether social responsibility can be profitable to a company, but how profitable a company can make social responsibility. "Every single social and global issue of our day is a business opportunity in disguise," Drucker told Cooperrider, echoing comments he had first made decades earlier. The insight helped spur Cooperrider to launch the Center for Business as an Agent of World Benefit, which is advancing the concept through research and action.

Let's just hope he resists the temptation to rename his venture the Center for Business as an Agent of Authentic World Benefit.

December 4, 2009

6

The Public and Social Sectors

Getting from Giving

’Tis the season for giving. Yet, as Peter Drucker knew so well, the rewards from such actions flow two ways—not just to those in need, but to those who get a lift from making a difference in an all-too-troubled world.

That is why on Christmas Day I went over to a church not far from my house to help dish up dinner for the hungry and homeless. Dozens of volunteers from my synagogue and elsewhere passed out about 1,000 plates of food. Many others, of course, will participate in similar activities today—and every day. Volunteering across the nation is at a 30-year high, according to the Corporation for National and Community Service, with 27 percent of adults donating their time and talent to a wide range of nonprofits. That's up 15 percent from 1974 and more than 20 percent from 1989.

What Makes Volunteers Tick

None of this would have surprised Drucker. Although best known for advising top executives from major corporations, the father of modern management counseled numerous social-sector organizations such as the Girl Scouts, forcing them to wrestle with the same fundamental questions that every enterprise—profit or nonprofit—should confront: What is our mission? Who is our customer? What does the customer value? What are our results? What is our plan?

Drucker, like all of us, saw the importance of lending a hand in what he termed "a rapidly changing and turbulent America"—one where, economists estimate, as much as a third of the population doesn't earn enough to cover basic necessities. But as Drucker approached the end of his life, he became convinced that this jump in volunteer participation wasn't being driven by the exigencies of the disadvantaged. "The main reason for this upsurge," he wrote in a workbook for nonprofit managers, published in 1999, "is the search for community, for commitment, and for contribution.

"Again and again when I talk to volunteers, I ask, 'Why are you willing to give all this time when you are already working hard?' Again and again I get the same answer, 'Because here I know what I am doing. Here I contribute. Here I am part of a community.'"

Drucker once had high hopes that people would find such fulfillment and a sense of belonging at their factories and offices. But this ideal, Drucker explained in his 1993 book, *Post-Capitalist Society*, "never took root." So while most volunteers are, as he observed, "well-educated, affluent, busy," and "enjoy their jobs," they are also yearning for a different sort of outlet that confers "civic pride."

Doing Well While Doing Good

With astonishing swiftness, however, this picture of two distinct arenas—one in which people go to their day jobs and try to do well, the other in which they leave work and try to do good—is getting fuzzy. More and more, as America Online founder and philanthropist Steve Case has pointed out, "the lines that divide the business, government, and charitable sectors are blurring."

On the one side, a mounting number of companies are paying attention to the so-called double bottom line: their effect on society as well as to their financial returns. Case's own Revolution Health is a good example. It's a for-profit business that seeks to make money in part by selling Internet advertising. But Revolution Health partners with nonprofits, broadening their visibility and helping them sign up new members and supporters, and the company has a social purpose: to assist people in leading healthier lives by building a "consumer-centric" market for medical and wellness information.

Is much of the talk about the double bottom line (or the triple bottom line, if you also consider environmental impact) pure public-relations hooey? You bet. But does much of it reflect a movement toward a genuinely new approach to business? Absolutely.

Creative Capitalism

"We can make market forces work better for the poor," Microsoft Chairman Bill Gates told a group of Harvard graduates, "if we can develop a more creative capitalism"—one in which it's possible to "make a profit, or at least make a living, serving people who are suffering from the worst inequities."

On the other side, the ranks of nonprofits are exploding. There are now about 1.5 million such organizations in the U.S., up from 1 million or so a decade before, the Urban Institute's National Center for Charitable Statistics reports. With growth has come opportunity—and not just for volunteers. An analysis this year by the Johns Hopkins Center for Civil Society Studies found that between 2002 and 2004, the paid nonprofit workforce grew by more than 5 percent, while overall employment declined slightly during the same period.

Nonprofits Attract Top Talent

In all, charities employed 9.4 million paid workers, more than those in the utility, wholesale trade, or construction industries. What's more, as the sector expands, it is attracting the best and the brightest. By all accounts, MBAs are increasingly eager to apply their acumen in finance, strategy, and marketing not to get rich, but to change the world.

Tom Tierney, the chairman of Bridgespan Group, a nonprofit that provides consulting services to foundations and other nonprofits, noted at a conference recently that his firm saw 110 applications for every entry-level spot it had open this year. Tierney, who used to be the chief executive of the corporate consultancy Bain & Co., stressed that these weren't second-rate candidates. "That talent pool is every bit as good—and I might argue better—than any talent pool Bain & Co. has even seen," Tierney said. "And Bain pays a lot more."

Why would anybody seek out a slimmer paycheck? It's for the very same reason Drucker identified: a deep desire to engage in "the civic responsibility that is the mark of citizenship." Only now, the trend is transcending volunteering and moving to the place that Drucker had always wished it would thrive: the realm of nine to five.

December 27, 2007

What Obama Shouldn't Do

Presidentelect Barack Obama has made plenty of promises about what he's going to do: provide tax relief to the middle class, rebuild our crumbling infrastructure, invest in renewable energy, ensure that all children receive a first-rate education, and make health care accessible and affordable for every American—all while taming the nation's monstrous deficit.

But as Peter Drucker made clear, Obama's success may well hinge on what he chooses not to do.

It is absolutely crucial, Drucker wrote in a 1993 piece in which he dispensed a little management advice for the Oval Office, that any new President "not stubbornly do what he wants to do, even if it was the focus of his campaign."

He noted that Harry Truman came into the Presidency convinced, "as were most Americans," that he should begin tackling a string of domestic problems, what with the end of World War II at hand. "What made him an effective President," said Drucker, "was his accepting within a few weeks that international affairs, especially the containment of Stalin's worldwide aggression, had to be given priority whether he liked it or not (and he didn't)."

"There seems to be a law of American politics," Drucker continued, "that the world always changes between Election Day and Inauguration Day. To refuse to accept this—as Jimmy Carter tried to do—is not to be 'principled.' It is to deny reality and condemn oneself to being ineffectual."

Of course, in Obama's case, the upending of the world has already happened. Strengthening the economy, and especially bringing some relief to battered homeowners, has to be his No. 1 aim. Should Obama splinter his efforts and concentrate on much more at the outset than fixing the financial system, he is likely, as Drucker put it, to "achieve nothing."

No "Sure Thing"

Another what-not-to-do rule for the President-elect: "Don't ever bet on a sure thing," Drucker wrote. "It always misfires." Drucker recalled that no President has enjoyed more of a popular mandate than did Franklin Roosevelt heading into his second term. Indeed, he had "every reason to believe that his plan to 'pack' the Supreme Court and thereby remove the last obstacle to . . . New Deal reforms" would be a slam dunk. His move, however, immediately backfired—"so much so," Drucker pointed out, "that he never regained control of Congress."

Obama's gracious victory speech, in which he reached across the aisle and expressed "a measure of humility and determination to heal the divides that have held back our progress," was a good and important first step. As he moves along in the months ahead, he must continue to take that same tack in both words and deeds.

What else shouldn't Obama do? "An effective President," Drucker wrote, "has to say no to the temptation to micromanage." The most promising paradigm, he suggested, might be FDR's cabinet, where "nine of 10 members (all but the Secretary of State) were what we would now call technocrats—competent specialists in one area." "I make the decision," Drucker quoted Roosevelt as saying, "and then turn the job over to a cabinet member and leave him or her alone."

By contrast, Drucker asserted, trying to have a single White House chief-of-staff spearhead an administration's biggest programs "has never worked" very well. Neither, he said, does the Clintonesque model of bringing into the room "dozens and dozens of deputy secretaries, under-secretaries, assistant secretaries, special assistants, and so on." That merely turns the highest levels of government "into a perpetual mass meeting."

Of all the things for the President not to do, though, Drucker left little doubt: He must never assume that government can—or should even try to—solve every ill.

Government Ineffectiveness

"There is mounting evidence that government is big rather than strong; that it is fat and flabby rather than powerful; that it costs a great deal but does not achieve much," Drucker wrote 40 years ago in *The Age of Discontinuity*. Three decades later, in an article in *The Atlantic*, Drucker's frank assessment hadn't changed much: "Government everywhere—in the United States, the United Kingdom, Germany, the former Soviet Union—has proved unable to run community and society."

Drucker didn't just lash out, however. He also offered up his share of prescriptions. Among them: building "the habit of continuous improvement" into all federal departments and introducing "benchmarking," in which the performance of various agencies would be compared annually, "with the best becoming the standard to be met by all the following year."

But, as Drucker saw it, the thing that government needs to do, most of all, is to stop doing. "The purpose of government is to make fundamental decisions and to make them effectively," Drucker declared. "The purpose of government is to focus the political energies of society. It is to dramatize issues. It is to present fundamental choices. The purpose of government, in other words, is to govern.

"This, as we have learned in other institutions, is incompatible with 'doing.' Any attempt to combine government with 'doing' on a large scale paralyzes the decision-making capacity. Any attempt to have decision-making organs actually 'do' also means very poor 'doing.' They are . . . not equipped for it."

Obama, for his part, seems to have embraced this philosophy. It makes no sense to push for "an era of no government," he told *The New York Times Magazine* last summer. "What we need to bring about is the end of the era of unresponsive and inefficient government and short-term thinking in government, so that government is laying the groundwork, the framework, the foundation for the market to operate effectively and for every single individual to be able to be connected with that market and to succeed in that market."

In the end, the surest route to "Yes We Can" will be for the President sometimes to say, "No, I'm afraid I can't."

November 7, 2008

Solving the
Health-Care Conundrum

President Barack Obama began this week to push hard on health-care reform. Whether any legislation gets passed will depend, of course, on how well he navigates the treacherous politics of Washington in the months ahead. But whether the medical system actually improves will hinge on something else altogether: how effectively it is managed in the years ahead.

This is something that Peter Drucker understood very well. "Drucker championed the twin principles of management by objective and management by measurement—two driving forces behind the modern quality revolution in health care," the University of Toronto's Neil Seeman and Adalsteinn Brown declared a few years ago in the journal *Health Quarterly*.

But the revolution has yet to make it past the barricades, at least in the U.S. To begin with, quality is not what it should be. A government report issued earlier this month found that 40 percent of recommended care is not received by patients. Meanwhile, infections that people acquire during the course of their stay in a health-care facility, such as a nursing home or a hospital, stand among the nation's top 10 causes of death. It's little wonder that Health & Human Services Secretary Kathleen Sebelius has said, "The status quo is unsustainable."

At the same time, costs are out of control. The U.S. spends far more per person on medical care than any other country. In 2007, we plunked down $2.2 trillion on medical expenditures, and government analysts predict the figure will climb by more than 6 percent annually through the next decade. That would boost the share of the gross domestic product going toward health care from 17.6 percent this year to 20.3 percent in 2018. All the while, some 45 million Americans remain without medical coverage.

A Complex Web

That the system is in such rotten shape is not totally surprising. The world of medicine has gotten more and more complicated over time. Drucker, for one, identified the hospital as "the most complex human organization ever devised," with its web of doctors and nurses and technicians. Insurance companies aren't inclined to simplify matters, either, having discovered that opacity and obfuscation can help bring in enormous profits.

So how do we make things better?

The White House believes there are several keys, including beefing up prevention and wellness programs so people don't get so sick in the first place. They're also hoping to spur the revamping of financial incentives for health providers so they're rewarded—rather than penalized—for delivering excellent care.

But much of the Administration's efforts are centered on something straight from the Drucker playbook: measuring results. Peter Orszag, the director of the Office of Management & Budget, is fond of citing a body of research from Dartmouth that shows how health-care spending varies widely between regions of the country, often with little correlation to outcomes.

By zeroing in on these discrepancies, as well as methodically determining which drugs and treatments work best, it should be possible to save oodles of money while enhancing quality. At least that's the theory.

What Drucker knew, however, is that measuring anything is far from a straightforward proposition. For starters, he wrote, "what we measure and how we measure determine what will be considered relevant and, thereby, determine not just what we see, but what we—and others—do." Beyond that, the more we measure, the more we risk flooding the system with data. What's needed, instead, is genuine information: what Drucker defined as "data endowed with relevance and purpose."

"A View of the Whole"

This is especially difficult to do, he added, in an organization filled with specialists—and no area has more specialists than medicine. "Each specialty," Drucker noted, "has its own knowledge, its own training, its own language."

A big challenge that management faces in such a situation, Drucker explained, is creating "a common vision, a view of the whole." Only when that's established can individuals begin asking the questions that Drucker deemed a matter of professional responsibility: "Who in this organization depends on me for what information? And on whom, in turn, do I depend?"

"Each person's list will always include superiors and subordinates," Drucker wrote in a 1988 piece in *Harvard Business Review*. "But the most important names on it will be those of colleagues, people with whom one's primary relationship is coordination.

"The relationship of the internist, the surgeon, and the anesthesiologist is one example," he continued. "But the relationship of a biochemist, a pharmacologist, the medical director in charge of clinical testing, and a marketing specialist in a pharmaceutical company is no different."

What is absent today is precisely the common vision and sense of coordination that Drucker called for. As Seeman and Brown pointed out, "health-care leaders have embraced measurement." That's not the problem. What "often goes missing," however, is Drucker's exhortation that "all collected data should be tied to a strategy that serves the patient."

In the end, Obama's team must remember that measuring is only half the battle. They must also make sure that the findings are diligently managed, just as Dr. Drucker ordered.

May 15, 2009

Boredom, Not Rigor, Dampens Volunteers' Spirits

Michelle Obama strode across the podium in San Francisco this week and, staring out at thousands of nonprofit leaders and volunteers assembled in front of her, took note of an unmistakable trend sweeping the country: These days, it's hip to help.

"You've done everything in your power," the First Lady declared at the start of the 2009 National Conference on Service & Volunteering, "to make giving back cool again."

Somewhere, Peter Drucker is smiling.

When I last wrote about the surge in volunteerism in America, a year and a half ago, I noted Drucker's influence in the field both as an adviser to numerous social-sector organizations and as an observer of people's hunger to find something in their lives that brings them fulfillment. "What the U.S. nonprofits do for their volunteers may well be just as important as what they do for the recipients of their services," Drucker wrote in his 1993 book, *Post-Capitalist Society*. "Citizenship in and through the social sector . . . restores the civic pride that is the mark of community."

Today, propelled by this way of thinking, volunteering is fast becoming a full-blown cultural phenomenon. Surveys suggest that Millennials—those born between 1980 and 2000—are more civic-minded than any generation since the 1930s. The nation's 77 million baby boomers are also getting into the act, as more and more folks in their 40s, 50s, and 60s look to take up a so-called encore career that's centered on volunteering and public service.

A Wave of Doing Good

Meanwhile, technology is enabling people, in a click, to find a multitude of avenues to get involved and do their part in tackling some of society's most pressing problems. Among those leading the wave is All for Good, a new Web site hosted by Google.

Nothing, though, has given the National Service Movement more of a lift than the words and deeds of the Obamas. From the President's signing in April of the $5.7 billion Serve America Act to his launching this month of United We Serve—an initiative designed to have all Americans make volunteering a part of their daily lives this summer—he has delivered on his campaign promise to make community service a centerpiece of his Administration.

Yet despite all of the momentum and the palpable excitement in San Francisco, nonprofits need to be careful or they'll wind up squandering the remarkable opportunity before them.

Earlier this year, the *Stanford Social Innovation Review* published a piece that noted how poorly most nonprofits manage their volunteers. As a result, more than a third of the 60 million-plus Americans who donate their time and talents one year don't do so the next—not only at the organization where they'd signed up, but at any nonprofit at all. Some call this "the leaky bucket of volunteerism."

There are a host of reasons for this pullback, according to the analysis, including nonprofits inadequately recognizing the contributions of their volunteers and a lack of training among volunteers and their managers.

But Robert Grimm, director of research and policy development at the Corporation for National and Community Service and one of the authors of the article, believes there's a more fundamental issue to grapple with: It isn't so much that volunteers have nightmarish experiences at nonprofits, he says; it's that they have "bland" ones.

Matching Needs and Skills

Nonprofits, says Grimm, must "find out what people's passions are"— and do a better job of meeting those interests. They also need to take far greater advantage of the skills that volunteers bring. There's no reason for an attorney, say, to paint a fence when the organization he wants to assist could put him to work on an urgent legal matter. Why have a retired marketing executive stuff envelopes when she could be helping to devise the nonprofit's new media campaign?

The ability of nonprofits to match needs and skills effectively becomes all the more critical as an increasing number of corporations, including consulting firms such as Deloitte and PricewaterhouseCoopers, donate millions of dollars worth of pro bono services to nonprofits.

The necessity of keeping workers engaged and bestowing upon them a feeling of pride is hardly exclusive to the social sector. Drucker taught that all managers must offer their employees a way to make a meaningful contribution. For it is this, even more than money, that motivates people.

"Personal satisfaction of the worker without productive work is failure," Drucker wrote in his 1973 classic, *Management: Tasks, Responsibilities, Practices*. "But so is productive work that destroys the worker's achievement" and his or her sense of having made a real difference. "Neither is, in effect, tenable for very long."

When it comes to volunteers, the instinct among some managers is not to demand too much from them for fear that they'll walk away if they're overworked. But, in fact, Drucker believed that volunteers are hoping to be pushed hard—as long as it's into something that can supply a big emotional payoff at the end.

"Volunteers have to get more satisfaction from their work than paid employees, precisely because they don't get a paycheck," Drucker wrote. "They need, above all, challenges."

Nonprofits must quickly begin to provide them. Or the nation's burgeoning ranks of volunteers will no longer feel cool. They'll simply grow cold.

June 26, 2009

Health-Care Reform:
The Right Kind of Compromise

This week's brouhaha over whether the White House is ready to give up on a public insurance plan as part of health-care reform provides a fascinating window into the give-and-take of capital politics. But it's also a window into what Peter Drucker called "the elements of decision making."

In that sense, the dustup in D.C. is instructive for any leader charged with implementing a difficult decision. Invariably, he or she will be forced at some point to take a step that many people instinctively resist: compromise.

"The leader sets the goals, sets the priorities, and sets and maintains the standards," Drucker wrote in his 1992 book, *Managing for the Future*. Yet he also "makes compromises, of course; indeed, effective leaders are painfully aware that they are not in control of the universe."

"But before accepting a compromise," Drucker added, "the effective leader has thought through . . . whether the compromises he makes with the constraints of reality—which may involve political, economic, financial, or people problems—are compatible with his mission and goals or lead away from them."

It was many months ago, back on the campaign trail, that President Barack Obama made the fundamental decision to move full steam ahead in trying to overhaul the nation's health-care system. In doing so, he seemed to follow to a tee Drucker's counsel regarding one of the most crucial questions that any executive should ask: "Is a decision really necessary?"

After all, as Drucker pointed out, "one alternative is always the alternative of doing nothing." And this is precisely the course that should be taken "if the condition, while annoying, is of no importance and unlikely to make much difference."

In this case, however, inaction was not a possibility—not with health-care costs soaring and not with 45 million-plus Americans uninsured and as many as 15,000 more losing their coverage every day, by some estimates.

But now has come what the President himself recently described as "the hard part." This is the inevitable stage, Drucker observed, when "it becomes suddenly quite obvious that the decision is not going to be pleasant, is not going to be popular, is not going to be easy."

Making it all the tougher for Obama is that lies are being spread about his beliefs: that he favors "socialism," government "death panels" for the elderly, and other nonsense. Maddening though this may be, the President needs to be extremely careful in the way that he and his surrogates push back, lest they stifle legitimate debate over the details of reform.

Conflict Can Produce Good Solutions

That would be a disaster because, as Drucker knew, the best outcomes emerge from sharply conflicting points of view. For starters, he explained, dissent "safeguards the decision maker against becoming the prisoner of the organization" he or she is in. In addition, it can present other ideas to fall back on should something later go wrong with the initial effort.

"Above all," Drucker wrote in *Management: Tasks, Responsibilities, Practices*, "disagreement is needed to stimulate the imagination" and come up with truly "creative solutions" that require "a new and different way of perceiving and understanding."

In the end, the key is to avoid what Drucker termed "the trap of 'being right.'" Rather than beginning "with the assumption, 'I am right and he is wrong,'" Drucker wrote, a great leader "starts out with the commitment to find out why people disagree" and is then prepared to yield where it makes sense to do so.

Earlier this week, as members of the Administration took to the Sunday morning talk shows, this is exactly what appeared to be happening. They suggested that they were not completely wedded to a "public option"—that is, setting up a government-run medical insurance plan that would compete with private insurers. Such flexibility is wise. All along, opponents have painted this proposal as a federal "takeover" of health care, and it's this kind of rhetoric that most threatens to derail reform.

At the same time—and even more important—Obama's advisers stressed that their openness to other approaches doesn't in any way mean that the President is forsaking certain essential aims: heightening competition (which should help curb costs) and offering choice. These, though, can conceivably be met through other avenues, including the establishment of health-care cooperatives.

How all of this will shake out is far from clear. Some of the Administration's closest allies are insisting on keeping the public option. More broadly, voters remain deeply skeptical of what the President and congressional Democrats are trying to achieve.

But know this: If we do ultimately get real reform, it will be because the Administration has forged what Drucker characterized as the right kind of compromise—one best expressed, he said, in the old proverb "Half a loaf is better than no bread."

On the other hand, if too much is bargained away—if the President, in desperation, gives up not only the public option but its underlying goals as well, he will have made a very different kind of compromise, expressed in the story of the Judgment of Solomon: "Half a baby is worse than no baby at all." As Drucker noted, half a baby "is not half of a living and growing child. It is a corpse in two pieces."

And one, we can be sure, whose parents couldn't afford any insurance to begin with.

August 21, 2009

Big Solutions Should Start Small

Even if Harry and Louise hadn't killed off President Clinton's health-care reform initiative in the planning stages, Peter Drucker believed it would have been doomed in practice by two other culprits: enormity and complexity.

"You have to start small," Drucker remarked during a 1996 interview, as he zeroed in on "the problem" with ClintonCare. "The big cure-alls never work."

It is this very insight that likely would have made Drucker a fan of the historic health-care legislation that Congress is in the final stages of passing. And it is an insight that managers far beyond the medical world should take note of, as it applies to practically every kind of organization.

The notion that the health-care package now on Capitol Hill is, in fact, based on a "start small" paradigm has gained currency in recent weeks, thanks to the publication in *The New Yorker* of a compelling article by Atul Gawande, a Boston surgeon and former Clinton adviser. Despite all the critics who have warned of a "big government" take-over of medicine, Gawande points out that nearly half the 2,000-plus pages in the Senate health-care bill are devoted to relatively small-gauge pilot programs that would "test various ways to curb costs and increase quality."

Avoiding Grandiosity

"There is a pilot program to increase payments for doctors who deliver high-quality care at lower cost, while reducing payments for those who deliver low-quality care at higher cost," Gawande writes. "There's a program that would pay bonuses to hospitals that improve patient results after heart failure, pneumonia, and surgery. There's a program that would impose financial penalties on institutions with high rates of infections transmitted by health-care workers. Still another would test a system of penalties and rewards scaled to the quality of home health and rehabilitation care. Other experiments try moving medicine away from fee-for-service payment altogether."

It seems counterintuitive, in some respects, to take on a gargantuan task by trying a little of this and a little of that. But Drucker taught that this is the only way for a potential game-changer to get off the ground. "Grandiose ideas for things that will 'revolutionize an industry' are unlikely to work," Drucker asserted. At another point, while discussing the development of education policy, he put it like this: "We need innovation; therefore, we need experimentation."

Bill Pollard, the chairman emeritus of ServiceMaster, a pest-control, lawn care, and housecleaning company, says that one of the most valuable lessons he ever learned from Drucker was that "the potential for the new always requires testing and piloting."

"Worth Doing Poorly"

"For a new idea to be successful, it must get off the drawing board and beyond a market analysis or focus study group," explains Pollard, a Drucker consulting client and close friend. "It's important to get started—to start servicing a few customers to learn from the practical application of an idea. Ideas can be studied and analyzed until they are suffocated. If a thing is worth doing, it is worth doing poorly to begin with . . . to learn from experience."

Of course, truly learning from experience takes real effort. Drucker stressed that every new endeavor must have built into it from the beginning carefully considered tools for flagging when an undertaking has gone off course and isn't likely to pan out.

At the same time, Drucker made clear that such assessments must not become too sharply focused on what's broken. "The first aim," Drucker wrote, "is to find out what we are doing well, for one can always go ahead and do more of the same, even if we usually do not have the slightest idea why we are doing well in a given area."

In his piece, Gawande makes the case for advancement through trial and error by tracing how a series of U.S. Agriculture Department pilot programs revolutionized farming in the early twentieth century. "What seemed like a hodgepodge eventually cohered into a whole," Gawande reports. "The government never took over agriculture, but the government didn't leave it alone, either. It shaped a feedback loop of experiment and learning and encouragement for farmers across the country." The result: Food prices tumbled while productivity and quality soared.

Pilot Testing the New Deal

Drucker, for his part, drew similarly on history. He concluded that the parts of President Franklin D. Roosevelt's agenda that fared the worst—including, for instance, the National Recovery Administration—started out as overly ambitious conceits that spanned the country. By contrast, Drucker said, "it is no coincidence that practically all successful New Deal programs had been pilot tested as small-scale experiments in states and cities over the preceding 20 years—in Wisconsin, New York City, or elsewhere in New York State, or by one of the Chicago reform administrations."

Drucker certainly understood the limits of the federal government and would have insisted that the actual implementation of these pilot programs and any follow-ons be left, wherever possible, to local agencies, nonprofits, and businesses. As the saying goes, Uncle Sam has to steer more and row less.

Yet interestingly, Drucker also discerned the seeds of what Gawande just wrote about, commenting in that 1996 interview: "The outline of a new American health-care system is slowly emerging out of literally hundreds of local experiments."

If health-care reform becomes law and more of these pilot projects reach full flower, maybe we'll hear a different—and more uplifting—watchword coming out of Washington: It's too small to fail.

January 8, 2010

Facing the Wreckage Head-On

Detroit has declined immeasurably since Peter Drucker described it, more than a half-century ago, as "*the* industrial city per se." But even by today's diminished expectations, the past few weeks have been especially tough.

Former Mayor Kwame Kilpatrick, already in prison for probation violations, was arraigned in federal court on 19 counts of felony fraud and tax charges. The president of the local school board resigned and was hit with criminal charges after he allegedly fondled himself during a meeting with a colleague. And newly released Census figures show that Detroit continues to lose residents.

Yet despite all the setbacks, the Motor City may well have begun the very earliest stages of a turnaround. This is largely due to a trait that current Detroit Mayor Dave Bing displays and that every manager, especially during this uncertain age, should emulate: the resolve to look at the worst problems square in the face.

"A time of turbulence is a dangerous time," Drucker wrote, "but its greatest danger is a temptation to deny reality."

Prevalence of Denial

Indeed, many fall straight into this trap, often unconsciously. The inability to deal with unpleasant circumstances "is what Sigmund Freud described as the combination of 'knowing with not knowing.' It is, in George Orwell's blunt formulation, 'protective stupidity,'" Harvard Business School's Richard Tedlow explains in his book *Denial*.

"From the young child who insists that his parents haven't separated even though his father has moved out, to the alcoholic who swears he is just a social drinker, to the president who declares 'mission accomplished' when it isn't," Tedlow adds, "denial permeates every facet of life. Business is no exception. In fact, denial may be the biggest and potentially most ruinous problem that businesses face, from startups to mature, powerful corporations."

The 66-year-old Bing, who enjoyed a Hall of Fame basketball career and success as the owner of several manufacturing companies before moving into politics, is anything but in denial. His leadership style first caught my eye when I read a profile of him earlier this year in *Sports Illustrated*. Bing, writer Michael Rosenberg said, "seems almost to take pleasure in telling people what they don't want to hear."

Smaller and Leaner

A month or so later, he made headlines for doing just that. Rather than trying to juice Detroit's Census count, so as to puff up the city's pride and maximize federal funding—a tactic used by many municipalities—the mayor spoke openly about the need to embrace a city that is much smaller and leaner.

"Transformational issues have to be talked about," Bing told me, citing the steady hemorrhaging of high-paying blue-collar work that Detroit has witnessed for many years. "It's hard for people to grapple with the fact that those jobs are gone and they're not coming back. We have to prepare ourselves for something very different."

This, of course, is the real trick: not only to have the courage to contend with the most daunting challenges but also to possess the vision and skill to then turn the situation into something positive. As Drucker asserted, "A time of turbulence is also one of great opportunity for those who can understand, accept, and exploit the new realities."

In Detroit's case, this means slimming things down before building them back up. Bing, who inherited a $300 million-plus deficit when he came into office in May 2009, reached agreement with the city council last month on a $3 billion budget that includes more than $100 million in cuts.

Dwindling Tax Base

Getting pinched like that is always painful. But with a tax base supported by only about 900,000 people—not even half of what Detroit had at its height—there's simply "a whole litany of things we can't afford to do anymore," says Bing, as he rattles off reductions in "street paving . . . grass cutting, snow removal," and other services. "Nobody likes to hear that. But if we fight it, we're going to keep spiraling down." In a similar vein, the mayor has targeted 3,000 blighted homes for demolition this year.

Yet Bing also believes that amid all the rubble a little light can shine: The scaling back will allow the city to focus on revitalizing a select number of core neighborhoods. The mayor notes that a number of new construction projects are now under way, and he also sees a chance to develop Detroit's international riverfront.

In the end, though, Bing recognizes that ideas, not edifices, are what must save the city. Detroit, he points out, has a rich tradition of engineering excellence and entrepreneurship. The question is: How can the city rekindle that spirit and translate it into jobs?

Repairing the Schools

"How do we identify the next Berry Gordy?" Bing asks, referring to the founder of Motown Records. "How do we identify the next Henry Ford?"

The process must begin, he suggests, by accepting "that we have a broken, failing school system." Some are urging mayoral control of the city's schools in the hope of improving accountability, but it isn't entirely clear that Bing is eager to play that role. In any event, such plans are presently stalled.

Detroit has a long way to go before it is healthy again. And Bing isn't immune to criticism. The *Detroit Free Press*, for instance, has rapped him for "mincing words about what the city's educational future should look like."

Still, all in all, Bing appears to be slowly making progress by confronting many of Detroit's harshest realities head-on while not overpromising what he can deliver. If the city rises as a result, the man who collected more than 3,400 caroms during his time in the NBA will have claimed his biggest rebound by far.

July 16, 2010

7

Art, Music, and Sports

Drucker on . . . Radiohead?

Peter Drucker loved music—Haydn and Beethoven, Mozart and Mahler. Were the late management philosopher around these days, however, he would undoubtedly be grabbed by the newest offering from an altogether different sort of act: the British rock band Radiohead.

Not its synthesizer-driven sound. Drucker, rather, would be struck by Radiohead's bold focus on something that far too many businesses overlook: pricing. If effectively tied to an overall marketing strategy, it can be a powerful tool in helping an enterprise seize opportunities.

Last week, Radiohead began to distribute its latest album, *In Rainbows*. Consumers can download it off the Internet and—here's the twist—pay whatever they think it's worth: $2, $10, or nothing at all.

"It's up to you," the band tells visitors to its Web site. "No, really. It's up to you."

The Complexities of Pricing

Properly pricing a product is no easy exercise. It involves a complex bit of calculus that must take into account not only a business' up-front investment but also the ongoing costs it expects to incur (as it moves down the learning curve and, presumably, becomes more efficient); the position of its competitors; and the crucial interplay between price and volume.

It also requires a degree of self-restraint. "The first and easily the most common sin" among businesses, Drucker wrote in a 1993 article, "is the worship of high profit margins and of 'premium pricing.'"

Historically, many companies ignored these factors. They set the price of something simply by adding up all their expenses and then slathering on top as much profit as they thought the market would bear.

As Drucker pointed out, such "cost-driven pricing" was backward. In the end, he concluded, "the only thing that works is price-driven costing"—that is, figuring out what customers believe a product or service is worth and then designing the item accordingly (with a sufficient profit built in to support sustainability and growth, which does not necessarily equate to the highest price that could be obtained).

Trusting the Customer

"Cost-driven pricing is the reason there is no American consumer-electronics industry," Drucker asserted. "It had the technology and the products. But it operated on cost-led pricing—and the Japanese practiced price-led costing."

What Radiohead has done is take things to an even more sophisticated level. In effect, the band has embraced to the extreme the idea of "value-based pricing": charging customers what you believe they're willing to pay, given the benefits provided them. In the business-to-business market, in particular, this means establishing different prices for different consumers for the very same product, based on its value to each.

Since word of Radiohead's pricing plan broke earlier this month, reactions have ranged from nonplussed to nearly apoplectic, with some predicting that the band's take-it-to-the-people approach will help hasten the demise of the big record labels. (Radiohead recently ended its relationship with giant EMI Group.)

I'm far from convinced that the release of this one album, in and of itself, will prove ruinous for the industry. But I would bet on this: It's bound to help the band enhance its own bottom line.

A Concert Draw

Thomas Nagle, coauthor of the classic *The Strategy and Tactics of Pricing*, is also impressed by Radiohead's savvy. Twenty years ago, when the first edition of his book was published, he cited the wisdom of musicians who charged relatively little for their concerts because these live performances were what drove record sales—then the most lucrative part of the business.

Now, he says, "the world has flipped." By pricing *In Rainbows* so flexibly—including presenting the option of paying the ultimate bargain-basement price, nada—Radiohead may well attract new fans that will fill its concerts, which are the real money machines of music today.

Beyond that, Radiohead is selling a souped-up version of *In Rainbows* (featuring a pair of vinyl LPs, a CD with extra songs, and photos) for around $80. Some observers have suggested that the digital download may thus act as a kind of "loss leader," hooking in folks who'll then be inclined to fork over a mint for the more expensive package.

But here's the funny thing: The *In Rainbows* download could well turn out to be a leader at no loss.

Nagle notes that consumers are often willing to pay for something, even if they can get it for free, as long as they perceive that it's a fair deal. And sure enough, a poll conducted by the music magazine *NME* indicates that Radiohead fans are, on average, plunking down $10 for their digital copy of *In Rainbows*—right in line with what Apple's iTunes charges for most albums.

All of which, of course, validates a page right out of the Drucker songbook: "What the customer sees, thinks, believes, and wants, at any given time, must be accepted by management as an objective fact and must be taken as seriously as the reports of the salesperson, the tests of the engineer, or the figures of the accountant."

October 11, 2007

Peter Drucker's Winning Team

In the summer of 1985, an executive named Peter Bavasi pored over a *Harvard Business Review* article by Peter Drucker in which the great management thinker described the "widow maker"—a job so inherently impossible that it was apt to defeat even the best and brightest.

Drucker's warning—"Any job that ordinarily competent people cannot perform is a job that cannot be staffed"—was especially ominous for Bavasi. He had, you see, just become president of the Cleveland Indians, a sports franchise to which the word "hapless" seemed inextricably tied.

So Bavasi called Drucker to seek his counsel, and there began a relationship that, with the new baseball season just under way, is well worth revisiting for what it can teach all managers, whether on the diamond or off.

Wanted: Organizational Expert

The 1985 season, during which the Indians had lost 102 games and won a mere 60, had given way to 1986 by the time Drucker came aboard as a full-fledged consultant. The Austrian-born professor enjoyed watching America's national pastime, and he had even struck up a friendship with Hall of Famer Yogi Berra when the two oft-quoted figures were neighbors in New Jersey in the early 1970s. (Drucker: "The best way to predict the future is to create it." Berra: "Prediction is very hard, especially when it's about the future.")

Bavasi, though, wasn't looking for a baseball guy. He needed an organizational expert, someone who could help teach his entire operation, from the equipment manager in the clubhouse to the skipper in the dugout, how to be more effective at a broad range of tasks. In fact, Bavasi had long been a big believer in Drucker's concept of MBO, or management by objectives.

MBO—by which managers throughout the organization jointly identify goals, clearly define each individual's responsibility for meeting them, and figure out how to measure the results—has had its share of critics over the years. Some, for instance, say the system is difficult to implement and doesn't work well in rapidly changing environments. Drucker, who had introduced the idea in his 1954 landmark, *The Practice of Management*, himself pointed out that MBO was no silver bullet against inefficiency. It works, he emphasized, only "if you first think through your objectives." Yet he pointed out "90 percent of the time, you haven't."

Assembling the Right Staff

Bavasi, however, found MBO was perfect for a baseball team, in part because the objectives were so unmistakable. "It's a business of absolutes," he told me. "It's win-lose, ball-strike. There's no in-between. There's no maybe." And so he drew up a 450-page strategic and operating plan, which was based on MBO and covered every department of the Indians.

Drucker tempered it slightly, advising Bavasi to make the objectives more qualitative and less quantitative as he moved from areas such as ticket sales to the ball club itself. To hold the manager to an exact number of wins, Bavasi explains, "would have put too much pressure on everybody." Instead, Drucker suggested the Indians concentrate on putting together the right kind of coaching staff that would ultimately lead to more victories.

To that end, he prompted Bavasi and his inner circle—the Indians' manager, general manager, and player personnel director—to think not only about honing the squad's physical skills, but tending to its emotional and intellectual development as well. With Drucker's guidance, Bavasi brought on a Spanish-speaking coach who could relate to his young Latino players. He made sure that one of his coaches was an avuncular sort the players could lean on, while another was tough enough to give them the occasional kick in the butt. "What he reminded us was that if we managed the human aspect," Bavasi says, "it would lead to productivity on the field."

The Hard-to-Manage Players

Drucker (who charged $5,000 a day) wasn't a constant presence. He was teaching in California at the time and would meet with Bavasi and the boys only when they traveled to Anaheim to play the Angels. Nor did he decree anything. Mostly, says Bavasi, "he consulted by probing, asking layers of questions, our answers to which began to reveal new ways of approaching old problems."

Drucker was also "a master," Bavasi recalls, at "creating discussions about certain hard-to-manage players." Among them was relief pitcher Ernie Camacho, who had a penchant for turning in a terrific season, only to follow up with a lousy one.

"Well," Drucker said, "looking at his statistical history we can conclude that he is a regressive personality. We see a lot of that among top-flight computer programmers. They will be given a very complex assignment and write brilliant code. Their next assignment will end up mediocre, sometimes even a disaster. Then they'll write something brilliant. Up, down. On, off. Just like your pitcher."

Turnaround Ace

Bavasi remembers Manager Pat Corrales perking up, sensing Drucker "was about to reveal the answer" to stabilizing the erratic reliever. "Peter," Corrales asked, "what can we do to get this guy to be more consistent?"

"Patrick," answered Drucker, in his formal manner, "the way I see it, there's only one thing you can do." Finally, after a long pause, he said, "You should consider trading this man as soon as you can." (Camacho lasted another year with Cleveland before joining the Astros.)

Bavasi left after the '86 season, and Drucker didn't consult for the team anymore. But while he did, the turnaround was undeniable: The Tribe won an impressive 84 games, and attendance at Cleveland Stadium soared to nearly 1.5 million from just 655,000 the year before.

"Peter had a lot to do with getting us focused as an organization," Bavasi says. "He had us look at everything we were doing to see if there was a good rationale behind it. . . . Peter was our MVP."

April 10, 2008

Organizations Need
Structure and Flexibility

There is certainly no shortage of management lessons to be gleaned from Michael Phelps' record-shattering performance at the Beijing Olympics—the importance of setting firm objectives and staying sharply focused perhaps chief among them.

Nevertheless, I suspect that Peter Drucker would have been more intrigued by the blows suffered in the boxing ring than by the gold gathered in the swimming pool. It was there, in the square circle, that the U.S. turned in its worst-ever showing, winning but a single bronze medal and sending disheartened fans scurrying to figure out what went wrong.

Interestingly, the answer appears to have relatively little to do with the fighters' athletic prowess and quite a lot to do with the way the team was run. Those in charge of the nine-man Olympic squad ignored a couple of basic principles that Drucker—though more a student of social science than of the sweet science—pounded home: the need for clear direction and yet, at the same time, a certain degree of organizational flexibility.

Too Many Coaches

In large part, the pugilists' problems can be traced to a move made last year: Members of the U.S. team had to leave their homes—and the care of their personal coaches—to live and train for 10 months as part of a new residency program at the U.S. Olympic Committee facility in Colorado. This, in turn, led to several major miscues—the kind that can plague any enterprise, if it's not careful.

The first was that, once in Beijing, at least several U.S. boxers didn't seem to know whom to listen to: the Olympic coach, Dan Campbell, or their longtime personal coaches. The Olympic staff told light flyweight Luis Yanez, for instance, to be aggressive from the opening bell of his big bout. But his hometown coach, to whom he felt tremendous fidelity, counseled patience. "You have the kid caught in between," Campbell told reporters. Yanez lost.

Drucker, for one, wouldn't have been surprised at the outcome. "In any institution, there has to be a final authority," he wrote in his 1999 book, *Management Challenges for the 21st Century*, "someone who can make the final decisions and who can expect them to be obeyed."

Conflict of Loyalties

But unless it's made plain whose role that is, confusion can arise. To be successful, any organization "has to be transparent," Drucker explained. "People have to know and have to understand the . . . structure they are supposed to work in. This sounds obvious—but it is far too often violated in most institutions (even in the military)."

The toughest situation, he added, is when people feel pulled in two directions, the way the boxers did. "It is a very old principle of human relations that no one should be put into a conflict of loyalties," Drucker asserted, "and having more than one 'master' creates such a conflict."

Yet Drucker recognized that rigidity isn't the right course, either—and it's here that those directing the U.S. boxing team (and surely a great many other managers) could profitably reconsider their approach.

Organize Flexibly

A common mistake in both management theory and practice, Drucker noted, is that we tend to become fixated on organizing things one way—and one way only. Depending on the era, we make it all about collaboration or all about decentralization or all about command-and-control.

But in truth, "there is no such thing as the one right organization," Drucker wrote. "There are only organizations, each of which has distinct strengths, distinct limitations, and specific applications. It has become clear that organization is not an absolute. It is a tool for making people productive in working together. As such, a given organization structure fits certain tasks in certain conditions and at certain times."

Frequently, it's assumed that "institutions are homogenous and that, therefore, the entire enterprise should be organized the same way," Drucker continued. "But in any one enterprise . . . there is need for a number of different organization structures coexisting side by side."

Tricky Coordination

For the boxers, this suggests that the best way forward may well be a blend, with weeklong periods of training at the Olympic site combined with personal coaching at home that is designed to reinforce the strategy set by the national team. Making this work would require deft coordination—and constant communication—among the different coaches to ensure that everyone is on the same page, but there's no doubt that it's doable. In fact, the women's gymnastics team operates under just such a model.

Jim Millman, the chairman of USA Boxing, has already indicated that he's interested in making some changes—though just how extensive remains to be seen. If Drucker is any guide, Millman and his colleagues shouldn't hesitate to be bold, especially given how high expectations were for the U.S. boxing team in Beijing. Some observers even thought this group might snare the most medals since 1984, when the U.S. collected 10 golds and two silvers in the ring.

"Unexpected failure . . . should be taken as seriously as a 60-year-old man's first 'minor' heart attack," Drucker wrote. What's more, good leaders "do not dismiss unexpected failure as the result of a subordinate's incompetence or as an accident but treat it as a symptom of 'systems failure.'"

That's vintage Drucker, never pulling a punch.

August 29, 2008

Making Music with Drucker

A s rockers, rappers, and country crooners scoop up their Grammy Awards this weekend, you can be certain that they'll thank all kinds of people for helping to make them stars: producers, agents, the fans, and, of course, many a mom.

But there's one Grammy winner of years past that feels it owes a debt to a very different sort of influence: Peter Drucker.

Pasadena (Calif.)–based Southwest Chamber Music has long drawn on Drucker's insights to help it manage the enterprise effectively, as well as to tailor its musical selections. By constantly questioning which programs and strategies have become obsolete, Southwest offers some valuable lessons that can help any organization—no matter what kind of business it's in—hit the right notes. "Reading Drucker became this incredible lightbulb for me," says Jan Karlin, the executive director of Southwest, which snared Grammys in 2003 and 2004 for the first two volumes of the Complete Chamber Music of Carlos Chavez.

Verdi Influenced Drucker

That an outfit such as Southwest would have a strong affinity for Drucker's work is not surprising, really. Drucker, who saw "management as a liberal art," peppered his books and articles with references to music. "The key to greatness" in any organization, Drucker wrote in a 2002 essay for *Harvard Business Review*, "is to look for people's potential and spend time developing it. . . . To build a world-class orchestra requires rehearsing the same passage in the symphony again and again until the first clarinet plays it the way the conductor hears it. This principle is also what makes a research director in an industry lab successful."

Notably, Drucker counted Giuseppe Verdi, the nineteenth-century Italian composer, as having a tremendous impact on him. In the late 1920s, Drucker lived in Hamburg, where he worked as a trainee at a cotton export firm. Every week, he'd escape the drudgery of his job by going to the opera, and it was there that he heard Verdi's *Falstaff.* "I was totally overwhelmed by it," Drucker recalled.

But what impressed him most was when he later discovered that Verdi's masterpiece—"with its gaiety, its zest for life, and its incredible vitality," as Drucker put it—had been written by a man of 80. "All my life as a musician," Verdi declared, "I have striven for perfection. It has always eluded me. I surely had an obligation to make one more try." Drucker said that these words from Verdi became his "lodestar," helping inspire him to write into his nineties.

Defining a New Mission

For Southwest, Drucker's teachings form a basis to examine all kinds of things, including the most fundamental aspects of the organization. Karlin, for instance, says that her grounding in Drucker made it clear that after Southwest had won its Grammys, it needed a new mission statement. The old one—"to energize and renew the standard chamber music repertory by integrating the best of contemporary world and early music in programs and concerts"—had largely been fulfilled.

"We started thinking, what are we going to do next?" says Karlin, displaying an entrepreneurial orientation that demands certain initiatives be abandoned to make way for the future. Southwest's new mission: "to provide the Southern California and international music communities with concert, recording, and educational programming that reflects the vast diversity of art music from around the world."

This fresh approach has led Southwest to focus on the rich cultural diversity in its own backyard—particularly in the Latin and Asian communities—and has opened the door to new adventures abroad.

Asking the Right Questions

Next year, Southwest will take part in a State Department–sponsored cultural exchange with Vietnam that will involve both musical performances and workshops on arts management featuring Drucker's principles.

Today, amid a difficult financial environment, Karlin and her husband, Southwest Artistic Director Jeff von der Schmidt, are asking a Drucker-like question that is meant to help them spot further opportunities, even with all the challenges: "If we were to begin Southwest now, what would it look like?"

"Peter would have encouraged us to rethink the organization—and that's what we're doing," says Karlin, who has produced a balanced budget for each of the 22 years Southwest has existed.

No One Is Immune

For his part, von der Schmidt says Drucker's writings have given him a way to consider the tough artistic choices he must make between embracing new music and sticking with classical compositions. "There really does have to be a balance of continuity and change," says von der Schmidt, pointing to one of Drucker's central themes.

In 2007, Southwest hired Michael Millar, who received his doctorate from Claremont Graduate University, where he studied both musical performance and arts administration. For the latter, his professors included none other than Peter Drucker.

Karlin and von der Schmidt were already familiar with Drucker when Millar arrived, but he has ensured that Drucker's emphasis on mission, customer, results, and plan has been embedded deeper throughout the organization. No one is immune. "It's about making everybody—even the musicians—more effective in what they do," says Millar, Southwest's development director and bass trombone player.

Connecting with Strengths

Millar invokes Drucker, as well, when he shows young people how to play. The typical way to teach an instrument, he says, is for the instructor to listen and then say, "Here's what you did wrong." Millar flips it around, asking, "Now tell me what you did—and start with what you did right."

"Students are able to connect with their strengths and make their weaknesses irrelevant," he explains. "Everybody needs to understand what they do well."

For Southwest itself, that's been turning Drucker into beautiful music.

February 6, 2009

Management Lessons
on Nothingness, Drawn from Art

———————

Some of the world's sharpest minds on management and leadership—
Warren Bennis, Ken Blanchard, Charles Handy, Stephen Covey,
Frances Hesselbein, and Jim Collins, among them—came to Southern
California last week to lecture and help commemorate what would have
been Peter Drucker's hundredth birthday. The speakers' remarks, in
which they linked Drucker's ideas and ideals to their own, were chock-
full of insight and inspiration.

And yet it was another Drucker Centennial event—the Monday night
opening of a Japanese art exhibition—that left the biggest impression
on me.

The Sanso Collection, as it's known, contains about 200 paintings,
roughly half of which are associated with Zen Buddhism. Drucker, who
in addition to being a management professor once taught Japanese art,
loved these pieces. And he'd often use them as an excuse to pause and
ponder and see the world in a different way.

Lots of Empty Space

Similarly, "he encouraged viewers to look, and look again," says the show's
curator, Bruce Coats, a professor of art history and the humanities at
Scripps College and a longtime friend of Drucker's.

But what Drucker hoped people would zero in on was more than
the images, which include fifteenth-century landscapes and nineteenth-
century sketches of monks and deities. He wanted them to observe, if not
revel in, the art's omnipresent nothingness. "The Japanese paintings are
dominated by empty space," Drucker wrote in *Song of the Brush*, a book
about the collection. "It is not only that so much of the canvas is empty.
The empty space organizes the painting."

The same, of course, holds true for ourselves and our enterprises: It's
the creation of empty space—moments when we shut off all outside dis-

tractions and give ourselves the opportunity to think—that can determine whether we're organized effectively and whether we'll move forward successfully.

Nevertheless, we clutter our canvases instead. Punch the term "information overload" into Google and you get more than 1.4 million hits—itself a sign of the problem. In his book *The Ten Commandments for Business Failure*, former Coca-Cola President Donald Keough cites one analysis that found the typical corporate employee is besieged by 133 e-mails every day.

Omnipresent Cacophony

Beyond that, Keough writes, "they deal with multiple communications—a fax here, a text message there—attend a meeting here and teleconference with another meeting there—watch a PowerPoint presentation here, watch a video report there. Phones ringing on the desk and vibrating in the pocket. The average human nervous system is not built to process material at anything approaching this blinding rate of speed and volume."

Some systematically fight off this onslaught. For instance, when Patty Stonesifer became CEO of the Bill & Melinda Gates Foundation, she made a point of keeping her Fridays unscheduled so she could study, learn, and refresh herself.

Keeping the calendar blank isn't easy, however, even for the most well-intentioned executive. Often, Drucker warned, "within a few days or weeks, the entire discretionary time will . . . be gone again, nibbled away by new crises, new immediacies, new trivia." That's why the most able time managers, he explained, "keep a continuing log and analyze it periodically," pruning additional activities as necessary.

Still, it's not just "inbox shock" and meeting fatigue that one must guard against. Put any project or deal into motion, and "it's difficult to stop," Keough asserts. "There is a tendency toward group wishing in decision making wherein everyone is so eager to make something happen that straight thinking becomes almost impossible."

Time to Think

Keough's advice for any leader: Cease what you're engaged in every now and again and chew on it for a while. "Time to think is not a luxury," he says. "It is a necessity. . . . Unless somebody stops to think . . . it's easy to make the same mistakes over and over."

This isn't simply a matter of focus. As I've noted in this column previously, Drucker was a big advocate of doing one thing at a time, and doing it well. But he also believed in not doing, so as to make time for pure contemplation. "Follow effective action with quiet reflection," Drucker said. "From the quiet reflection will come even more effective action."

Tellingly, this is a theme that cropped up several times during last week's Drucker Centennial celebration. In his keynote address, author Jim Collins urged people—especially young people—to "turn off your electronic gadgets," put "white space on your calendar," and take advantage of these "glorious pockets of quietude." And during his introduction of British social philosopher Charles Handy, Kai Ryssdal of public radio's "Marketplace" mentioned a scheme that Handy once had: to substitute his own "Thoughts for Today" on the BBC with a "Silent Pause for the Day."

Handy's notion, Ryssdal recalled, was to give listeners two minutes in which they could sit quietly and ruminate before heading out "into the hurly-burly of everyday life." Handy's producers nixed the idea, recognizing, as Ryssdal pointed out, that "two minutes of complete silence is not great radio."

It is, though, great management.

November 13, 2009

Japanese Baseball
and Management Revelations

Last week's official start for Major League Baseball brought with it some of life's most joyful sounds: the crack of the bat, the snap of the mitt, and the flutter of the printed page.

For Opening Day invariably means not only a new season but also a shelf full of new books about the game, including this year's MVP (most valuable publication): *Willie Mays: The Life, the Legend* by James Hirsch. For those whose tastes run more to the business section, meanwhile, there is an improbable title bound to pique even their interest: *What If a Female Manager of a High School Baseball Team Read Drucker's "Management"?*

Currently available only in Japanese, the novel has become a sensation overseas. It has sold more than 300,000 copies in just a few months and currently sits as the No. 3 best seller on Amazon's Japanese list. There is talk of an English translation. (The book's author, Natsumi Iwasaki, is donating some of the royalties to the Japan Drucker Workshop and the Peter F. Drucker & Masatoshi Ito Graduate School of Management; both are affiliated with the Drucker Institute, which I run.)

Corporate executives, more than diehard baseball fans or curious teens, have proven so far to be the primary audience for the narrative, as they consider its key lessons. One crucial insight: "The organization starts with the customer," Iwasaki told me. Or as Drucker put it: "'Who is the customer?' is the first and the crucial question in defining business purpose and business mission. It is not an easy, let alone an obvious, question. How it is being answered determines, in large measure, how the business defines itself."

Management Story

In Iwasaki's story, a student named Minami Kawashima unexpectedly becomes the manager of the baseball team at Tokyo's Hodokubo High—a position in Japan that's roughly one part clubhouse attendant and one part team caretaker. When she assumes this role, she doesn't know much about the job or the players with whom she must now work.

What she quickly realizes, however, is that they're a bunch of under-achievers, talented athletes who are unmotivated and not performing up to par.

Then one day, Minami stumbles across a version of Drucker's 1973 classic, *Management: Tasks, Responsibilities, Practices*. She devours it and begins taking action. Among Minami's first steps: setting clear objectives, just as Drucker prescribed. "Objectives are not fate; they are direction," Drucker wrote. "They are not commands; they are commitments. They do not determine the future; they are means to mobilize the resources and energies of the business for the making of the future."

In Minami's case, her ultimate goal is for the squad from Hodo-kubo to claim Japan's high school baseball crown, the Koshien National Championship. To get there, she embraces a number of Drucker's basic principles, all hinted at by the names of the book's chapters: "Minami Addresses Marketing," "Minami Tries to Harness People's Strengths," "Minami Takes on Innovation," "Minami Thinks About What Integrity Is."

Primary Customers

Many readers seem to be inspired by the protagonist. Even though Minami is a young woman—not exactly a position of high stature in traditional Japanese society—and occupies a lowly position within the organization, "she found a way to make a big difference," says Emi Makino, who is studying at the Drucker School (and who served as my translator when I chatted with Iwasaki). "It shows that anyone can be empowered to make a contribution."

Perhaps the biggest revelation for the team comes about when Minami helps them figure out who their primary customers are. The answer: the boys' parents, a realization that spurs them to live up to their abilities.

"They first have to give back a sense of satisfaction to the parents," Iwasaki explains. "That's what those customers value: touching moments" on the field. The team then "galvanizes around that mission, and the wheels start turning."

The 41-year-old Iwasaki is a relative newcomer to this way of thinking, having discovered *Management* in 2006, a year after Drucker died. At the time, the online gaming enthusiast was trying to figure out how to more effectively organize people to play. A blogger noted that he was reading Drucker to help him with this, and so Iwasaki decided to do the same.

He soon found that he wasn't just interested in Drucker's ideas; he also was deeply moved by them. "*Management* is really a work of art, a historic achievement," says Iwasaki, who himself has written for Japanese television and produces comedy events for stage and screen.

Sense of Community

Iwasaki suggests that his book's popularity may reflect a change in Japanese culture. After a period in which people became "scattered all over the place" and "lost a sense of community," he believes that a collaborative spirit may be coming into vogue again. "There are signs of people wanting to work together," Iwasaki says. "In that context, Drucker's words really sink in."

As crazy as all this may seem, Drucker would have very likely appreciated Iwasaki's book. He loved Japan and had a close relationship with some of the nation's leading companies for many years. He also loved baseball. In the mid-1980s, Drucker advised the Cleveland Indians and helped revive the then-struggling franchise.

Through the exploits of Minami Kawashima, Iwasaki has put the two pieces together, a literary double play.

April 13, 2010

Index

About the Author

Rick Wartzman is the executive director of the Drucker Institute at Claremont Graduate University. The Institute seeks to better society by stimulating effective management and responsible leadership. It does this, in large part, by advancing the ideas and ideals of the late Peter F. Drucker.

Rick is also a columnist for *Bloomberg Businessweek* online. And he was the editor of *The Drucker Lectures: Essential Lessons on Management, Society, and Economy*, which was published in June 2010 by McGraw-Hill.

Rick's book, *Obscene in the Extreme: The Burning and Banning of John Steinbeck's The Grapes of Wrath*, was published in September 2008 by PublicAffairs. It was named by the *Los Angeles Times* as one of its 25 favorite nonfiction books of the year and chosen as a finalist for the Los Angeles Times Book Prize in history and a PEN USA Literary Award.

Rick is the coauthor, with Mark Arax, of the bestseller *The King of California: J.G. Boswell and the Making of a Secret American Empire*, which was selected as one of the 10 best books of 2003 by the *San Francisco Chronicle* and one of the 10 best nonfiction books of the year by the *Los Angeles Times*. It won, among other honors, a California Book Award and the William Saroyan International Prize for Writing.

Before joining the Drucker Institute, Rick spent two decades as a newspaper reporter, editor, and columnist at the *Wall Street Journal* and *Los Angeles Times*.